Resting among Us

Resting among Us

Authors' Gravesites
in Upstate New York

Steven Huff

Syracuse University Press

∞ The paper used in this publication meets the minimum requirements
of the American National Standard for Information Sciences—Permanence
of Paper for Printed Library Materials, ANSI Z39.48-1992.

For a listing of books published and distributed by Syracuse University Press,
visit https://press.syr.edu.

ISBN: 9780815638070 (hardcover)
      9780815611608 (paperback)
      9780815656890 (e-book)

Library of Congress Cataloging-in-Publication Data

Names: Huff, Steven, author.
Title: Resting among us : authors' gravesites in upstate New York / Steven Huff.
Description: First edition. | Syracuse, New York : Syracuse University Press, 2023. |
    Includes bibliographical references.
Identifiers: LCCN 2023020975 (print) | LCCN 2023020976 (ebook) |
    ISBN 9780815638070 (hardcover) | ISBN 9780815611608 (paperback) |
    ISBN 9780815656890 (ebook)
Subjects: LCSH: Authors—New York (State)—Biography. | Authors—Tombs—
    New York (State)—Guidebooks. | Authors—New York (State)—Guidebooks. |
    New York (State)—Biography. | LCGFT: Biographies. | Guidebooks.
Classification: LCC PN452 .H84 2023 (print) | LCC PN452 (ebook) | DDC 809—
    dc23/eng/20230803
LC record available at https://lccn.loc.gov/2023020975
LC ebook record available at https://lccn.loc.gov/2023020976

Contents

Acknowledgments

I wish to thank numerous people without whom this project might never have been completed. First, and foremost, my life-partner Betsy Gilbert, for her work and encouragement and belief in my project. Keith Mc-Manus, who traveled with me to several cemeteries, and was essential help in organizing and preparing photos. David White and Tim Madigan who toured Forest Lawn, Buffalo, and other cemeteries with me. Bill Kauffman, for reading the manuscript and for advice and encouragement, M. J. Iuppa for reading the manuscript and making many suggestions. Sally and Lou Ventura, and Paul Spaeth who showed me Robert Lax's grave, with special thanks to Paul Spaeth for giving me a tour of the Lax archive. Jane Sutter for her help when this project was but a blog. Kelly Balenske, my editor at Syracuse University Press. And many others who have given me directions along the road.

I wish to acknowledge the following rights-holders for permission to reprint:

A. Poulin Jr., Lines from "A Momentary Order" from *Selected Poems.* Copyright © 2001 by the Estate of A. Poulin Jr. Reprinted with the permission of The Permissions Company, LLC, on behalf of BOA Editions Ltd., boaeditions.org.

Anthony Piccione, Poem, "Looking at the Stars and Falling Outward" from *Seeing It Was So.* Copyright © 1986 by Anthony Piccione. Reprinted with the permission of The Permissions Company, LLC, on behalf of BOA Editions Ltd., boaeditions.org.

Kathleen Farrell for the sketch of Charles Hoy Fort, chapter 1.

Getty Images for the photo of Frederick Douglass.

"Ithaca, N.Y." Copyright © 1966 by A. R. Ammons, from *Collected Poems 1951–1971* by A. R. Ammons. Used by permission of W. W. Norton and Company, Inc.

Library of Congress for photos of Edna St. Vincent Millay (chapter 3); James Fenimore Cooper (chapter 4); John Burroughs (chapter 6); Alexander Woollcott (chapter 10); Mark Twain (chapter 11); Shirley Chisholm (chapter 29); Louise Brooks (chapter 36).

Oneida County History Center for permission to reprint photo of Harold Frederic.

Saratoga Springs History Museum for permission to reprint photo of Mansfield Tracy Walworth.

The Matilda Joslyn Gage Center for permission to reprint photo of Matilda Joselyn Gage.

Paragraph beginning, "These 'poetic essays' or 'essayistic poems' . . ." by Deborah Tall and John D'Agata, from *The Seneca Review* Fall 2017 with permission of the editors.

Untitled lines from the inscription on the grave of Robert Lax, with the permission of the Robert Lax Literary Trust.

"Your Absence Has Already Begun," by Deborah Tall, from *Afterings*. Geneva, NY: Hobart and William Smith Colleges Press, 2016, with the permission of David Weiss.

Jean Webster Papers, Archives and Special Collections, Vassar College Library, Collection: Benedict / Folder 35.11 for the photo of Adelaide Crapsey (chapter 36); and the photo of Adelaide Crapsey and Jean Webster (chapter 32).

Resting among Us

Introduction

In the spring of 2015 I went to Los Angeles for the annual conference of the Associated Writers and Writing Programs, fondly known to authors as AWP. I flagged a taxi outside my hotel to the convention hall and I got an Iranian driver. He wanted to know what the conference was about. When I explained, he said, "You mean there are poets?" I said yes, there were. That got him excited.

I said, "You love your poets in Iran, don't you? How about Omar Khayyam?" And I recited a few verses from the *Rubaiyat* that I knew in English, which pleased him grandly. He said that in Iran he made pilgrimages to Khayyam's tomb, and that many others do as well.

I thought about that encounter for a long time. Americans go a-pilgriming too. Thousands go to Graceland every year, to the DC monuments, or to the Gettysburg battlefield. Many travel to monasteries to stay as guests to pray or meditate in silence. I had visited the graves of Robert Frost and Kenneth Rexroth. My Massachusetts cousins graciously took me to Emily Dickinson's plot in Amherst. Those were pilgrimages too. But many of us have an aversion to cemeteries, for a variety of reasons. We associate them with our personal grief, or maybe we have not reconciled ourselves to the reality that our own lives have an end date, and some of us are afraid of ghosts.

My friend the poet Mihaela Moscaliuc told me that in her native Romania people commonly go on Sundays directly from church to a cemetery, bringing their picnic lunches, and spend a good share of the day communing with the spirits of their dead family members. Here, some never visit the graves of their elders. In fact, among the things that people of older cultures find puzzling in America are our disconnection from our

1

history and a passivity toward our ancestors. Some know little about their great-grandparents. Many could not name a living American poet, far less a dead one. Yet, I think if we did, if we did recognize those singers and storytellers and cultural shamans who came before us, if we noted not only what they wrote, but when they lived and where their remains went to rest, it would help us preserve a sense of ourselves, instill a sense of lineage in our young and wavering culture.

It occurred to me that someone needed to write a travelogue for literary pilgrims. I was driving through New York's Finger Lakes region with my partner Betsy, and we decided to take a detour to a cemetery on a back road in Lakemont where I had heard that Paul Bowles, American novelist, translator, and composer, is buried. I was a little astonished to find him in a rather lonely little cemetery, three hundred miles from his birthplace in New York City and thousands of miles from Tangier where he lived most of his life and died. I left a small stone on his marker, where someone else had left a bronzed pinecone on a slender stick. When I told my literary friends in Rochester where Bowles is buried, they were, every one of them, surprised. Why was he buried there? What was his connection to Upstate?

It was just such questions that I set out to answer when I decided to take on this project. I would concentrate on Upstate New York, my home ground. I would search for the graves of Upstate authors and record my finds. I would search out not only the celebrated writers buried in New York soil, like Bowles, Mark Twain, John Gardner, and James Fenimore Cooper, but also the lesser-known who also deserve our reverence and respect. Moreover, I would call this book an account of journeys rather than of pilgrimages since, while a trip to the grave of an author whom you love and who may have had a profound influence on your life could certainly be called a pilgrimage, the discoveries that I hope this book leads you to—of writers you may be only slightly aware of, or only discover through this book—will be perhaps not pilgrimages except by the broadest definition. But, by going to their graves, and being introduced to their works, they may become part of *your* journey through New York literature.

So, I want this book to do more than revere the writers and their resting places; I want it to help raise Upstate New Yorkers' awareness of our literary heritage. I am an Upstater by identity, and this is an Upstate book.

Had I included New York City, its exurbs and Long Island, those regions would have dominated it and made it just another guide to the big city. I have included one person, Edward R. Crone, who was not a writer, but as the real-life model for the character Billy Pilgrim in Kurt Vonnegut's *Slaughterhouse-Five* he is an icon of modern American literature. He is in his family's plot in Mount Hope Cemetery in Rochester.

Without a doubt, I will find that I have left someone out. Probably more than one. My readers will let me know, I hope. But here I want to lay before the reader my criteria for inclusion. The writer must have published at least one significant full-length book, play, or screenplay (recognizing, of course, that a full-length book of poems is usually slim by comparison to most other genres; recognizing also that screenplays are often written by two or more authors). Pamphlet writers then, and those whose works have appeared only in journals or magazines, are not here. I include some individuals who are not remembered primarily as writers, yet produced an unarguably important book, such as US Rep. Shirley Chisholm, author of *Unbought and Unbossed*. Lastly, the author, or the author's ashes, must be interred in Upstate New York. While cemeteries are not museums, they are often a microcosm of an area's history and culture, and for that reason I often make mention of other notables interred therein.

This book makes no pretension to in-depth biography or literary criticism. I do *not* call myself a scholar, nor a historian, only a writer in search of the ancestors of my tribe. Nor is this truly a travelogue. However, I hope you will consider it a pathway to the works of those included here. All of them are worth further exploration. All had reputations that extended far beyond the borders of our state, and yet they have made the ground of our Upstate New York heritage richer.

As I was to learn in my research, internet helpers such as findagrave. com will get you to the right town and to the right cemetery, and will usually feature a picture of the grave, and section and plot number. But unfortunately, many cemeteries do not have clearly posted sections. Some bigger cemeteries have an office and a helpful someone behind a desk. But I knew I would have to develop a strategy for finding the actual graves, since even small graveyards can be frustrating, especially ones where the essential information has eroded from the stones. My solution from my earliest searches was simple: I divided a cemetery, or a section, into quadrants, and in each of the four I started at one side and walked the rows until I hit bingo. It may seem ponderous, but it worked, and it had the added advantage that I got some much-needed exercise. That said, my hope is that with the directions provided in this book, and its photos, you will find the graves without difficulty.

This book is for the curious traveler who needs no excuse to search out-of-the-way Upstate New York, its back roads, rivers, bars, diners, parks, and other places worth a short sojourn. It is also for anyone who shares my compulsion to explore books. In my research I drove thousands of miles and visited local libraries, town halls, delis, and bookstores; places that also add to our sense of home ground. Off-the-path Upstate New York is a soulful place, not the "colorless hinterland" that Norman Mailer once called it. Many times, I swept the gravestones clean of dirt and scraped off the moss and bird-droppings. Often, I talked to local people who were unaware that a noted author is buried in their neighborhood, but usually they seemed intrigued and happy to find out. I met wonderful people who cheerfully gave me directions to remote cemeteries, and where to get a beer and a burger afterward.

Traveler, consider my Upstate, my home ground.
Steven Huff
Rochester, New York

East

1　Albany

Charles Fort

Albany has some of the richest history in Upstate New York. Named by the British for the Duke of Albany, it began its life in 1624 under the Dutch who called it Fort Nassau, not gaining its English name for another forty years. Although the fur trade gave it its initial economy, its position on the Hudson River, near where the Mohawk River joins, as well as being the eastern terminus of the Erie Canal, made it an important northeastern trade hub. "We know every step of the way / from Albany to Buffalo," went the old Tin Pan Alley song, although the bulk of freight was going the other direction, as the canal linked Albany and New York Harbor with the Great Lakes for midwestern grain, lumber, and coal, as well as salt from the Syracuse region, and fruit from Western New York counties. It has the oldest continuous city charter in the United States. After moving to various locations up and down the Hudson, the state capital settled permanently in Albany in 1797.

It has a long literary heritage. Herman Melville's boyhood home still stands in Clinton Square. And many of Henry James's family members are buried in Albany Rural Cemetery. Albany is the setting for William Kennedy's Albany series of novels *The Ink Truck* (1969), *Legs* (1975), *Billy Phelan's Greatest Game* (1978), *Roscoe* (2002) *Changó's Beads and Two-Tone Shoes* (2011), and *Ironweed* (1983) which won the Pulitzer Prize for fiction and became a celebrated movie by Hector Babenco, starring Jack Nicholson and Meryl Streep. But one other writer buried in Albany Rural Cemetery, more peculiar than the others, was Charles Hoy Fort.

1.1: Charles Hoy Fort. Image by Kathleen Farrell.

Charles Hoy Fort (1874–1932): On the Contrary

Once the world's most notable contrarian, Charles Hoy Fort was a cataloger of oddities. He made a career of taking science to task on all reigning theories, proposing that what science advances as theory always leaves human experience out of the equation. Born in Albany, he educated himself in New York Public Library in Manhattan.[1] He collected testimonials of bizarre and unexplained events and phenomena and published them in four witty books, *The Book of the Damned* (1919), *New Lands* (1923), *Lo!* (1931), and *Wild Talents* (1932), attracting a considerable following of intellectuals and literary lights in addition to ordinary readers.[2]

He did not, however, offer a theory for any phenomenon that he himself reported, instead saying that a skeptic walks a path around all theories, since, according to Fort, there is no reliable hierarchy of truth: one theory is no better than another. What greater skeptic than one skeptical even of himself? He was convinced that scientists, and indeed any theoreticians, suppress inconvenient evidence. He was happy to advance evidence of the paranormal (teleportation, out-of-the-body-travel, odd things that fall from the sky such as frogs, and spontaneous human combustion), but would not affirm any belief thereof. According to Robert Todd Carroll, "His real purpose seems to have been to embarrass scientists by collecting stories on 'the borderland between fact and fantasy' which science could not explain. . . . Since he did not generally concern himself with the reliability or accuracy of his data, this borderland also blurs the distinction between open-mindedness and gullibility."[3]

In a review in the *New York Times* in 1931, Maynard Shipley damns *Lo!* with faint praise, along with Fort's other books, as "among the freaks and curiosities of literature." But he adds, "he is perhaps the enzyme orthodox science most needs. . . . He is the enfant terrible of science, bringing the family skeletons to the dinner table when distinguished guests are present."[4]

But the novelist, actor, and screenwriter Tiffany Thayer, undoubtedly Fort's most ardent defender, insisted that he was not a crank. "Charles Fort," he wrote, "was the arch-enemy of dogma—not of science. . . ." In his introduction to *The Books of Charles Fort*, he asserts, "for twenty-one

---

1. New Netherland Institute, "Charles Hoyt Fort."
2. Carroll, "Fort, Charles (1874–1932)," 148.
3. Carroll, 149.
4. Shipley, "Enfant Terrible of Science," 35.

years I have used its parts—each of the four volumes here collected—as an acid test for drinking companions, and this has tended to keep me sober."[5]

Certainly, his skepticism about the shape and construction of the universe and his dubiousness about Darwinian evolutionary theory have been outstripped by science since his time. But in his own day, he attracted prominent followers such as Theodore Dreiser, who became his friend and helped him publish his books, and Thayer, who founded the Fortean Society which drew a cabal of notable members including architect Frank Lloyd Wright, futurist and architect Buckminster Fuller, popular novelist Booth Tarkington, writer and film director Ben Hecht, journalist H. L. Menken, and two famous members of the Algonquin Round Table, Alexander Woollcott and Dorothy Parker.[6]

His problems with authority, scientific or otherwise, began in childhood. He was born in Albany to well-to-do Dutch immigrant parents who lived in the upscale Lower State Street section; his mother died shortly after his birth. His father was a terrifying disciplinarian, and his punishments wreaked on Charles and his brothers, according to Jim Lippard, "ranged from beatings to imprisonment in a dark room for days at a time." Not the sort of upbringing that shapes a well-rounded personality.[7]

While still in his teens Fort became a feature writer for the Albany *Democrat* and the Brooklyn *World*. For a time, he worked as a travel writer for newspapers, touring South America, Europe, and South Africa where he contracted malaria. Returning home, he married an English servant in his family's house named Anna Filing.[8]

For the next ten years the couple lived in New York City's Hell's Kitchen and the Bronx, sometimes nearly destitute, surviving on odd jobs and his freelance writing. They were a devoted couple, however, and Anna's chief problem with him was his reclusiveness which did not moderate with age. But in 1916 Fort's fortunes changed when he inherited

---

5. Thayer, "Introduction," vii.
6. Dunning, transcript, "Skeptoid #488"
7. Lippard, "Charles Fort," 277.
8. Rickard, "Fort: His Life and Times."

1.2: The Fort Family Plot, Albany. Charles Fort's footstone is second from right.

his share of his grandfather's estate. Now he had enough money to live independently, investing his time in research at New York Public Library.

A bulky, muscular, imposing figure who reminded some of a walrus, he was also a man of prodigious output. In addition to his four volumes of anomalies, he wrote ten novels, although publishing only one, *The Outcast Manufacturers* (1906), and an autobiography, *Many Parts* (1901).

He died on May 3, 1932, just days before the publication of his last book, *Wild Talents*. His health had been in decline that year, and his eyesight had been failing. When he finally checked into Royal Hospital in the Bronx complaining of weakness, he died after only a few hours, possibly from leukemia.[9] But his influence marches on in such incarnations as the

9. Rickard.

Fortean Society; the International Fortean Organization, which publishes *INFO Journal*; and another periodical publication, the *Fortean Times*. All of these are dedicated to the unknown, the unexplained, the anomalous. Said Thayer, "He was one sane man in a mad, mad world—and for that reason very lonely."[10]

Certainly we have our doubters today who point their fingers at so-called "fake news." Usually they have a political axe to grind, if not an ideological one. Charles Hoy Fort was a gadfly, a rebel, but one without an ideology; and anyway, he was brave and brilliant. You do not have to be anti-science to appreciate the spirit of his career. Didn't Thoreau tell us to question everything? Didn't Thomas Kuhn warn us that our beloved paradigms would shift beneath our feet? Maybe that is why Fort attracted so many writers to his battlements. Maybe we need a few Charles Forts, lest we fall into lockstep. Or fall asleep.

Finding the Grave

Fort is buried in Albany Rural Cemetery, a little north of the capital city, actually in the village of Menands. The cemetery is four hundred acres and is the final resting place of dozens of notable people, including President Chester A. Arthur; Erastus Corning, founder of New York Central Railroad, and his great-grandson Erastus Corning who was Albany's longest-serving mayor (forty-one years); numerous congressmen; several cabinet members; Thurlow Weed, a nineteenth-century newspaper publisher and New York political kingmaker; and Fort, of course.

The best way to get to the cemetery is to take Route 90, the non-toll extension from the Thruway that goes to Albany. Get off on Route 787 North, and in just a short distance exit onto Route 378 West, then quickly exit onto Route 32, which is Broadway. Turn right (north), and in about half a mile, turn left through the portals of the tree-lined Cemetery Avenue. When you cross the railroad tracks you will see St. Agnes Cemetery

10. Thayer, xxi.

on the left; Albany Rural Cemetery is straight ahead. Or key Cemetery Avenue, Albany, NY, 12204 into your GPS.

The office is on the left as you enter the cemetery (closed on Sundays), and if you get lost you will find the folks there helpful. But there are also cemetery maps available in an outdoor box. Make the next left onto South Ridge Avenue, and drive up the hill. The road is narrow, so drive carefully. At the very top, turn left onto Cypress Avenue. In a few thousand feet you will come to a fountain in a circle. You should park at this point. The Fort family plot is on the outer perimeter of section 28, facing slightly away from the fountain. Charles H. and Anna Fort's names and dates are on the imposing monument, as well as on the two footstones farthest to the right.

Sources

Carroll, Robert Todd. "Fort, Charles (1874–1932)." In *The Skeptic's Dictionary*, edited by Robert Todd Carroll, 148–50. John Wiley and Sons, 2003.

"Charles Hoyt Fort (1874–1932): Arts and Letters." New Netherland Institute. Accessed April 18, 2023. www.newnetherlandinstitute.org/history-and-heritage/dutch_americans/charles-hoyt-fort.

Dunning, Brian. Transcript of podcast "Skeptoid #488: Who Was Charles Fort?" August 13, 2015. https://skeptoid.com/episodes/4488.

Lippard, Jim. "Charles Fort." In *The Encyclopedia of the Paranormal*, edited by Gordon M. Stein, 277–80. Prometheus Books, 1996.

Rickard, Bob. "Charles Fort: His Life and Times," with Chronology. Charles Fort Institute (1995, 1997). www.forteana.org/fortbiog.html.

Shipley, Maynard. "Charles Fort, Enfant Terrible of Science." Review of *Lo!*. *New York Times*, March 1, 1931.

Thayer, Tiffany. "Introduction." *The Books of Charles Fort*. New York: Henry Holt and Co., 1941.

2   Auriesville

Daniel Berrigan

Auriesville is a rural hamlet in Montgomery County, a little west of Amsterdam, or about forty miles west of Albany, near the Mohawk River. It's the site of the Jesuit National Shrine of the North American Martyrs, also called Our Lady of Martyrs Shrine. The 158-acre ground is the reputed site of the Mohawk village of Ossernenon where Jesuit missionaries were tortured and killed: René Goupil in 1642, Isaac Jogues and Jean de Lalande in 1646, all of whom were raised to sainthood for their pains. The village paid dearly for this twenty years later in 1666 when a French raid under the Marquis de Tracy destroyed the village. After the carnage, they made the Mohawks an offer they couldn't refuse, and the natives agreed to accept Jesuit missionaries. A mission was established somewhere in the area that is now Auriesville. By that time, however, the tribe had been devastated by a smallpox epidemic, another gift from Europe.

The Jesuit shrine is also the reputed site of the birth in 1660 of Kateri Tekakwitha, a Mohawk woman who was devoted to the church and canonized in 2012 as the first Native American saint. I've been using the word "reputed" because the actual location of the Mohawk village is in dispute. Some archeologists place it some miles away. But, in God's eyes, it's not far off.

The largest structure on the site is the Coliseum Church, a church-in-the-round, and the largest sanctuary I have ever seen. I found the main door open, which is on the west side. It must hold thousands, and it's a little

14

startling to find such a place so far out in the sticks. At a small museum you will find a "Pilgrimage/Tour Coordinator." The former Jesuit retreat house, just over the fence from the cemetery and mortuary chapel, was sold to the World Peace and Healing Organization some years ago, which has turned it into Holy Mountain Buddha Land, a colorful and imposing presence.

Daniel Berrigan (1921–2016): A Man of Peace and Defiance

One day in the early 1970s, I was on a Trailways Bus heading home, Upstate, after a short period of hanging about in Greenwich Village trying to be a singer. My guitar was in the luggage compartment under the bus, and my backpack was under my feet. The bus stopped in a town in the Hudson Valley, probably Poughkeepsie. In fact, I was feeling glum about my failure to excite the New York coffeehouse crowds, and I didn't care what town we were in. I saw a crowd of people on the sidewalk saying goodbye to a priest. He was shaking hands and laughing with them before he climbed aboard carrying a rolled newspaper. Apparently, he was no *ordinary* priest. He took the aisle seat next to me. It was a crowded bus and I think it was the only seat left open, because in those years many people were still hesitant to sit next to a hippie.

We talked for a bit. He asked me what I was doing and I told him about my bad luck in New York, and he was sympathetic. We talked about the Vietnam War, and the ongoing anti-war protests. Then he relaxed and read his newspaper, and we said goodbye when he got off in another town. I got off in Batavia, and then hitchhiked south to my studio apartment in Attica, where I settled in to contemplate my next move.

It was later that I saw a picture in a magazine of Daniel Berrigan which looked spot-on like my traveling companion on the bus. Like most notorious people, he was probably glad not to be recognized—especially on a bus where he couldn't break away if things got too thick. Besides, in those years he was often pursued by the law. But he traveled light, with nothing but a backpack. "Dan owned nothing," his niece Frida Berrigan said. "He carried nothing. Whenever I traveled with him, to conferences, speaking engagements, retreats, family occasions, he'd bring that little backpack of nothing. I'd pick him up and ask, 'Is that all you have?' He'd say: 'Yes, that's it. Let's go.'"[1]

Born in Minnesota, Berrigan grew up one of six brothers in an Irish family, the son of a warm and caring mother and a father who was emotionally distant and occasionally violent. While the boys were still young, they moved to a farm near Syracuse. Although he felt that the church condoned his father's abuse of his mother, he decided while still in his teens that he wanted to be a priest.[2]

He was ordained in 1952 after earning a bachelor's degree from a Jesuit seminary in Hyde Park, New York, and a master's from Woodstock College in Baltimore. Berrigan returned to Syracuse to teach New Testament studies at Le Moyne College from 1957–63. His radicalism finally ran him afoul of Cardinal Francis Spellman of New York, who exiled him briefly to a "fact-finding" mission to South America.[3]

He was a pacifist, but a complicated one. He and his brother Philip, also a priest, would go to radical lengths, arguably violent, to promote peace. In Catonsville, Maryland, in 1968, he and Philip and seven others entered the Selective Service office, removed the 1-A files (men tagged fit for military service), carried them to the adjacent parking lot, and set them afire with homemade napalm.[4] He and the others went to prison for it, although Daniel first went on the lam for a few months, for which J. Edgar Hoover honored him with inclusion in the Ten Most Wanted list.[5] Not many priests get that kind of recognition. FBI agents, posing as bird watchers, finally caught up with him at the Block Island home of his friends William Stringfellow and Anthony Towne, and he was off to Danbury Prison in New York State.[6] He got out in 1972.

Even before the stunt in Catonsville, he was a major figure in the Vietnam era peace movement. In 1968 he received a phone call from peace

1. Dwyer, "He Traveled Light," 1.
2. Lewis, "Daniel Berrigan Dies at 94," 7.
3. Lewis, 7.
4. Lewis, 7.
5. Keane, "Lessons from Berrigan's FBI Evasion," 3.
6. Lewis, 7.

activist David Dellinger asking him to join historian and social activist Howard Zinn on a flight to Hanoi to receive three American fighter pilots that the North Vietnamese government was offering to release, but only to members of the American peace movement.[7] They flew to Hanoi and the American pilots were released to them, but the US government was not about to let these men land at an American airport and face the press along with two peaceniks. When the plane landed in Laos, US Ambassador William Sullivan came aboard the plane, took command of the three men, and accompanied them home in an Air Force plane.[8]

Other notable episodes of civil disobedience followed. Daniel and Philip and six others in 1980 entered a nuclear facility in King of Prussia, Pennsylvania, damaged warheads with hammers, and doused files with blood, racking up ten felony counts and more jail time.[9] Their act inspired the movie *In the King of Prussia* which dramatized and reconstructed the act and the following court drama, with Martin Sheen playing the judge and the defendants playing themselves. The film is based on actual court transcripts, well worth seeing. The judge disallowed defendants to call expert witnesses to testify to the justification of their acts, which naturally meant lengthy appeals.

But Berrigan, rebel though he was, remained in the priesthood to the end of his life. He played a small role as a Jesuit brother in Roland Joffé's *The Mission*, with Robert DeNiro, Jeremy Irons, and Liam Neeson, and also served as a consultant on the film.

He is included in this book because he was a writer, and an important one. He wrote more than fifty books of theology, memoir, and poetry. In 1957 he won the Lamont Poetry Prize from the Academy of American Poets, one of the most coveted prizes in poetry (now called the Laughlin Award, named for James Laughlin, founder of New Directions Publishing, the publisher of Berrigan's poetry).[10] He wrote books on the Old Testament: *No Gods but One* (on Deuteronomy), *Isaiah: Spirit of Courage*,

7. Zinn, "Introduction," ix.

8. Berrigan, *Night Flight to Hanoi*, 136–38.

9. Lewis, 7.

10. Lewis, 7.

Gift of Tears; Exodus: Let My People Go; Minor Prophets, Major Themes; and on the New Testament: *Whereon to Stand: The Acts of the Apostles and Ourselves.* Other books include his memoirs: *The Dark Night of the Resistance; Night Flight to Hanoi; To Dwell in Peace: An Autobiography;* and poetry: *Time Without Number,* which won the Lamont; *Prison Poems; Tulips in the Prison Yard: Selected Poems of Daniel Berrigan; And the Risen Bread: Selected and New Poems 1957–1997.* Not bad for such a busy fellow. When he wasn't getting arrested (he has often been photographed smiling as he is led away in handcuffs), or working with the poor, or caring for the dying, or protesting against an impassive government, he was writing.

Finding the Grave

Daniel Berrigan is buried in the Jesuit cemetery at Our Lady of Martyrs Shrine (where he'd gone as a boy when he decided to be a priest), under a simple stone, exactly like hundreds of other stones for priests like himself in the same burial ground.

To get to Auriesville, from east or west, take Thruway Exit 28. Once past the exit, you will see a sign for Auriesville, four miles to the east. This is State Highway 920P. In a little less than two miles you will turn left on New York Route 5S. In another few miles watch for a small sign for the martyrs shrine. You'll see a stone structure near the road that might lead you to believe it's the whole show. But it's not. Drive up the hill to the grounds. A large parking lot is to the east of the church. Or set your GPS for 136 Shrine Rd., Fultonville, NY, 12072, which is its official postal address.

To reach the cemetery, find the small, shady circle in the center of the grounds where signs identify the spot as the site of Ossernenon. From this point follow the path of brick edifices with painted plaster stations of the cross, about a hundred feet apart, which lead to the top of a wooded hill where you will encounter a life-size sculpted crucifixion. Beyond that, and a bit to the left, is the mortuary chapel, and from there you can see the cemetery sloping down the hill. The nearly identical stones are arranged according to the date of death of the interred. That makes it easy. Berrigan died April 30, 2016, and his stone is in the last row, across a path, about in the center.

2.1: The grave of Daniel Berrigan in the Jesuit Cemetery in Auriesville.

Interestingly, he is about fifty feet from the grave of the staunchly conservative Avery Cardinal Dulles (whose stone is significantly larger), the son of the saber-rattling Secretary of State John Foster Dulles and nephew of CIA Director Allen Dulles (see Central, chapter 24, Watertown), who in their time advocated for flexible use of nuclear weapons such as against North Korea. The cardinal's stone is bedecked with flowers. I began to pull the long grass stems from around Berrigan's stone. But then I stopped. I think he would have liked them.

Sources

Dwyer, Jim. "He Traveled Light: Just a Backpack and Beliefs." *New York Times*, May 6, 2016.

Keane, James T. "Lessons from Daniel Berrigan's FBI Evasion," *America: The Jesuit Review*, February 1, 2016.

Lewis, Daniel. "Daniel J. Berrigan, Defiant Priest Who Preached Pacifism, Dies at 94." *New York Times*, April 30, 2016.

Zinn, Howard. "Introduction." In *Night Flight to Hanoi: War Diary with 11 Poems*, by Daniel Berrigan, ix–xii. New York: Perennial Library, 1968.

3   Austerlitz

Edna St. Vincent Millay

Austerlitz is a mountainous town in largely rural Columbia County. It borders the state of Massachusetts on its east side. In 1818, Martin Van Buren, the future president who was a state senator at the time, conferred the name Austerlitz on the town to honor the place in the Czech Republic where Napoleon won one of his greatest battles.

In a land dispute during the winter of 1882, an axe murder occurred in Austerlitz. Oscar Fritz Allan Beckwith delivered the blow to one Simon Adolphus Vandercook, after which he used the same instrument to chop Vandercook into bite-size pieces, and then devoured him. With the law in pursuit, Beckwith fled on foot to Canada where he was finally arrested in Parry Sound, north of Toronto, and brought back to stand trial. He was hung in 1888 on gallows erected in front of the Columbia County Courthouse in Hudson. He was almost eighty years old.

Beckwith might have remained Austerlitz's most enigmatic figure, had not the Ambrose Cook property on East Hill Road sold in 1925 to a famous poet, Edna St. Vincent Millay, and her husband.

Edna St. Vincent Millay (1892–1959): A Poet Like No Other

The woman who would one day be called America's most beloved poet, who would fill theaters and lectures halls mesmerizing audiences with her dramatic readings, was born in rural Rockland, Maine, in 1892. The name of the New York City hospital where once her uncle's life was saved was given to her for a middle name, lending her at birth a bit of mysterious

3.1: Edna St. Vincent Millay. Genthe photograph collection, Library of Congress, Prints and Photographs Division, LC-DIG-agc-7a10216.

elegance.[1] But her family was scratching to get by in rural Maine. The road ahead of her was going to be rugged.

1. Epstein, *What Lips My Lips Have Kissed*, 14.

She was nine years old when her mother Cora threw her father out of the house and divorced him for gambling and unspecified abuses, and the family went through years of moving from place to place, sometimes taken in for short stays by tolerant relatives, finally landing in a rented house in Camden, Maine. Cora was a nurse for private families and worked long hours, often away from home for days at a time. Vincent, as her family called her, was the eldest of three daughters, her mother's favorite; but in that position she assumed responsibilities that often fall on eldest daughters—all of the cooking, housework, laundering, gardening, and snow shoveling, *plus* raising her two younger sisters, Norma and Kathleen. According to biographer Daniel Mark Epstein, Vincent was "a vulnerable, neurasthenic girl who life had dealt a difficult hand."[2]

When they received notice that her estranged father was on his deathbed, it was Vincent—now twenty years old—who got on the train to Kingman, to sit by his bed and read to him. To the surprise of everyone, he recovered.[3] But things were about to change again for Vincent. She was a rebel, and on that trip to Kingman she met a young woman named Ella, the daughter of her father's doctor; they became infatuated with each other, and she extended her stay for so many days that her mother became frantic trying to reach her, fearing she was sick. According to biographer Nancy Milford, "She wasn't sick, she was having fun. The gloom that had engulfed her at home was lifting."[4] What finally drew her home was a letter from her mother telling her about a poetry contest that she wanted her daughter to enter. The winning poems would be published in *The Lyric Year* anthology, and there were cash prizes.[5]

Now Vincent had two things going for her that gave her life a sense of ebullience and strength: love and poetry. She would have many lovers in her life, and she would be a major American poet.

Vincent entered "Renascence," a poem of over two hundred lines that she had been working to finish. The poem is now regarded as not only

2. Epstein, 6.
3. Milford, *Savage Beauty*, 58–59.
4. Milford, 60–61.
5. Epstein, 58.

one of the finest of her career, but one of the best American poems of that period. When it won only an honorable mention, it touched off a chorus of protest from readers who felt that it should have won first place. Even Orrick Johns, the first-place winner, said he felt embarrassed that his own poem should have won over "Renascence," and declined to attend the celebratory banquet.

> All I could see from where I stood
> Was three long mountains and a wood;
> I turned and looked another way,
> And saw three islands in a bay.
> So with my eyes I traced the line
> Of the horizon, thin and fine,
> Straight around till I was come
> Back to where I'd started from;
> And all I saw from where I stood
> Was three long mountains and a wood.[6]

In the poem, she begins to experience infinity, and yet, "The sky, I said, must somewhere stop." And "For my omniscience I paid a toll / In infinite remorse of soul." Loathing the dreary state of earth and her transgressions against her own soul, she is pushed into the grave by the weight of the world's sorrows. Then under a revivifying rain, she wishes to rejoin "Beloved beauty" in the living world. She cries to God to bring her back to earth, and He grants her reentry to life, with a rebirth of wonder. It is a romantic poem of euphoria at being alive, of an ecstatic spirit conjoined to God and nature.

That "Renascence" did not win may have had less to do with the editors' literary judgment than the fact that Vincent had been writing seductive letters to Ferdinand Earle, the editor who was in charge of the competition, and he'd been a fool, writing thinly veiled letters in return. His wife had discovered Vincent's letters, resulting in a breach in their marriage.[7]

6. Millay, *Collected Poems*, 3.

7. Epstein, 66.

For Vincent, the letdown was more than literary disappointment. Either because she was sure that she'd submitted an unbeatable poem, or because she'd thought her wiles put her over the top, she was counting on the $500 prize. Her family was also counting on it—Cora's annual salary as a nurse was only about $800.[8]

But the public hubbub over "Renascence" drew more readers to it than would have noticed it otherwise. It was taught in classrooms. And it inspired some wealthy patrons to send Vincent to Vassar College.[9] A new literary celebrity, she moved to New York, she got fan mail, she hung out with the big city literati before she'd even registered for college.

She drank and smoked her way through rigid, dour Vassar, went AWOL, smashed the rules into fractions, and got away with it by means of charm and scholastic brilliance. Vassar President Henry MacCracken said many years later,

> She cut everything. I once called her in and told her, "I want you to know that you couldn't break any rule that would make me vote for your expulsion. I don't want to have any dead Shelleys on my doorstep, and I don't care what you do." She went to the window and looked out and she said, "[W]ell on those terms I think I can continue to live in this hellhole."[10]

According to Epstein,

> With Arthur Hooley [an older man and love interest] occasionally available for heterosexual trysts in New York City and Mamaroneck, and a harem of sex-starved Vassar girls eager for same-sex experiments right there on campus, Millay found herself at the center of a four-year bacchanal, an early-twentieth-century clinic in the art of love.[11]

8. Epstein, 66.
9. Milford, 78.
10. "MacCracken Remembers St. Vincent Millay," 55–56.
11. Epstein, 83.

But the faculty and administration, in a parting strike, expelled her shortly after her final exams. It looked as if she wouldn't be allowed to cross the platform to receive her diploma. However, her popularity with the student body won out when it took up a petition that got her reinstated—with MacCracken's support.[12]

In Greenwich Village, she was a central figure in the bohemian culture—openly bisexual, feminist, pacifist, and championing idealistic political movements, all of which required considerable audacity. Her house in the Village at 75½ Bedford Street, where she lived from 1923–25 with her new husband, coffee importer Eugen Jan Boissevain, was noteworthy for being only nine and a half feet wide.[13] Indeed, from the outside it seems a sliver of a place. And it was only a few steps from Chumley's, a pub that operated as a speakeasy during Prohibition.

She won the Pulitzer Prize in 1923 for her book *The Ballad of the Harp-Weaver*, published in 1922. It was her fourth book of poems, following *Renascence and Other Poems* (1917), *A Few Figs From Thistles: Poems and Four Sonnets* (1920), and *Second April* (1921).

But life in the hive of activity that is New York was making it hard for her to write. In 1925 they bought the three-hundred-acre farm in Austerlitz. On narrow East Hill Road, their nearest neighbor was a mile away. She named it Steepletop for the fields of steeplebush that she loved, and where blueberries also proliferated, and all was surrounded by woods. She brought trees from her native Camden to plant around the shed that became her writing cabin. And the house nearly sagged with her bookshelves. She and Eugen installed a tennis court and a swimming pool and fountain that was fed by a pipeline from a cistern on a mountain several miles away. She spent endless hours in her kitchen garden—a rather large one.[14]

It was a bucolic paradise where she could write unimpeded, supported by her husband, and visited by a stream of artists and writers. Next to the pool was a bar. The rule was, you must be dressed to drink at the bar, but

12. "MacCracken Remembers St. Vincent Millay," 55–56.

13. Epstein, 182.

14. Conversation with caretaker Haley Prescott at Steepletop, September 2021.

nudity was de rigueur in the pool. However, her years there were also marred by personal problems: her alcoholism, and injury from an automobile accident that lead to morphine addiction, contributed to the slow decline of her health.

But even in strife and ill health she remained a prolific poet turning out a string of books: *The Buck in the Snow, and Other Poems* (1928), *Fatal Interview* (1931), *Wine from These Grapes* (1934), *Huntsman, What Quarry?* (1939), *There Are No Islands, Any More: Lines Written in Passion and in Deep Concern for England, France, and My Own Country* (1940), and *Mine the Harvest* (1950) posthumously published, edited by her sister Norma.

The property caretaker found her dead at the foot of her stairs on the afternoon of October 1950 (a year after her husband's death), when he came to light the fire for the evening. Her doctor said that she had suffered a heart attack; the Columbia County coroner said she had been dead for about eight hours.[15] Norma, who took up residence at Steepletop after Vincent's death, was a singer and actress and had been a constant correspondent with her sister. She established the Millay Colony for the Arts across the road from the house, where artists and writers still come to stay and do their work in relative solitude. Later, she established the Millay Society to preserve both Millay's legacy and Steepletop, which became a National Historic Landmark in 1972.

Edna St. Vincent Millay was not only one of America's best-loved poets but one of the country's most famous persons. She was one of the few poets America has had who would be recognized if she walked into a restaurant anywhere in America. There may never be another.

Finding the Grave

The graves of Edna St. Vincent Millay, her husband Eugen, and her mother are in the woods near the house. Unfortunately, as of this writing, the grounds are not open, but hopefully may reopen at some point. The following paragraph is from the Millay Society:

---

15. "Edna St. Vincent Millay Found Dead."

3.2. The grave of Edna St. Vincent Millay and Eugen Jan Boissevain, Austerlitz.

Steepletop is currently closed to the public, however, there are times when the house and grounds will be open for special events and activities. To learn more about these events, visit millay.org where you can sign up for email communications to keep you informed.

Sources

"Edna St. Vincent Millay Found Dead at 58." *New York Times*, August 20, 1950.
"Edna St. Vincent Millay Residence." NYC LGBT Historic Sites Project. Accessed April 18, 2023. https://www.nyclgbtsites.org/site/edna-st-vincent-millay-residence/.

Epstein, Daniel Mark. *What Lips My Lips Have Kissed: The Loves and Love Poems of Edna St. Vincent Millay*. New York: Henry Holt, 2001.

Marchese, Allison Guertin. *Hidden History of Columbia County*. Charleston, NC: History Press, 2014.

Milford, Nancy. *Savage Beauty: The Life of Edna St. Vincent Millay*. New York: Random House, 2002.

Millay, Edna St. Vincent. Collected Poems. Edited by Norma Millay. New York: Harper Perennial Modern Classics, 2011.

"President MacCracken Remembers Edna St. Vincent Millay." *Vassarion: Vassar Encyclopedia* (1967), 51–55.

4   Cooperstown

James Fenimore Cooper,
Susan Fenimore Cooper

I like walking in Upstate villages, and Cooperstown is one of my favorites. It is prosperous and quaint in the best sense: it is old (established in 1786) and has not allowed its treasured architecture to tatter and fall. People are friendly, there are good restaurants, and a downhill walk to the shore will give you cool breezes in the summer. It can be frustratingly crowded in the summer since it is home to the Baseball Hall of Fame, and there are endless small shops pushing souvenirs and paraphernalia, popcorn and hot dogs—all things baseball. Parking on the street in the center of the village is often difficult, but in the busy seasons there are parking lots outside the village where you can catch a shuttle to where the action is.

Cooperstown lies at the southernmost point of Lake Otsego, the same lake that is called Glimmerglass—the place of the main action in James Fenimore Cooper's *The Deerslayer*—and the name survives in the famous opera house in Cooperstown. There are a couple of good approaches to the village, from the south or northwest via Route 28 or from the watery north by birchbark canoe. From a southern approach, you pass through what seems like an ordinary plaza district. But never fear, the lovely village of Cooperstown is ahead.

Besides baseball and opera, Cooperstown is also famous for the Farmers' Museum, and for the aura of Cooper, one of the most prolific and influential novelists in all of American literature. It is hard to think of another American writer whose image so predominates in a village. For

4.1: James Fenimore Cooper. Photo by Mathew Brady. Library of Congress, Prints and Photographs Division, LC-USZ62-8222.

a small fee, docents provide "Cooper Walks," taking in every site relevant to the author of the Leatherstocking Tales. In recent years there has been renewed interest in the life and works of the famous author's daughter, Susan Augusta Fenimore Cooper, most famous for *Rural Hours* (1950), regarded as the first book of significant nature writing by an American woman, and a forerunner of Thoreau's *Walden* (1854).

James Fenimore Cooper (1789–1851):
Leatherstocking Romantic

James Fenimore Cooper's name is almost synonymous with the American Historical Romance, a category that requires no historical accuracy, much less plausibility. In fact, the weaving of implausibility is method, since romance requires that good must triumph over evil (a few good people get bumped off in the process, but that is to be expected) and love over inhumanity, and the reader must be ready to suspend reasonable disbelief. But since his books were so widely and avidly read in his own time, he helped create the white European and East Coast urban notions of Native Americans; their ethos, personalities, and general proclivities, ranging from the almost regal dignity of his character Chingachgook to the utterly debased and bloodthirsty Magua. The crown of all his creations in the Leatherstocking novels is Natty Bumppo, the mythical woodsman and trail guide, a man of almost unerring decency, who adopts a new moniker in each novel: Hawkeye, Deerslayer, Pathfinder. I have judged him a little lower than the angels since he does occasionally shoot someone.

Cooper is a good storyteller, however you may feel about his portrayals of Indians, women, the French, or the Dutch, or his innuendoes against book-learning (the latter primarily to reinforce Natty Bumppo's natural innocence). As for romance, we must still need a little of it since his books remain popular. One morning I was sitting in a waiting room reading *The Pathfinder* while my car was being repaired. Across from me I noticed a well-dressed businessman reading *The Last of the Mohicans*, which led to an interesting discussion.

Reading through his novels as I researched this book was a pleasure. That's right, I had not read them before. Everyone has a few gaping holes in their reading experience, and that was one of mine. I don't know why, I'm not shy of long books. I find lengthy stretches of exposition in fiction dull, but that wouldn't keep me away from a real classic. Maybe it is because in college long ago I read Mark Twain's essay, "Fenimore Cooper's Literary Offenses," in which he rakes Cooper over the coals for clumsy writing. Not that what he said is entirely untrue, it's just that, for all the faults that Twain finds in the Leatherstocking Tales, they still provide a warm fire on a cold evening.

Yet one of Twain's complaints bears repeating since it confronts idiosyncrasies in Cooper's style that a contemporary reader should be forewarned of before diving into his novels. According to Twain, one of the eighteen rules governing fiction that Cooper violates is that "The talk shall sound like human talk, and be talk such as human beings would be likely to talk in the given circumstances, and have a discoverable meaning, also a discoverable purpose, and a show of relevancy, and remain in the neighborhood of the subject at hand. . . ."[1]

Ouch! It is true that Natty Bumppo is given to lofty philosophical and even theological speeches at every turn of the tale—especially in *Deerslayer,* and even when under hostile attack by "savage" Hurons, as if he had time to wax while in a desperate struggle to save his own skin and those around him. And bear in mind that Mr. Bumppo is illiterate. One wonders why his almost constant companion Chingachgook doesn't whack him over the head.

On the other hand, more authentic colloquial language in popular American fiction doesn't begin until somewhat later; Twain's own *Adventures of Huckleberry Finn* was one of the first, published many years after the author of the Leatherstocking Tales was dead. Prior to that (and to some degree after), characters in novels were expected to speak like well-bred and respectable people, even if they were illiterate, ill-bred, and up to no good. Yet, I do not think that I am going too far out on a limb to claim that Cooper was giving his readers, in The *Deerslayer,* The *Last of the Mohicans,* The *Pioneers, Pathfinder,* and *The Prairie,* what they were most hungry for. European readers were hungry for the same; Cooper became the first American writer to gain wide popularity there,[2] and had a marked influence on French Romanticism.[3]

He wrote other books besides the Leatherstockings: *The Spy,* and his novels of the sea: *Ned Myers or A Life Before the Mast, The Red Rover,* and *The Sea Lions.* Thirty-seven books in all.

1. Twain, "Fennimore Cooper's Literary Offenses," 72.
2. Wasserman, "Cooper and the Image of America."
3. Partridge, "Cooper's Influence on French Romantics," 174.

4.2: Susan Augusta Fenimore Cooper. Photo by W. G. Smith, Cooperstown, NY, c. 1855, via Wikimedia Commons.

One of the things that I like about the Leatherstocking Tales is the settings in New York's wilderness of the eighteenth century: the lake he calls Glimmerglass; the Adirondack woods; Lake Ontario, which he calls the Inland Sea; the fort at Oswego. What a marvelously wild place, with moose, leopards, bears, hostile tribes of Iroquois and Hurons, and the noble Mohicans, of whom there is but one left. The forest was a magnificent pantry wherein if you got hungry you just shot the next deer that wandered by.

Perhaps only his nemesis, Mark Twain, left more of a mark on our literature in the nineteenth century.

Susan Augusta Fenimore Cooper (1813–1894): At Home in Nature

Like her father, Susan Augusta Fenimore Cooper was an American original. She is regarded as the first woman nature writer, most famous for her book *Rural Hours*, a journal of natural observations in the environs of Cooperstown, in seasonal sections, spring through winter. Strongly attached to her father, she served as his amanuensis and first reader. She never married, apparently because her father's disapproving shadow fell upon all would-be suitors.[4]

When her father's house Otsego Hall burned a year after his death, she built her own house in Cooperstown with bricks recovered from the rubble. What greater tribute can a daughter give? She planned to write a biography of him, but he discouraged that idea.

While few have read her single novel *Elinor Wyllys*, her *Rural Hours* has gone through multiple editions since it appeared first in 1850. William Cullen Bryant called it "a great book—the greatest of the season."[5] According to Anne Perrin, the book is a jeremiad which, while it hesitates to criticize the disruptions to nature by new and expanding settlements and even praises the dominion of man over the earth, it yet cautions against wanton exploitation and loss of the spiritual dimensions of nature.[6] More books followed: *Rhyme and Reason of Country Life* (1885) and *Mt. Vernon to the Children of America* (1859). She also published numerous articles to rally support among Episcopalians for the welfare of Oneida Indians.[7]

---

4. Rademaekers, "Susan Fenimore Cooper."
5. Cunningham, "Child of Genius," 340.
6. Perrin, "Subversion of Style in Cooper's *Rural Hours*," 79.
7. Hauptman, McLester, and Hawk, "Another Leatherstocking Tale," 10.

4.3: The grave of James Fenimore Cooper (left) and his wife Susan Augusta de Lancey in Cooperstown.

In later life she founded an orphanage in Cooperstown,[8] and was one of the town's reliable philanthropists. Clearly, she was a big-hearted woman.

Finding the Graves

To visit the graves of novelist James Fenimore Cooper and his daughter Susan Fenimore Cooper, we need a starting point in town. Let's suppose that you managed to find a parking place on Main Street, or you've arrived there via shuttle from one of the lots outside of town, or you arrived from Lake Otsego by canoe. In any case, a traffic circle in the middle section

8. Gundrum, "Memorializing Mothers," 42.

4.4: The grave of Susan Fenimore Cooper in Cooperstown.

of Main Street is a good place to anchor our directions. From there, walk east for a short distance. The Baseball Hall of Fame is on the right, but visit it later—remember, we are on a mission. Immediately after passing the Hall of Fame, turn right through the portal into Cooper Park. You'll be facing the regal sculpture of Cooper himself in the middle of the thoroughfare.

A short walk on that road takes you directly to Church Street and its intersection with Fair Street. Walk up Fair Street a short distance to No. 69, on your left, Christ Church (Episcopal). Immediately to the left of the church you will find a path that will take you back to Christ Churchyard. If you prefer, there is a Church Street entrance, and another entrance via a flowered path around the corner on River Street. Whatever entrance you take, look for the cemetery map mounted on a pedestal near to the church; it is very well done, showing points of interest in the cemetery, and if you refer to it, you'll easily find the two stones for James Fenimore Cooper and his wife Susan. Just to their left is Susan Augusta Fennimore Cooper's grave.

Sources

James Fenimore Cooper

Partridge, Eric. "Fenimore Cooper's Influence on the French Romantics." *Modern Language Review* 20, no. 2 (1925): 174–78. https://doi.org/10.2307/3714204.

Twain, Mark. "Fenimore Cooper's Literary Offenses." *Litigation* 24, no. 2 (1998): 72–70. http://www.jstor.org/stable/29759984.

Wasserman, Renata R. Mautner. "James Fenimore Cooper and the Image of America." In *Exotic Nations: Literature and Cultural Identity in the United States and Brazil, 1830–1930,* 154–85. Cornell Univ. Press, 1994. http://www.jstor.org/stable/10.7591/j.ctt207g5v4.9.

Susan Fenimore Cooper

Cunningham, Anna K. "Susan Fenimore Cooper: Child of Genius." *New York History* 25, no. 3 (1944): 339–50. http://www.jstor.org/stable/23163066.

Gundrum, Amy R. "Memorializing Mothers: Stained-Glass Windows, Female Empowerment, and Religion in Cooperstown, New York." *New York History* 88, no. 1 (2007): 33–53. http://www.jstor.org/stable/23183552.

Hauptman, Laurence M., L. Gordon McLester, and Judy Hawk. "Another Leatherstocking Tale: Susan Fenimore Cooper, the Episcopal Church, and the Oneida Indians." *New York History* 94, nos. 1–2 (2013): 9–39. https://www.jstor.org/stable/newyorkhist.94.issue-1-2.

Perrin, Anne. "Subversion of Narrative Style in Susan Fenimore Cooper's *Rural Hours.*" In *James Fenimore Cooper: His Country and His Art, Papers from the 1999 Cooper Seminar (No. 12)*, edited by Hugh C. MacDougall, 79–84. Oneonta, New York: The State University of New York College at Oneonta, 1999.

Rademaekers, Justin King. "Susan Fenimore Cooper: Biography." *Quotidiana*. Accessed April 18, 2023. http://essays.quotidiana.org/cooper_s/.

5   Kingston

Walter B. Gibson

In 1777, during the Revolutionary War, the new state of New York set up its government in Kingston, judging it to be a relatively safe distance from the advancing British army under Gen. William Howe, who had taken control of Manhattan. Here, in June, the state organized a governing body, with George Clinton sworn in as first governor (later to be the fourth US vice president), and John Jay its first chief justice (later to be the first US supreme court chief justice and a signatory of the Treaty of Paris in 1783). Thus Kingston rightly claims status as the first New York state capital. It was an extraordinary moment in history.

Earlier that spring, Howe sent a force of seven thousand soldiers by sea to the St. Lawrence River under General Burgoyne, with orders to circle around and attack the colony from the north and secure the vitally strategic Hudson River, cutting New England off from the rest of the colonies. It was the age-old divide-and-conquer tactic. But the colonial forces scored a major victory over the British at Saratoga and Burgoyne surrendered his army to Gen. Horatio Gates on October 17.

However, while the battle was raging in the north, British forces under General Vaughan sailed north on the Hudson from Manhattan, taking aim at Kingston. They burned about three hundred homes and buildings, and left the city a smoldering ruin. Those buildings that were built in the Dutch era were built of stone, but their interiors were burned to ash. With winter coming, residents rigged up lean-tos against the stone walls.

To the surprise of many, the Brits under Vaughan did not continue north to join Burgoyne's army in the north, but called their work in

Kingston a job well done, and turned tail back to the warmth of New York. They would have been too late to help Burgoyne anyway. And the British never did gain control of the Hudson.

When the revolution ended in 1783, a crew of white men and numerous enslaved people began cutting west from Kingston through the mountains and backwoods to establish the Schoharie Road, hoping to rebuild the city as a trade center. In 1828, the Delaware and Hudson Canal connected the Delaware River with the Hudson at Rondout, now part of Kingston, and became a critical passage for coal from northeastern Pennsylvania. More roads and railroads followed. Kingston regained some of its prominence in the Hudson River Valley, becoming the main river port between Albany and New York City. In 1861, the *Mary Powell*, the largest, fastest, and most elegant steamboat on the Hudson River, began carrying passengers between Kingston and New York City. A three-hundred-foot sidewheeler, it ran for fifty-five years until it was sold for scrap.

Over the years, Kingston has had its ups and downs. The IBM plant, which opened in 1956 and employed more than 7,000 people at its peak, closed in 1995 and transferred its 1,500 remaining jobs to Poughkeepsie. And unlike some other eastern New York communities, such as Woodstock and Saratoga Springs, it has never been a holiday destination. But in recent times it has seen a rebirth, mostly owing to the gravitation of artists to set up their studios in the lofts of old mills and factories.

Naturally, a city that has been such a focal point of history has bragging rights on a long list of distinguished people, more than just Clinton and Jay; for example, Charles Dewitt, delegate to the Continental Congress; Alton Parker, Democratic nominee for president in 1904; Peter Bogdanovich, movie director and film historian—the list is too long to grant it justice here. But there was one person, Walter B. Gibson, an author, quite unlike the rest.

Walter B. Gibson (1897–1985): Bard of the Shadow

Walter Gibson may have been the most prolific writer of his or any other generation. The author of more than 280 novels for his series *The Shadow*,[1]

---

1. Knowles, "Wizard of Words."

he wrote well over 175 other books—many on psychic phenomena, manuals of magic tricks, martial arts, spiritualism, card games, hypnotism, true crime, and his theory of dreams. He wrote puzzles for newspapers. He once said that he couldn't remember all the books he'd written. And he was a professional magician.

He was born in Germantown, Pennsylvania, in 1897. Like most magicians, his fascination with sleight-of-hand happened early. But his love for writing—and writing fast—would dominate most of his life. Fortunately, the two elements worked together. While attending Colgate University in Hamilton, New York, he wrote more than two hundred articles for a variety of publications on magic—an enormous output for a student carrying a full load of classes. Still in his youth, he joined a carnival performing as a magician, touring New Jersey and Long Island. His magic performances and mastery of a variety of tricks drew the attention of some of the most famous magicians of his day—which also led to his first book contracts.

He joined the Society of American Magicians in 1919. This led to his association with famed magician Howard Thurston, who was too busy wowing audiences to write his own books on magic, and contracted with Gibson to play ghostwriter. Harry Houdini himself was impressed with Gibson's feats of magic, but also with his skill at cranking out Thurston's books, and wanted him to do the same for him. Unfortunately, before Gibson could show him the two books he'd written for him, still in manuscript, Houdini died of a ruptured appendix after famously collapsing on stage October 31, 1926. Gibson then showed them to Houdini's widow Bessie, who, however, was consumed with managing the estate of her late husband and didn't want the added headache of seeking a publisher. She suggested he publish them under his own name, and one of the two did publish, *Popular Card Tricks*.[2]

For many years Bessie held annual seances attempting to reach her husband's spirit, but passed the responsibility on to Gibson in 1936, who continued until his own death.[3]

2. Shimeld, *Gibson and The Shadow*.
3. Trav, "Magic behind The Shadow."

Gibson would write several books on Houdini, his tricks, and his art of escape. In 1927 he published *First Principles of Astrology* under the pen name Wilber Gaston. Over the years he used enough pen names, seventy-nine, to make a hefty invitation list to a soiree. Yet, according to his son Robert, "Walter Gibson, in fact, did the work of seventy-nine people in his lifetime."[4]

Gibson was already writing fiction for such magazines as *Tales of Magic and Mystery* and *True Strange Stories*, when pulp magazine publishers Street and Smith contracted with him to write novel-length stories on a character called The Shadow, which had already been created for radio. He was to produce one for each issue of *The Shadow Magazine*, using the pen name Maxwell Grant. The first one appeared in their April–June issue, 1931. They became so popular that the magazine went to a monthly format, and eventually to twice each month, demanding twenty-four novel-length stories each year, a pace that would kill most writers. But he did it.[5]

Gibson liked chain-smoking and pounding typewriter ribbons to shreds, hour after hour. He was reputed to turn out as many as 10,000 to 15,000 words on a good day, or well over a million words per year for more than fifteen years. To put that number in perspective, most fiction writers call 1,200 words a good day's work for a rough draft. Later drafts and revisions can be glacially slow; whole chapters might be thrown away, or the writer might become dispirited and stop for a while. Sinclair Lewis claimed to write three thousand words per day. Hemingway said that anyone is lying who claims to write more than five hundred per diem. Gibson didn't revise, rewrite, or throw away chapters. But he did find time to research, even traveling to other cities to get a feel for whatever locale he planned to cast in his next Shadow adventure.[6]

He moved to Maine with his second wife Julia in 1936,[7] yet even in that pastoral setting he kept up the hammering pace. He did not write the

4. Gibson, "Foreword," in Shimeld, *Gibson and The Shadow*.
5. Shimeld.
6. Shimeld.
7. Shimeld.

5.1: The grave of Walter B. Gibson in Kingston.

famous *Shadow* radio plays. In fact, he felt that the radio Shadow lacked the complexity of his character. But those shows, with Orson Welles as The Shadow and Agnes Moorehead as his companion Margot Lane, helped sales of the pulp version.

With 282 of his Shadow novels in print he left the series to other writers (they eventually numbered 325). He concentrated on writing books on whatever subject tickled his inventive wit: *Houdini's Escapes and Magic*; *The Complete Beginner's Guide to Magic*; *Hypnotism*; and many more, including *The Complete Book of Divination and Prophecy*—although, as he grew older, not at the pace that he drove when he was a young man.

After time in New York City, he moved with his third wife Litzka (who coauthored *The Complete Book of Divination*) to Putnam Valley, New York, and finally settled in 1963 in Eddyville, near Kingston.[8] He and Litzka were local celebrities, performing magic shows, even making appearances on national TV. He died on December 6, 1985, after a debilitating stroke suffered the previous month.

Finding the Grave

Gibson is buried with Litzka in Montrepose Cemetery, 75 Montrepose Ave., Kingston, block D, section 2. From Broadway, which runs through the center of town, take West Chester Street south, all the way to the end. On your left will be Montrepose Avenue, and to your right you will see the cemetery gates. Or key the above address into your GPS. Once inside the gates, take the paved car path more or less straight ahead. In a few hundred feet you will see an unpaved car path to the right. On the corner is a double-bowed tree. About a hundred feet down the unpaved path, you will see his stone near the path under a small evergreen tree.

Sources

Gibson, Robert. "Foreword." In *Walter B. Gibson and The Shadow*, by Thomas J. Shimeld. Jefferson, NC: McFarland and Co., 2003. Kindle.

8. Shimeld.

Knowles, George. "Walter B. Gibson (A Wizard of Words)." Controversial.Com (2008). https://www.mysticlightpress.com/index.php@page_id=131.html.

Shimeld, Thomas J. *Walter B. Gibson and The Shadow.* Jefferson, NC: McFarland and Co., 2003. Kindle.

Trav, S. D. "Walter B. Gibson: The Magic behind The Shadow." *Travalanche.* Accessed April 18, 2023. https://travsd.wordpress.com/2020/09/12/walter-b-gibson-the-magician-behind-the-shadow.

6 Roxbury

John Burroughs

I love driving in the Catskills. The air is sweet, and I keep my windows down even in the cold. The temperature changes smartly from one elevation to another. It still has its old wooden barns, well-maintained—they haven't torn them down and replaced them with ugly aluminum buildings. Any town is worth stopping in, having lunch, and looking around. It will be good for your mental health.

The people of the Delaware County town of Roxbury, which includes the hamlet of Roxbury and the hamlet of Grand Gorge, seem enthused with keeping the past alive (they are a Preserve America Community). The Roxbury Nine is a "vintage" baseball team that plays by the 1898 rules of the game and wears the uniforms of that era: only the catcher is allowed to wear a mitt, and the rest have to make do with bare hands. And Kirkside Park, after years of neglect, has recently been restored to its nineteenth-century splendor. Jay Gould, the noted railroad magnate and Gilded Age robber baron, was born here, of humble beginnings, in 1836. His young neighbor and classmate, John Burroughs, could hardly have been more different from him.

John Burroughs (1837–1921): The Catskills' Great Naturalist and Philosopher

> We can use our scientific knowledge to improve and beautify the earth, or we can use it to deface and exhaust it. We can use it to poison the air, corrupt the waters, blacken the face of the country,

46

6.1: John Burroughs, 1837–1921. Library of Congress, Prints and Photographs Division, LC-USZ62-86843.

and harness our souls with loud and discordant noises, or we can use it to mitigate or abolish all these things.
—John Burroughs *The Summit of the Years*

In the 1980s I began to hear the phrase "sense of place." Poets talked about it. It seemed that every distractedly lonesome person longed for such a sense. It is inherently hard to define, but I'll give it a shot: a psychic rootedness, a familiarity with a place so deep that one knows not only the local people and who cooks the best stew, but the flora and fauna, the early signs of coming seasons, the geology, and what people were here before us—more or less what you get from reading Susan Augusta Fenimore Cooper (see East, chapter 4, Cooperstown).

John Burroughs, who certainly possessed that sense, did not live his entire life in the Catskill Mountains, but, as he said himself, he never truly took root anywhere else. Essayist and poet, he is most often described as a naturalist, but that hardly describes his capacity for observation: to read him is to know what grows in the Catskill Mountains, and its uses; the habits and quirks and songs of every species of bird; the animals (fox, beaver, skunk) and the hunt. His essay, "Phases of Farm Life," is essential reading for anyone who wants to know what a sense of place is, or was, in the Catskills in the nineteenth century—the hand-mowing and threshing of grain, cow and sheep raising, sugaring in the spring when the sap ran, the varieties of cottage manufacturing. To my lights he is the observer of record for the kinds of farming that predominated at various elevations in those mountains, for barn raisings, for farmers who dropped everything to help another farmer get in his crop.[1] He wrote:

> When the produce of the farm was taken a long distance to market,—that was an event too; the carrying away of the butter in the fall, for instance, to the river, a journey that occupied both ways four days. Then the family marketing was done in a few groceries. Some cloth, new caps and boots for the boys, and a dress, or a shawl, or a cloak for the girls were brought back, besides news and adventure, and strange tidings of the distant world.[2]

As the above indicates, Burroughs was already writing of the past; he was a witness for a world that was already changing. Indeed, he counted among his friends men who were major agents of change: Thomas Edison,

---

1. Burroughs, "Phases of Farm Life."
2. Burroughs.

Henry Ford, E. H. Harriman, and Theodore Roosevelt.[3] In a letter to Clara Barrus, his late-life companion and biographer,[4] he rhapsodizes over his love for the family farm, and pines for his deceased siblings and parents:

> We used, too, in my boyhood to make over two tons of butter annually, the care of which devolved mainly on her [his mother], from the skimming of the pans to the packing of the butter in tubs and firkins, though the churning was commonly done by a sheep or a dog . . . I can remember Mother's loom pounding away hour after hour in the chamber of an outbuilding where she was weaving a carpet, or cloth. I used to help do some of the quilling. . . . [5]

Catskills historian Alf Evers wrote, "As Burroughs climbed and walked, camped and fished among the Catskills, he wrote essay after essay. And these essays still have the power to let us see the Catskills through Burroughs's understanding eyes."[6]

In one of her books on Burroughs, Barrus points to essential differences between him and the better-known Henry David Thoreau; not only that Thoreau had a tendency to preach,[7] but that Thoreau became identified with Concord "almost to the exclusion of other fields,"[8] although this unfairly ignores Thoreau's writings on Maine and his excursions on Grand Island in Western New York.

But anyone looking to Burroughs to bear the standard for the environment and for preservation must sooner or later countenance his Faustian friendships with Gilded Age barons. He especially admired Ford, whom he judged an idealist,[9] for his appreciation of nature, for his interest in the

3. Renehan, *An American Naturalist*, 7.
4. See Central, chapter 20, Port Byron.
5. Barrus, "Ancestry and Family Life," in *Our Friend John Burroughs*.
6. Evers, *Catskills*, 548.
7. Barrus, "John Burroughs: An Appreciation," in *Our Friend John Burroughs*.
8. Barrus, "The Retreat of the Poet-Naturalist," in *Our Friend John Burroughs*.
9. Renehan, 275.

Transcendentalists, and for opening his purse to poor people he encountered—although he battled with the auto baron for his antisemitism.[10] Burroughs was a complex man. He deplored natural history museums for their stuffed animals and artificial representations of nature. And it is possible that if he could have seen ahead to what mass industrialization would cost the natural world—the polluted lakes, the bad air, the frightening indications of our changing climate, and how it would put humanity at an even greater psychic remove from the earth than he witnessed in his own time—he might have felt differently about Ford and his other wealthy friends, although he might have pronounced it inevitable. One has only to read Hayden Carruth, one of the most rural of recent American poets, to understand what has befallen the beloved family farms (see *Brothers, I Loved You All*). Burroughs's reputation, his gift to all of us who love the natural world, is his stunning body of writing. And there he sits, atop such a pile of books as would have exhausted most writers. Nor did he stick only to writing about farming, hunting, and the natural world. He was one of the earliest champions of Walt Whitman, and wrote two books about him. He was a poet himself, by the way, though not a particularly successful one.

He knew Ralph Waldo Emerson (and referred to him as his "spiritual father"),[11] John Muir,[12] and of course Whitman.[13] And as Evers writes, "He did not deny the cruelty and hostility that often face the individuals who make up the earth's living population but, like his master Ralph Waldo Emerson, he had faith in the essential goodness of life."[14] Or as Burroughs himself put it, "As a whole or in the long run, nature is good. The universe has not miscarried. . . . It is good to be here, and it must be equally good to go hence."[15]

10. Renehan, 276.
11. Joan Burroughs, director of John Burroughs Association. Email, May 19, 2022.
12. Renehan, 210–14.
13. Renehan, 154.
14. Evers, 548–49.
15. Burroughs, "Good Devils," 463.

He died in 1921 at the age of eighty-four, while on a train home from a sojourn out west.

Somewhere Wendell Berry has written that all it takes is one generation to stop performing some old task, such as making butter, weaving wool, or making soap, for us to forget how it is done, and some of us have a hell of a time trying to relearn it. My mother was the last person I knew who actually made butter at home with a hand churn, when she was a girl on a farm in Ohio, and she certainly regarded it as drudgery. When I decided that I was tired of insipid commercial butter, I had to go in search of how to make it with the electric utensils that I have in our home kitchen. (It was worth the trouble, by the way.) Burroughs's work, entertaining as it is, tells us not just quaint stories about what used to be, how things were done, but how things idyllically should be. And for that, he is not only a tall member of the pantheon of New York authors, but a national treasure.

His Books

Here is a short selection of his thirty-two books: *Locusts and Wild Honey* (1879), *Fresh Fields* (1884), *Signs and Seasons* (1886), *Whitman: A Study* (1896), *Squirrels and Other Fur Bearers* (1900), *Camping and Tramping with Roosevelt* (1906), *Leaf and Tendril* (1908), *The Summit of the Years* (1913), *Accepting the Universe* (1920), *The Last Harvest* (1922). It doesn't matter which book you start with. All his writing is lucid and absorbing. They are in many libraries in the state and readily available online from used bookstores. And of course, they are offered on Kindle—his soul rocks in the bosom of Amazon. But also, a fourteen-minute hand-colored silent film from 1914 that YouTube has made available, *A Day with John Burroughs*, will delight any of his admirers.

Finding the Grave

To get to Roxbury, take US 88 to Oneonta, then take Route 23 east to Route 30 and turn south; or you can take Route 23A northwest from Route

6.2: The grave of John Burroughs in Roxbury.

87 through Catskill Park to Route 30, and turn south. You're looking for Hardscrabble Road off Route 30, on your right, which will take you to Burroughs Memorial Road. Or you can set your GPS for 1067 Burroughs Memorial Rd., Roxbury, New York.

You'll see a small roadside park: the John Burroughs Memorial State Historic Site. There is no parking lot, but plenty of space to pull off. The main feature of the park is a two-sided sign with illustrations from Burroughs's life. His old house, Woodchuck Lodge, is nearby, well-maintained and open to visitors the first weekend of each month, May through October, but I wasn't lucky enough to land on one of those dates. It's an easy walk to his grave. From the park, you'll see a trail leading up the mountain ridge. In a short distance you'll find a gigantic black stone, which was his favorite perch and lookout point when he was a boy, which presents a marvelous panorama of mountain and valley. Nearby, and looking like a stone-made four-post bed, is the philosopher's grave.

Sources

Barrus, Clara. *Our Friend John Burroughs*. Public Domain Book. 1914. Kindle.

Burroughs, John. "The Good Devils: An Essay on Nature Optimism." *Art World* 3, no. 6 (1918): 463–66. https://doi.org/10.2307/25588372.

Burroughs, John. "Phases of Farm Life." In *Catskills: Selections from the Writings of John Burroughs*. Boston and New York: Houghton Mifflin, Riverside Press Cambridge, 1910. E-book.

Evers, Alf. *The Catskills: From Wilderness to Woodstock*. New York: Doubleday and Co., 1972.

Renehan, Edward J. *John Burroughs: An American Naturalist*. Post Mills, VT: Chelsea Green Publishing Co., 1992.

7　Saratoga Springs

Mansfield Tracy Walworth, Charles Brackett

I'll use any excuse to travel to Saratoga Springs. It has great restaurants and bars and a good used bookstore or two, plus the historic Revolutionary War battleground sites where the American rebel forces defeated Gen. John Burgoyne in 1777. Caffe Lena, on Phila Street, is the oldest continuously operating folk music spot in the United States, where Bob Dylan, Dave Van Ronk, Utah Phillips, and dozens of other folkies played in the early days of their careers—in the folk music world, it's hallowed ground. Saratoga is also home to Yaddo, perhaps the most famous artists and writers retreat in the country. Of course, most people come for the horseraces, resorts, and spas.

And once it was home to a novelist, more notorious than famous; and a screenwriter of Hollywood's golden age.

Mansfield Tracy Walworth (1830–1873):
Mad Leads to Madness

He was not the sort of fellow you would invite to a soiree, not a nice one anyway. Writers can often be complicated people, but Mansfield Tracy Walworth was far beyond the pale, even in literary circles. The son of New York State Chancellor Reuben Hyde Walworth, he was born into privilege in Saratoga Springs where the Walworths occupied a position of local royalty: a dignified old family with a lot of money. And a dark side that carried Mansfield to his early death.

What was a state chancellor, you might ask? The job was a carryover from British rule when New York State had a court of chancery like they

54

7.1: Mansfield Tracy Walworth. Courtesy of the Saratoga Springs History Museum.

have in Mama England. Reuben was the sixth chancellor, from 1826 until the post was eliminated in 1847 when the third New York State Constitution was adopted.[1] Chancellor Walworth held great power as head of the state judiciary, and acted as a kind of judge at large. He traveled the state judging cases from small claims to capital crimes, and in 1825 he left three murdering brothers dangling from gallows in Buffalo.[2] He sent a young New York City woman to the noose for the murder of her infant child, although there remained strong evidence that her lover was the guilty party.[3] But the chancellor also sat on the Court for the Trial of Impeachments and Correction of Errors, which could act as a court of appeals, so it was tough to challenge his decisions.[4] Like many prominent people of his time, he was a member of the Temperance Societies, as well as the Great Bible Tract. He was nominated to the US Supreme Court by President Tyler in 1844, but the senate did not act on the nomination. Four years later he ran unsuccessfully for New York governor.[5]

Reuben's own family was heading for sensational trouble, although the good chancellor, who died in 1867, was gone before the worst of it hit the paddle wheel.

His son Mansfield was a bright fellow who graduated from Union College in 1849 and became a lawyer,[6] and then a writer of sensationalist novels, low-brow stuff that would have disappeared long ago if they had not been written by such an infamous character. But in fact, *Warwick, or the Lost Nationalities of America*; *Hotspur*; *A Tale of the Old Dutch Manor*; and *Lulu: A Tale of the National Hotel Poisoning*, among others, are still available online in both print and e-book format. The last was a fictionalization of a mysterious miasma which in January 1857 struck some four hundred guests of the National Hotel in Washington, DC, resulting in more than thirty deaths, including several congressmen and

1. Historical Society of the New York Courts, "New York State Court of Chancery."
2. O'Brien, *Fall of the House of Walworth*, 55–56.
3. O'Brien, 58–59.
4. O'Brien, 60.
5. Walworth, *Walworths of America*, 120.
6. Walworth, 140.

the nephew of the new president-elect James Buchanan, who himself was taken ill. Arsenic poisoning was suspected as an attempt on Buchanan's life; water-born bacteria was also suspected, but the offending bug was never identified.[7] The *New York Times* commented that Walworth's novels were "intended for and only bought by the numerous class of persons who admire glittering and gaudy descriptions and sentimental storytelling."[8]

A Confederate sympathizer during the Civil War, he was arrested in Washington in suspicion of spying for the South. But wealth and privilege saved him from prison, and possibly even the gallows. He was released into the company of his father and ordered not to leave the house in Saratoga for the remainder of the war.[9] Or else.

But allow me to back up a few years. In 1852, Mansfield married Ellen Hardin Walworth,[10] a Kentuckian and the daughter of the chancellor's second wife's previous marriage—in other words, he married his stepsister. That was actually legal everywhere in the United States except Virginia.[11] To everyone's dismay, he turned out to be an abusive husband, both physically and verbally.[12] After having five children—three daughters and two sons—and after several attempts at reconciliation, the couple divorced. Mansfield moved to a boardinghouse in Manhattan, cut off from his family and his considerable inheritance.[13]

From there he wrote letters back to Ellen, threatening to beat and even kill her and the rest of his family. These were vile rants of a mentally ill and obviously dangerous man. Eventually their nineteen-year-old son Frank who suffered from epilepsy, and who was very close to his mother, began intercepting the letters and keeping them from her.[14] He decided to take matters into his own hands, and on the morning of June 2, 1873,

7. O'Brien, 135.

8. "Terrible Parricide," *New York Times*, 8.

9. O'Brien, 28.

10. Walworth, 141.

11. Mueller, "In What States Is It Illegal?"

12. O'Brien, 138, 160.

13. O'Brien, 163, 144–46.

14. O'Brien, 182–83.

he boarded a train in Saratoga bound for Manhattan. He left word for his father at the boardinghouse, asking him to come to his hotel room in the Sturtevant House.[15]

The following morning, June 3, Mansfield knocked on his son's door. What exactly was said between them no one knows, but Frank fired four shots into his father with his Colt revolver, and then walked promptly to the police precinct station on Thirtieth Street between Sixth and Seventh Avenue. Stepping calmly to the desk, he said to the officer in command, "My name is Frank H. Walworth; I have just shot and killed my father, Mansfield T. Walworth in the Sturtevant House, and here is my pistol," according to the New York Times which called it "a case of unusual repulsiveness."[16]

Frank was remanded to the Tombs awaiting trial. Only a month later, at the age of twenty, he received a life sentence for second degree murder.[17] But this is where the story takes another extraordinary turn.

His mother, Ellen, was determined to win a pardon for her son on grounds of insanity, and enlisted the aid of numerous doctors as well as poet William Cullen Bryant who had a solid reputation in the Republican Party.[18] Frank was pardoned in 1877 by Governor Lucius Robinson.[19] He was freed, but his life was short: he died in 1886 from a lung disease probably contracted while in prison.[20]

Yet, for all that, the murder of her husband liberated Ellen. She enrolled in New York University to study law, and after graduation, practiced in New York and Washington, DC. She lived a long life as a lawyer and public servant; she wrote numerous articles on science and historic preservation, became an authority on the Saratoga battlefields, raised funds for the restoration of George Washington's home in Mount Vernon,

---

15. "Terrible Parricide," 8.
16. "Terrible Parricide," 8.
17. "Walworth Tragedy," New York Times, 1.
18. O'Brien, 253.
19. Murder by Gaslight, "Walworth Patricide."
20. O'Brien, 276.

7.2: The general area of the unmarked grave of Mansfield Tracy Walworth in Saratoga.

and was one of the four principal founders of the Daughters of the American Revolution (DAR). She died in Washington, DC, in 1915 and was carried home to Saratoga for burial.[21]

Finding the Grave

You *can't* find the grave, not really. Several members of the Walworth family are buried in Greenridge Cemetery in Saratoga Springs, and in fact he is too. But according to cemetery staff, they are not entirely sure where

21. Sanders, "Kentucky Genesis," 364.

Mansfield Tracy Walworth is. They know he is buried in the old section A, near his older brother Clarence, who was a priest—in fact, one of the founders of the Paulist Priests. But either there is no marker remaining, or the grave is marked by one of a couple small stones nearby that are now illegible. Apparently, no one felt inspired to tend it, which speaks volumes.

But Ellen's grave is worth a visit. From South Broadway (Route 9), just a little south of the business district, turn east on Lincoln Avenue, and then very shortly turn right on Greenridge Place, a short cul-de-sac. At the very end of the street, you will see the portals of Greenridge Cemetery. Greenridge is part new section, and part old, which can be confusing, but these directions will get you to the spot.

Once through the front portals, turn left onto an unpaved path and stay on it as it takes a sharp turn to the left along the perimeter fence. Make a right turn passing behind the Civil War Memorial. Old section B will be straight ahead. Stay on the path and stop next to the sign for old section A. A few strides away, and to your left, is the modest spire for Ellen Hardin Walworth. From the sign, follow the lane back directly to the area near the fence. There you will see Fr. Clarence's crypt, and the area of grass under which lies the infamous Mansfield.

Charles Brackett (1892–1969): Of Hollywood's Golden Age

When was Hollywood's Golden Age? To most movie fans, including those of us who call ourselves cinephiles, it was the era in which our favorite films were made, whenever that happened to be. But to film critics and academics, it was the long stretch of years between the mid-silent era and the 1960s, the period when movies climbed from mere enchantment to art, when all the plastic elements of filmmaking were mastered and the pantheon of great actors and writers and directors was established in the chaos of Hollywood. One of the great names of that period was screenwriter and producer Charles Brackett, born in Saratoga Springs, New York.

Much of what has been written about Charles Brackett—books, articles, theses, and so forth—are dominated by the figure of movie director

Billy Wilder. This is because of a widely held notion that Brackett worked in Wilder's shadow. Sam Staggs, in a 2002 book on the making of the movie *Sunset Boulevard*, says that this is because of the prominence of the "auteurs," that is, directors who are seen as the dominant creative force in the making of any film.[22] But Wilder himself, Staggs said, "never suggested that Brackett was anything less than the perfect partner."[23]

Indeed, as a team they made most of their best films, with Wilder as director and Brackett as producer, often coauthoring the screenplays. For creative control of the finished work, it was the best combo possible. In their heyday they were called "Hollywood's perfect marriage," the kind of team rare in the industry, such as Ismail Merchant and James Ivory or Joel and Ethan Coen. Their auspicious meeting was on August 17, 1936. Brackett wrote in his diary that day that Paramount Pictures wanted to take him away from the screenplay for *Tightwad* to put him on another project, and he planned to stage a "grouchy refusal." But he "[l]earned that the other story is *Bluebeard's Eighth Wife*, for Claudette Colbert, Ernst Lubitsch directing. I am to be teamed with Billy Wilder, a young Austrian I've seen about for a year or two and like very much. I accepted the job joyfully."[24] Besides, any screenwriter in those days would jump at the chance to work with Lubitsch.

A match made in Hollywood, if not quite heaven. Wilder was not the smooth and eloquent writer that Brackett was, a Harvard Law grad who joined the staff of the *New Yorker* in the late 1920s as a drama critic and published four novels before being lured to Hollywood, landing there in 1930 just as the talkies were coming into their own.[25] Wilder needed Brackett's fluency with words.

Of the two men, Brackett was the conservative Republican, an impeccably mannered man, born to a Saratoga banking family. But, Staggs says, his novels demonstrate that he was no prude. *The Counsel of the Ungodly*;

22. Staggs, *Close-Up on Sunset Boulevard*, 37.
23. Staggs, 38.
24. Slide, *It's the Pictures That Got Small*, 86.
25. Staggs, 5.

Week-End, That Last Infirmity, American Colony; and one more while he was already gainfully employed in the film biz, *Entirely Surrounded*, "are urbane, edgy stories, impatient with bourgeois values, dark, and yes, cynical. They also have a surprising number of homosexual characters," which, at the time, would have been daring.[26]

But then came the divorce. In *Sunset Boulevard*, Gloria Swanson plays Norma Desmond, a has-been film goddess who traps William Holden as her screenwriter/gigolo in her pipedream of making an enormous comeback. Of all the Hollywood movies about Hollywood, this one was probably the greatest, and it was Wilder and Brackett's finest, their best collaboration, a true classic. It was also their last together. Sometime between the end of the shooting schedule and its release, Wilder told Brackett, almost casually, that it was time to end their partnership. Brackett was thunderstruck.[27] Yet, the split was amiable, at least outwardly. Wrote Tom Allen, "Like a truly 'happy couple,' even after the 1950 divorce, neither ever felt compelled to jealously ascribe sole inspiration for portions of dialogue or plot to himself."[28]

He and Wilder shared the Oscar for Best Adapted Screenplay for *The Lost Weekend* (1945), from the novel by Charles Jackson, which Brackett also produced and won Best Picture;[29] and they shared Best Original Screenplay with D. M. Marshman Jr. for *Sunset Boulevard* (1950). After his split with Wilder, Brackett shared another Best Original Screenplay for *Titanic* (1953) with Richard L. Breen and Walter Reisch.

In fact, he worked on many more films as writer and producer after the split, many of them memorable: *Niagara* (1953), *The Mating Season* (1951), *The Girl in the Red Velvet Swing* (1955), and *Teenage Rebel* (1956), although often he acted only as producer, such as on *The King and I* (1956) and *The Wayward Bus* (1957). The last film that he both wrote and produced was *Journey to the Center of the Earth* (1959), adapted from the Jules Verne classic.

26. Staggs, 44.
27. Staggs, 45.
28. Allen, "Bracketting Wilder," 29.
29. See Central, chapter 18, Newark.

7.3: The spire of the Brackett family plot in Saratoga. Charles Brackett's footstone is in the foreground.

In 1957 he received the Honorary Oscar "For Outstanding Service to the Academy." He made his last film, *State Fair*, in 1962. It was time to retire.

Finding the Grave

From South Broadway (Route 9), just a little south of the business district, turn east on Lincoln Avenue, and then very shortly turn right on Greenridge Place, a short cul-de-sac. At the very end of the street, you will see the portals of Greenridge Cemetery. Shortly after entering the gates of Greenridge Cemetery, you will see a wood-frame storage building with a front porch straight before you. Park there, or drive up the hill. The Brackett family spire is visible almost straight ahead, and an easy walk. Charles Brackett's footstone is among those of his many family members around its base.

Sources

Mansfield Tracy Walworth

"F. H. Walworth Pardoned. Governor Robinson Orders His Release." *New York Times*, August 2, 1877.

"The Four Founders." Daughters of the American Revolution. Accessed April 18, 2023. https://www.dar.org/archives/four-founders.

Mueller, Jennifer. "In What States Is It Illegal to Marry Step-Siblings?" *Law for Families*. Accessed April 18, 2023. https://www.lawforfamilies.com/12307129 -states-illegal-marry-stepsiblings.html.

"New York State Court of Chancery." Historical Society of the New York Courts. Accessed April 18, 2023. https://history.nycourts.gov/court/court-chancery/.

O'Brien, Geoffrey. *The Fall of the House of Walworth*. New York: St. Martins, 2011.

Sanders, Robert Stuart. "The Kentucky Genesis of the Daughters of the American Revolution Manifested in the Life of Mrs. Ellen Hardin Walworth." *Register of Kentucky State Historical Society* 43, no. 145 (1945): 358–64. http://www.jstor.org/stable/23372482.

"A Terrible Parricide. Mansfield Tracy Walworth Killed by His Own Son—Surrender of the Murderer." *New York Times*, June 4, 1873.

Walworth, Clarence A. *The Walworths of America: Comprising Five Chapters of Family History with Additional Chapters of Genealogy*. Albany, NY: The Weed-Parsons Printing Co., 1897.

"The Walworth Patricide." *Murder by Gaslight*, May 25, 2013. http://www.murder bygaslight.com/2013/05/the-walworth-patricide.html.

"The Walworth Tragedy." *New York Times*, July 6, 1873.

Charles Brackett

Allen, Tom. "Bracketting Wilder." *Film Comment* 18, no. 3 (1982): 29–31. http:// www.jstor.org/stable/43452873.

Slide, Anthony, ed. *"It's the Pictures That Got Small": Charles Brackett on Billy Wilder and Hollywood's Golden Age*. Foreword by Jim Moore. New York: Columbia Univ. Press, 2015.

Staggs, Sam. *Close-Up on Sunset Boulevard: Billy Wilder, Norma Desmond, and the Dark Hollywood Dream*. New York: St. Martin's Griffin, 2002.

8   Stamford

Ned Buntline (Edward Zane Carroll Judson)

Stamford, New York, is a village in the lower elevations of the Catskill Mountains near the Delaware River. One gets the sense that it hasn't changed very much over many years, despite the presence of a few chain stores and ATMs. Small, comely, it would be a comfortable place to get snowed in. Part of the village is in the town of Stamford, part in Harpersfield. I drove south on Route 10 from the New York State Thruway Exit 29. You can approach it from Route 23, but I found that scenic Route 10 is rewarding. A little north of Cobleskill is a stone marker, "Near this spot, Catherine Merckley, on October 18, 1780, fleeing on horseback from the Indians was shot and scalped by Seths Henry." This event followed by two and a half years the Battle of Cobleskill, May 30, 1778, in which Loyalists and Iroquois led by Mohawk leader Joseph Brandt attacked and destroyed much of Cobleskill.

Stamford was founded in 1792, the first settlers having arrived ten years before. In 1814, when the nation was at war with Britain, little Stamford contributed more than twenty officers and around a hundred and twenty foot soldiers, which must have left farms and businesses short of strong-backed youth. But the war on the home front that year was with wolves encroaching on farmers' livestock, and a five-dollar bounty was paid for each wolf shot.

The oldest Stamford house on the west side of the Delaware River was the birthplace in 1823 of Edward Zane Carroll Judson, aka E. Z. C. Judson, aka Colonel Judson, later famous for his dime novels written under his penname Ned Buntline. His great-grandfather Samuel Judson was one

of the town's first settlers. Broad traveler, adventurer, luxury seeker, blo-
viator, and con artist though Ned was, the quiet bucolic Stamford would
remain his hometown where he would shelter from his life's storms.

Ned Buntline (1823–1886): Hero with Many Masks

Ned Buntline was about as complicated and flamboyant as any author
who ever lived, more complex than Walworth in chapter 7, but without
the malice. He campaigned for temperance, but alcohol was probably the
only thing that he was ever temperate about—and that only sometimes.
In fact, he was known to head to a saloon after giving a fiery temperance
speech, with some of the audience in tow who had signed the pledge.[1] In
addition to the above-mentioned virtues, he was also a bigamist, a bail
jumper, and a natural-born showman. In his best years he was, at least
by his own calculations, the wealthiest author in America; money he
earned from the sale of the dime novels that he cranked out, one after
another,[2] at least four hundred of them, mostly adventure yarns. Short,
quick reads.

Before he gained fame as a novelist he wrote stories for magazines,
most notably the *Knickerbocker*,[3] a respected literary journal, which is
curious considering the hack quality of his later work. But Buntline also
founded and published several magazines, as well as a scandal newspaper,
Ned Buntline's Own, which carried a regular feature about himself from
which many of the fables of his life gained currency,[4] and thus are hard to
corroborate as anything close to fact.

Many biographers have tried to nail down his personality and found
themselves in a thicket of contradictions. But all have agreed on his noted
bonhomie. According to the editor of one collection of his stories, Clay
Reynolds, "He seems to have been one of the most personally charming

---

1. Reynolds, "Great Rascal," in *Hero of a Hundred Fights*.
2. Reynolds, "Great Rascal."
3. Bradshaw, *So Much Larger Than Life*, 12.
4. Bradshaw, 18.

individuals of his era."[5] As biographer T. M. Bradshaw has written, "Actual crimes, schemes, and lying manipulations aside, he was known as pleasant company, a genial, good-natured, friendly man"; also, "intelligent and creative but completely heedless of real consequences."[6]

Historians have debated the old story that Buntline special-ordered the Colt company's long-barreled .45 revolver, gave it his name, the Buntline Special, and presented them as gifts to some of his western friends such as Wyatt Earp, Bat Masterson, and others. However, this story has largely been debunked as frontier mythology.[7]

When he was still a boy, his father moved the family from Stamford to Philadelphia so that he could study law. Ned, hating the cramped city, snuck aboard a West Indies fruit ship. He may have lied about his age to the captain who put him to work as a cabin boy, since he was only about twelve years old. It was the beginning of a short career working on merchant ships.[8] He must have lied about his age again when he joined the Navy in 1837, aged fourteen.

Most of his accounts of his heroic Navy years are probably yarns, but one bona fide adventure occurred one night aboard a small boat, on route to the Brooklyn Navy Yard with a load of sand when it capsized after colliding with a ferry in the dark, and seventeen men went overboard into the icy water of the East River. Ned's actions helping the men stay above water until rescue led to his appointment by President Martin Van Buren to midshipman aboard the warship *Boston*.[9]

His name on his gravestone in Stamford Cemetery is Col. E. Z. C. Judson, a rank that he never held. As a midshipman in the Navy during the Seminoles Wars he saw little action. He claimed that in the Civil War he fought on with General Sherman after Appomattox; in fact, he was once jailed for desertion, often cited for drunkenness and insubordination, and

5. Reynolds, "Great Rascal."
6. Bradshaw, 8.
7. Shillingberg, "Wyatt Earp and the Buntline Special Myth," 113–54.
8. Reynolds, "Great Rascal."
9. Bradshaw, 11.

dishonorably discharged in August 1864. While on furlough in Washington, he went to Mathew Brady's studio and, sitting himself in the famous chair in which Lincoln had been photographed, he posed in a colonel's coat—an act of impersonating an officer[10] that could have landed him in the brig again. But he claimed the rank of colonel for the rest of his days.[11]

His relationships with women were often tempestuous. He married at least nine times. According to biographer Julia Bricklin, he did not bother to divorce several of the women before remarrying.[12] In New York City, a woman named Kate Hastings accosted him on the street and thrashed him with a horsewhip for writing in his *Ned Buntline's Own* that she operated a brothel.[13]

One incident in which he was shot and wounded and lynched, and yet survived, made news far and wide. In 1846, he was in Nashville writing for one of his magazines when he became involved with Mary Porterfield, the teenage wife of Robert Porterfield, fireman and auctioneer's assistant. Both Buntline and Mrs. Porterfield claimed innocence, but various people had seen them together. Robert Porterfield, deranged with jealousy, went looking for Buntline with a gun, and fired several shots at him; Ned returned fire and mortally wounded Porterfield with a bullet to his head, and then turned himself over to the law.[14]

In an apparently unruly courtroom, he was shot and wounded by Porterfield's brother. He was released, but not before a crowd of outraged citizens dragged him from the jail and lynched him, only to be rescued when friends arrived and cut the rope.[15] A variety of somewhat conflicting accounts from the time describe him being chased from the courthouse and hiding in the nearby City Hotel, then leaping from a third-floor window, which apparently left him with a permanent limp.

10. Bradshaw, 44.
11. Reynolds, "Great Rascal."
12. Bricklin, "Many Wives of Ned Buntline," 1.
13. McIver, "Adventures of a Rogue Writer," 18.
14. Bradshaw, 19–21.
15. McIver, 1–15ff.

Following the incident, Buntline wrote in the *Knickerbocker,* "Mr. Porterfield was a brave, good, but rash and hasty man; and deeply, deeply do I regret the necessity of his death. His wife is as innocent as an angel."[16]

In the years following the Civil War, the United States had a fairly large standing army in the West engaged in the Indian Wars. Buntline knew that most of them were garrisoned for long periods of time with little to do, and so he gave them what he knew they'd love: sensational novels mythologizing white American heroism in the West, such as *Buckskin Sam the Scalp-Taker* and *Norwood, Or, Life on the Prairie.*

To many of his eastern readers the West was a mystery, and so they had little cause to doubt him. He is most identified with the western novels,[17] although he wrote far more sea adventures—*The King of the Sea: A Tale of the Fearless and Free; The Queen of the Sea, Or, Our Lady of the Ocean: A Tale of Love and Chivalry*—or hardscrabble and adventure novels—*The Virgin of the Sun: A Historical Romance of the Last Revolution in Peru.* Ned was especially fond of hunting and fishing, and his characters were also lovers of the open wilds, on land or sea.

In 1868, on a trip to Nebraska, he met a young man named William F. Cody who had been working as a civilian scout for the US Army under Gen. Philip Sheridan. Buntline liked his flamboyant personality. He wrote a purportedly nonfiction book about him and his supposed exploits among Indians, and gave him a name—Buffalo Bill. He didn't invent the name—it was a common moniker in the West at that time—but he made it stick to Cody. *Buffalo Bill, the King of the Border Men* was serialized in the *New York Weekly,* beginning in December 1869.[18] When Cody read the book, most of the heroics were news to him. Buntline also made him out to be a temperance advocate like himself, which was another stretch of imagination, since Cody was fond of his tipple.

But Bill too had a flair for show business, and Buntline made him famous, organizing and promoting a traveling show for him, *Scouts of*

---

16. Bradshaw, 21.

17. Reynolds, "Going West," in *Hero of a Hundred Fights*

18. Reynolds, "Going West."

the Prairie, beginning in Chicago in 1872. The entertainment consisted of western scouts on horseback, Indians—sometimes real, sometimes actors—and a rough, hurriedly written script for good old-fashioned western shootouts.

The show was a success, repeated many times over, moving around the eastern half of the country from one big top to another. But it hit one snag in St. Louis when Buntline was arrested in his hotel for jumping bail on a charge of incitement to riot in the city twenty years before, which he probably assumed had been forgotten. Authorities confiscated the cashbox before he skipped town again.

Buntline wasn't one to let adversity spoil his day. When Buffalo Bill decided to split with Buntline and run his own show, to be called *Buffalo Bill's Wild West*, casting none other than Wild Bill Hickock to play Buntline's part (after all, unlike Buntline, Hickock was a handsome fellow), Buntline started a rival show, bringing real Comanches instead of actors, and two white scouts, Arizona Frank and Dashing Charlie. And, anyway, he made easier money on Bill by writing the western novels *Buffalo Bill's Best Shot*, *Buffalo Bill's Last Trail*, and *Buffalo Bill's Last Victory*.

Certainly he helped to create the romantic and largely mythical images of the American West, perpetuated by authors like Zane Grey and Louis L'Amour and traded on by Hollywood actors and directors such as Tom Mix, William S. Hart, John Wayne, John Ford, Howard Hawks, and multiple TV shows of the 1950s. He surely made his mark.

Gravity caught up with Edward Zane Carroll Judson, aka Ned Buntline, on July 16, 1886, when he died of congestive heart failure in his Stamford home. In the last months of his life, he was confined to an "invalid chair," tended to by his last wife Anna Fulton. But the mayhem was not over. At least two former wives went after his Civil War pension. And Anna was forced to sell their house to make good on his debts.[19]

Another note of interest: Buffalo Bill Cody had a home in Rochester from 1873 to 1877 at 10 New York St. with his wife Louisa and their children, daughters Arta and Orra, and son Kit Carson; a home base for his

19. Bradshaw, 77–79ff.

8.1: The grave of Ned Buntline and family in Stamford.

family while he was on the road with his show.[20] According to historian James Hughes, Cody taught shooting skills to Kit in the backyard of the New York Street house.[21] However, Kit died of scarlet fever there, aged five, and was buried in Mount Hope Cemetery in the city. Later, while

20. Andjelic, "Mount Hope and Buffalo Bill Cody," 2–3.
21. Hughes, "Those Who Passed Through," 80.

they were living in North Platt, Nebraska, eleven-year-old Orra died of fever and was brought to Mount Hope for burial. Arta, twenty-eight, died of meningitis in Spokane, Washington, in 1904, and was also brought to Rochester to be buried next to her siblings.[22]

Finding the Grave

Follow Route 23 (Main Street) east out of the village. Turn right on Tower Mountain Road where you will find two cemeteries directly across from each other. Stamford Cemetery is on the right. The official address is 2 Mountain Rd., Stamford, NY, 12167, if you want to use your GPS. From the small parking lot inside the gate, follow the car path straight back for a couple hundred feet. When you see a stone for Grant, turn right; the tall brown spire is visible from there. As mentioned above, his name of the stone is Col. E. Z. C. Judson 1823–1886, also here are Irene A. Judson, "d. 1881 in her 4th year"; E. Z. C. Judson Jr. 1881–1894; and his last wife Mrs. Anna Judson [no date].

Sources

Andjelic, Milos. "Mount Hope and Buffalo Bill Cody." *Epitaph: The Friends of Mount Hope Cemetery* 31, no. 4 (Fall 2012).

Bradshaw, T. M. *Ned Buntline: So Much Larger Than Life.* N.p., 2019. Kindle.

Bricklin, Julia. "The Many Wives of Ned Buntline." HistoryNet.com. 2021. Accessed April 18, 2023. https://www.historynet.com/many-wives-ned-buntline.

Hughes, James. "Those Who Passed Through: Unusual Visits to Unlikely Places." *New York History* 89, no. 1 (2008): 76–81. http://www.jstor.org/stable/2318 3508.

McIver, Stuart. "The Adventures of a Rogue Writer." *South Florida Sun-Sentinel*, January 12, 1992. https://www.sun-sentinel.com/news/fl-xpm-1992-01-12-920 1030022-story.html.

Monaghan, Jay. *The Great Rascal: The Life and Adventures of Ned Buntline.* Boston: Little, Brown and Co., 1952.

22. Andjelic, 2–3.

Munsell, W. W. "The History of Delaware County: Town of Stamford," *Genealogy and Historical Site*. Accessed April 18, 2023. https://www.dcnyhistory.org/books/munstam.html.

Reynolds, Clay, ed. *Ned Buntline, The Hero of a Hundred Fights: Collected Stories from the Dime Novel King, from Buffalo Bill to Wild Bill Hickock*. New York: Union Square, 2011.

Shillingberg, William B. "Wyatt Earp and the Buntline Special Myth." *Kansas Historical Quarterly* 42, no. 2 (Summer 1976): 113–54. https://www.kshs.org/p/kansas-historical-quarterly-wyatt-earp-and-the-buntline-special-myth/13255.

9 Woodstock

Howard Koch, Hervey White,
Paula Danziger, Janine Pommy Vega

As a young musician enamored with the folk music movement in the 1960s, Woodstock was, to me, a kind of Mecca, an off-the-path place in the forested Catskill Mountains with a mysterious psychic magnetism that had drawn some of the song-makers I admired most. It had lured them there from the harried smoke of New York City to settle down in relative quiet. Here were Tim Hardin, John Herald, Peter Yarrow, Maria Muldaur, and of course Bob Dylan, as well as some electrified acts that drew from folk tradition: Paul Butterfield and his Blues Band, and Levon Helm, Robbie Robertson, and the others that made up The Band. Not that you'd expect to run into any of them hanging around in front of the drugstore. But they were there, in this little town, part of its artsy milieu. Others came just to perform: Dave Van Ronk, Patrick Sky, Mississippi John Hurt, Joan Baez, Pete Seeger, even Lead Belly himself.

But they were really just a new wave. Woodstock had been an art haven for longer than any living memory. Hudson River School painter Thomas Cole was here more than a hundred years before the folks with the banjos showed up. The Byrdcliffe Arts Colony was started in 1902 on the lower slope of Overlook Mountain; although much of its property was sold off long ago to keep the Byrd afloat, it is now the Byrdcliffe Arts Guild, a not-for-profit and the oldest continuously functioning arts and crafts colony in America. The Art Students League of New York came here in 1906, now called the Woodstock School of Art.

My girlfriend was studying at SUNY New Paltz in 1969, and one spring weekend day she impulsively rode her bicycle twenty-seven miles north to Woodstock. There, cycling around, she heard a band playing in a building. It sounded pretty good, so she peeked inside and found the Paul Butterfield Blues Band rehearsing. Friendly fellows, easy to hang out with. In fact, Paul Butterfield and his wife invited her home for dinner and to sleep over. The next morning, Butterfield put her bike in the trunk of his car and drove her back to college. She recalled that all the way, he kept saying, "I can't believe you rode your bike this far!"

It was the kind of thing that could only happen in Woodstock. But later that year the atmosphere changed because of the Woodstock music festival, although it was actually held in Bethel, some sixty miles away. Long after the revelers went home, and the trip tent folded up and all the garbage picked up, hordes of curious travelers and stargazers followed the signs to Woodstock and the nearby hamlet of Bearsville. If not for the publicity-storm from the festival, many of them would never have heard of the little town where living legends were now keeping out of sight, pulling their curtains tight, and sending errand boys for their groceries. To some degree that change has been permanent: sometimes it's called the most famous small town in America, although many of those deified stars of the '60s have died or moved on, to be replaced by a new generation of artists.

I first came to Woodstock with a friend on a long weekend in '69 to camp in the Catskills. The traffic in town was astonishing. A policeman told me that at midday it was averaging forty-five minutes for a car to get through town. That night we went to a free concert nearby, probably at Byrdcliffe, featuring the band Fear Itself with the amazing Ellen McIlwaine singing. Traffic notwithstanding, Woodstock was a beautiful place, with a current of psychic energy and mystique.

Many writers settled there and in surrounding towns, and some rest in the small Woodstock Memorial Society Cemetery, also called the Artists Cemetery, a short walk from the center of town. Route 212 runs through the middle of town, where it turns a corner at the small village green. At that point, turn north onto Rock City Road. On the right, shortly after you turn, is the large and prominent Woodstock Cemetery. Artists Cemetery is to the left side of the road, easier to miss, beyond a parking lot. Turn left on the short Mountain View Road, which runs along the perimeter of the parking lot and takes you directly to the cemetery. Or key 12 Mountain-view Ave., Woodstock, NY, 12498 into your GPS. Artists Cemetery occupies slopes behind and to the right of a traditional, older cemetery. Unlike the older cemetery, Artist's Cemetery graves are flat stones and plates (save for a couple marked by boulders and a shrine at the bottom of the back slope for the ashes of Radcliffe Whitehead, the founder of Byrdcliffe), and thus it is difficult to note precise landmarks.

It is the resting place of sports commentator Heywood Hale Broun, and of numerous artists, including Milton Avery, Petra Cabot, Bolton Brown, Frank Swift Chase, and Philip Guston. But writers' graves abound: Howard Koch, Paula Danziger, Janine Pommy Vega, and Hervey White.

Howard Koch (1901–1995): Forging Ahead

Howard Koch, best known as the principal screenwriter for the classic film *Casablanca*, settled in Woodstock with his family in the late 1950s. They had moved to Europe in 1951 because he was blacklisted for his work on the movie *Mission to Moscow*. When he was cleared to work in the United States again, Woodstock offered the quiet and easy surroundings that had eluded them in New York City and Hollywood.

He was born in New York, went to Bard College, and gave up a legal career to write plays, three of which were produced on Broadway,[1] before he was hired by John Houseman in 1938 to write radio scripts for Mercury Theater, the New York theater company run by Houseman and Orson Welles that was producing radio dramas adapted from literature.[2]

The best known of these, of course, was *The War of the Worlds*, which Koch had titled *Invasion from Mars*, and which was broadcast on the evening of October 30, 1938—Halloween. Welles and Houseman were demanding bosses, and Koch worked like the devil on the script, so much

1. Gossow, "Howard Koch Dies at 95," D17.
2. Koch, *As Time Goes By*, 3.

so that after the broadcast he went to bed and slept like a moon rock, unaware that the world outside was dissolving in panic over what they had heard on the radio. Many believed that extraterrestrials were really on the attack in New Jersey, while others thought that the war they had been worrying about was finally happening, and that Germany was striking New Jersey. Maybe New York and Washington would be next.[3]

Not until he saw a newspaper in a barbershop the next morning did Koch realize what he had helped to cause. According to him, "the submerged anxieties of tens of thousands of Americans surfaced and coalesced in a flood of terror that swept the country."[4] CBS switchboards had been jammed.[5] Police stations fielded hundreds of calls, and people fled in their cars in all directions.[6]

Fortunately, no one died of shock or committed suicide. And the country slowly got a grip on itself before Welles and company could be pilloried.[7] But Koch credited popular columnist Dorothy Thompson for putting it all in perspective. "[F]ar from blaming Mr. Orson Welles," she wrote, "he ought to be given a Congressional medal and a national prize for having made the most amazing and important contribution to the social sciences." She went on,

> If people can be frightened out of their wits by mythical men from Mars, they can be frightened into fanaticism by the fear of Reds, or convinced that America is in the hands of sixty families, or aroused to revenge against any minority, or terrorized into subservience to leadership because of any imaginable menace.[8]

After the infamous broadcast, Koch took another shot at play writing, and then moved on to Hollywood like Welles himself, and began

---

3. Koch, *Panic Broadcast*, 15, 16.
4. Koch, *Panic Broadcast*, 16, 24.
5. Koch, *As Time Goes By*, 5.
6. "Radio Listeners in Panic," 1.
7. Koch, *Panic Broadcast*, 24.
8. Koch, *Panic Broadcast*, 92.

working on screenplays.[9] One of his first was *Sea Hawk* (1940), an Errol Flynn feature directed by Michael Curtiz, which Koch wrote with veteran screenwriter Seton I. Miller. Later he worked on *Sergeant York* (1941)—the Cary Cooper classic about an American pacifist who becomes a World War I hero after deciding to "render unto Caesar that which is Caesar's."[10] On this venture he worked with three other writers, one of which was John Huston, whom he had worked with on the New York stage, and who would become famous later that year for directing *The Maltese Falcon*.

Koch's most famous effort was *Casablanca*, again working with Michael Curtiz. He was one of three screenwriters—twin brothers Julius and Philip Epstein and Koch—working from a never-produced play by Murray Burnett and Joan Allison. But partway into the project, the Epsteins were taken off and put on a different script. It was crisis time— little progress had been made, and shooting was about to begin. Koch had to take what he had, some one-liners and virtually no storyline or structure, and forge ahead full steam, making up scenes as he went along, barely keeping up with the filming schedule, hoping it wouldn't all fall apart.[11] At some point, Ingrid Bergman asked Koch, "Who will I end up with?" He couldn't tell her, because he hadn't gotten that far. He finished the script on the last day of shooting.[12] So, in that famous last scene when Bergman's Ilsa doesn't know if she is going to get on the plane or not?— it's possible that she really didn't know. *Casablanca*, which many now call the best movie ever made, and a beloved classic, was a helter-skelter rush job.

I used to teach a class at Rochester Institute of Technology called Writing about American Film, where I showed a number of classic movies. I always began with *Casablanca*, partly for the local connection: Bergman's home was in Rochester with her first husband Petter Aron Lindström (he was studying medicine at the University of Rochester) when she was in

9. Bard College Archives, "Howard Koch."
10. Bard College Archives, "Howard Koch."
11. Koch, "Casablanca," 3, 4.
12. Bard College Archives, "Howard Koch."

Hollywood playing the part of Ilsa,[13] and partly because many of my students had never seen a black and white film. I've never met anyone who didn't like *Casablanca*, and after I showed it to my students, I knew I could show them other black and white movies.

Howard Koch's blacklisting was a classic example of hysteria and political stupidity. President Franklin Roosevelt asked Warner Brothers to make a movie adapted from the novel *Mission to Moscow*, a story sympathetic to the Soviet Union and Stalin, to soften America's heart toward Russia and help generate support for the USSR in the war against Germany. Koch wavered. Jack Warner insisted.[14]

Years later, in 1951, the House Committee on Un-American Activities turned its focus on the entertainment industry, and studios developed the Hollywood Blacklist to keep themselves out of trouble. Entertainment careers were ruined because of alleged Communist associations. The so-called Hollywood Ten went to jail for refusing to cooperate and name names. Koch in the early '50s was himself barred from employment, largely, he understood, because of his work on the afore mentioned *Mission to Moscow*. Never mind that Roosevelt had wanted it, had all but ordered it.[15]

But Koch was resilient. He and his family moved to England, where he continued working under an assumed name. When they returned in the late '50s and settled in Woodstock, he went back to work in both TV and films, and acting under the name Peter Howard.[16]

Finding the Grave

Walk to Artists Cemetery from the center of town or drive from Route 212 to Rock City Road to Mountain View Road. Park on Mountain View Road at the foot of the traditional cemetery, which is on a hill. The part called

13. Memmott, "Bogart and Bergman Had Casablanca and Rochester."
14. Bard College Archives, "Howard Koch."
15. Bard College Archives, "Howard Koch."
16. Bard College Archives, "Howard Koch."

9.1: The grave of Howard Koch and family in Woodstock.

Artists Cemetery is on the far side of the hill, and also on the right side slope. Walk directly over the hill. Howard Koch's grave, where he is buried with his wife and family members, is among other flat stones to the lower right as you face the woods.

Paula Danziger (1944–2004): Bard of Girls' Lives

By the time Paula Danziger died in 2004 at age fifty-nine, she had written more than thirty books, mostly young adult novels. Her first, *The Cat Ate My Gymsuit*, about a teen girl with weight, home-life, and school problems who is inspired into a better self-image by a sympathetic teacher, set a tone for later works: adolescent and teen girls who fight back brazenly. These were fictions that grew from her own unhappy childhood under the thumb of an explosive father, and all the maladjustments of a dysfunctional family.[17]

She was born in Washington, DC, and grew up in Metuchen, New Jersey. Her young life resembled the teen girls she wrote about. The local library became her sanctuary.[18] Some of her other books are classics, such as *The Divorce Express* and the fourteen books in the Amber Brown series. In all, she wrote thirty books, translated into thirteen languages. She was especially popular in England, where she spent a lot of her time and was often a guest on the children's TV show *Live and Kicking*.[19] She received numerous awards, including the International Reading Association's Children's Award and Read-a-Thon Author of the Year.

Later in life she split her time between New York City and Woodstock, and toured her books, giving talks to grade-schoolers and teens. In early June of 2004 she suffered a heart attack and was hospitalized, but she did not recover and died a month later.[20]

Finding the Grave

Walk to Artists Cemetery from the center of town or drive from Route 212 to Rock City Road to Mountain View Road. Park on Mountain View Road at the foot of the traditional cemetery, which is on a hill. The part called

17. Manelius, "Paula Danziger."
18. Manelius.
19. Manelius.
20. Manelius.

9.2: The grave of Paula Danziger in Woodstock.

Artists Cemetery is on the far side of the hill, and also on the right-side slope. Paula Danziger is on the slope to the right of the older cemetery.

Janine Pommy Vega (1942–2010): Poet of a Changed Consciousness

I can think of moments when I've tried to explain to a younger person what Jack Kerouac meant to my generation in the 1960s, at least to those of us who read his novel *On the Road*. Quite understandably, the response is often something like, "Okay, so he bummed around the country and hung out with crazy people—what's the big whoop?" Well, in the 1950s and the early '60s most Americans didn't just quit their jobs and hit the pavement—at least not until hippies started doing it en masse. But many of us yearned to break from the staid, middle-class, postwar world of identical front yards, sitcoms, whitewall haircuts, and neckties that felt like harnesses. Kerouac pointed the way, as did his Beat pals Neal Cassidy and the poet Allan Ginsburg, to intense, unblushing experience, often gritty, sometimes epiphanous, with poetry and jazz and "tea" (marijuana).

The book had a life-altering effect on Janine Pommy Vega, who read it when she was still a teenager. Thus inspired, she caught a bus to New York City where, in Greenwich Village, she quickly fell into the company of the Beats, especially Gregory Corso, Allen Ginsberg, Herbert Huncke, and Peter Orlovsky who became her lover.[21] She said, "It was [Kerouac's] idea of the desire to go. You know, for years, geez, that's mainly what I did."[22] She told an interviewer that leaving New Jersey for New York "was a complete and total change of consciousness in itself."[23]

Her first book, *Poems to Fernando*, for her husband Fernando Vega, a Peruvian painter who had died of a drug overdose in Ibiza, was published by City Lights Books in San Francisco in 1968 when she was twenty-six, relatively young for a poet. Restless after Fernando's death, she traveled in Europe and Israel for more than three years, working through a staggering grief, before returning to New York.[24] Many of her books of poetry—there are more than a dozen—are reflective of her spiritual journeys in the Himalayas, the Amazon, and other places. She lived for a time as a hermit on the Isla del Sol in Lake Titicaca.[25]

Later in life, while acknowledging the influence of the Beats on her poetry, she no longer identified with that literary movement. According to Nancy M. Grace and Ronna C. Johnson, authors of *Breaking the Rule of the Cool: Interviewing and Reading Women Beat Writers*, "Pommy Vega's

---

21. Grimes, "Janine Pommy Vega Dies at 68," A22.
22. Grace and Johnson, *Breaking the Rule of Cool*, 244.
23. Grace and Johnson, 246.
24. Grace and Johnson, 232, 235.
25. Grimes, A22.

9.3: The grave of Janine Pommy Vega in Woodstock.

work articulates the refraction of feminist politics through New Age spirituality, romanticism, liberation theology, and open sexuality."[26]

She was part of the New York Poets in the Schools program, and taught poetry in prisons through the program Incisions/Arts, which she directed, and through a degree program with Bard College for inmates. In the last years of her life, she lived with her companion, poet Andy Clausen, near Woodstock in the hamlet of Willow, where she died from a heart attack on December 23, 2010.[27]

26. Grace and Johnson, 244.
27. Grimes, A22.

Finding the Grave

Walk to Artists Cemetery from the center of town or drive from Route 212 to Rock City Road to Mountain View Road. Park on Mountain View Road at the foot of the traditional cemetery, which is on a hill. The part called Artists Cemetery is on the far side of the hill, and also on the right-side slope. Her stone is on the right-side slope, easier to find than many there because its red marble stands out.

Hervey White (1866–1944): Founder of the Fest

Hervey White may have been the nearest thing that a later generation of Woodstock revelers could call a patriarch—if indeed they knew who he was. The gravestone in the Woodstock Artists Cemetery for White, poet, novelist, natureman-philosopher, and amateur builder, seems untended. That is, you don't find the little stones, coins, or trinket memorabilia on his grave that I often find on those of writers who were cultural icons.

Yet White was one of the principal founders of the art culture that blossomed in Woodstock when he started the Maverick art and literary colony in 1905. Earlier, in 1902, he helped found the eponymously named Byrdcliffe Arts Colony with Ralph Radcliffe Whitehead and his wife Jane Byrd McCall.[28] But White had his own vision. The Radcliffe-Byrds were a bit too well-heeled and structured for his comfort, so he left. He bought some farmland on borrowed money and called it Maverick. He built a variety of shacks and cabins and invited artists and writers to come to Woodstock to live cheaply and simply. And come they did. The digs were simple, rough, and unpainted, and White himself was there to cheer them on. He also built a theater, although tree-trunk support posts blocked audience view of the stage.[29]

28. Rhoads, *Ulster County*, 7.
29. Rhoads, 311.

"Hervey White has always been a poor man," said novelist Henry Morton Robinson. "[He] would not be Hervey White and be any other kind of man."[30]

The real revelry and jollification began at a critical moment in 1915 when Hervey needed a well to supply water to the cabins. The drillers presented Hervey with a bill for $1,500, a lot of money in those days.[31] Local artists decided to hold a festival to raise the cash, and a stone quarry was quickly made into an open-air theater, with seating and an orchestra pit.[32]

"Those attending," according to the *New York Times*, "have been asked to come in fancy costume, or at least to dress comfortably without regard for convention, and to bring articles to sell." At night, following a pageant and afternoon concerts in the theater, "Lada, a dancer, who has performed professionally in New York, will give a program of dances by moonlight."[33]

It was so successful that they did it again the following year, and the year after that—there were always creditors who came after Hervey post-festival for the proceeds. Robinson wrote, "The local grocery man, butcher, lumber dealer and builder were on hand just as Hervey finished his morning coffee. They stood in a long line . . . I have seen him start the day with $3,500 and at nightfall would not have a penny." But the festival itself, Robinson said, "expanded enormously; it became the only thing of its kind in America, a frankly bacchanalian rout at which most of the ordinary inhibitions were slipped off, revealing the merrymakers as something the Greeks had plenty of words for."[34] It finally petered out in 1931.

In 1908 he built a printing shop called Bearcamp for the Maverick Press, which published some of his later works: *The Ship of Souls* (poems) and *Man Overboard: A Naughty Novel*. Earlier books included novels *Noll and the Fairies* and *Differences*. Some of his books can be had in facsimile copies; others are scarce, and hard to get at affordable prices.

30. Robinson, "The Maverick," 73.
31. Robinson, 74.
32. Evers, *Catskills*, 635–36.
33. "Theatre in Stone Quarry," 11.
34. Robinson, 75.

Born in Iowa, Hervey was descended from William and Susanna White, voyagers on the *Mayflower*, whose child Peregrine White traveled in utero and was born before the boat reached Plymouth. Similarly, Hervey's body and soul searched for a place to root. He and his siblings were abandoned by their father and orphaned after the death of their mother. But he was adept at finding wealthy people to help him along, and he attended Stockton Academy, the University of Kansas, and Harvard, although he had also traveled the country and toured Mexico working as a minerologist.[35]

According to his granddaughter, Christie White Dauphin, he was a "brilliant, hard-working, generous, Quaker/Puritan, sexually inexperienced bisexual . . . so loved and misunderstood that at one point in the history of the Maverick, he had a reputation as the 'Jesus Christ of Woodstock.'"[36] In 1904 he married Vivian Bevans, a young ceramicist and artists' model, who had been lured from the Art Institute of Chicago to Byrdcliffe by Whitehead. They had two children, Caleb and Dan. But it was a stormy marriage; he was apparently abusive at times, and Vivian moved back to Chicago with the boys.[37] Her divorce lawyer was Clarence Darrow.

In the last years of his life, he built a tiny cabin for himself—six feet by eight feet—where he lived in accomplished simplicity that reminds one of Thoreau's cabin on Walden Pond. Except that for Thoreau it was an experiment in living deliberately. For White this was *place*, and *final*.[38]

Finding the Grave

Walk to Artists Cemetery from the center of town or drive from Route 212 to Rock City Road to Mountain View Road. Park on Mountain View Road at the foot of the traditional cemetery, which is on a hill. The part called Artists Cemetery is on the far side of the hill, and also on the right-side

35. Dauphin, "Hervey White and Vivian Bevans."
36. Dauphin.
37. Dauphin.
38. Rhoads, 57.

9.4: The grave of Hervey White in Woodstock.

slope. Walk directly over the hill. On the back slope of the cemetery, as you face the shrine, White's grave is in the last row on the left, near the top of the slope. The Canadian flag pictured in the accompanying photo is a mystery. Bevans had a Canadian in her family tree, but it is doubtful that White identified with that country.

Sources

Howard Koch

Gossow, Mel. "Howard Koch, a Screenwriter For 'Casablanca,' Dies at 95." *New York Times*, August 18, 1995.

"Howard Koch." Bard College Archives and Special Collections. May 28, 2011. https://www.bard.edu/archives/voices/koch/koch.php.

Koch, Howard. *As Time Goes By: Memoirs of a Writer.* New York: Harcourt Brace Jovanovich, 1979.

Koch, Howard. "Casablanca." *Bard College Alumni Magazine* (May 1967): 3–4.

Koch, Howard. *The Panic Broadcast: Portrait of an Event.* With an Introductory Interview with Arthur C. Clark. Boston: Little, Brown and Company, 1970.

Memmott, Jim. "Humphrey Bogart and Ingrid Bergman Had Casablanca and Rochester in Common." *Democrat and Chronicle* (Rochester, NY), April 23, 2019. https://www.democratandchronicle.com/story/news/2019/04/23/humphrey-bogart-ingrid-bergman-lived-rochester-ny/3539095002/.

"Radio Listeners in Panic, Taking War Drama as Fact." *New York Times*, October 31, 1938.

Hervey White

Dauphin, Christie White. "Hervey White and Vivian Bevans—The Family Story." Hervey White: The Maverick of Woodstock. 2012–2014. https://herveywhite.com/family-story/.

Evers, Alf. *The Catskills: From Wilderness to Woodstock.* New York: Doubleday and Co., 1972.

Rhoads, William B. *Ulster County, New York: The Architectural History and Guide.* Delmar, New York: Black Dome Press, 2011.

Robinson, Henry Morton. "The Maverick." In *Remembering Woodstock*, edited by Richard Heppner. Charleston, SC: The History Press, 2008.

"Theatre in Stone Quarry. Mavericks to Hold a Festival Near Woodstock, N.Y." *New York Times*, August 11, 1915.

Paula Danziger

Manelius, Lauren. "Paula Danziger." Pennsylvania Center for the Book, 2019. https://pabook.libraries.psu.edu/literary-cultural-heritage-map-pa/bios/Danziger__Paula.

Janine Pommy Vega

Grace, Nancy M., and Ronna C. Johnson. *Breaking the Rule of the Cool: Interviewing and Reading Women Beat Writers.* Jackson: Univ. Press of Mississippi, 2004.

Grimes, William. "Janine Pommy Vega, Restless Poet, Dies at 68." *New York Times*, January 2, 2011.

Guide to the Janine Pommy-Vega manuscripts, 1967–1980. University of Delaware Library—Special Collections. Accessed April 18, 2023. https://library .udel.edu/special/findaids/view?docId=ead/mss0456.xml;tab=notes.

Central

10 Clinton

Alexander Woollcott

Nestled in the hills a little to the west of Utica in Oneida County is the village of Clinton, not to be confused with the town of Clinton in Duchess County, or the town of Clinton in Clinton County up north on the Canadian border. It is named for George Clinton, the first governor of New York. Its first settlers were Revolutionary War veterans and their families who started arriving in 1787, although it didn't actually incorporate as a village (in the town of Kirkland) until 1846.

Grover Cleveland lived briefly in Clinton; Clara Barton, founder of the American Red Cross, attended the Clinton Liberal Institute, 1850–52; and Elihu Root, who was born in 1845 in a house on the Hamilton campus, went on to serve as secretary of war and secretary of state under presidents McKinley and Theodore Roosevelt. His daughter Edith married Major General Ulysses S. Grant III, and both are buried in the Root family plot in Hamilton College Cemetery.

Iron ore was mined here and two blast furnaces produced untold tons of cast iron until 1900, when competing iron production in the Mesabi Range in Minnesota put them out of business, much as it did in Furnaceville, closer to Rochester.

Clinton is home to Hamilton College, named for Alexander Hamilton who was on the college's board of trustees. Founded in 1793 as the Hamilton-Oneida Academy, it enrolled both white and Native American students, and received its formal charter in 1812 as a liberal arts college. Ezra Pound enrolled at Hamilton in 1903, and graduated in 1905. It was here that he studied Dante, and may have developed his early ideas for his

10.1: Portrait of Alexander Woollcott. Library of Congress, Prints and Photographs Division, Carl Van Vechten Collection, LC-USZ62-121914.

Cantos. Another student, Alexander Woollcott, who graduated in 1909, would shake up the theater world.

Alexander Woollcott (1887–1943):
Brilliant (and Beloved) Smart Aleck

Long regarded as one of New York's (and hence the nation's) most influential drama critics, as well as a journalist, playwright, actor, and radio commentator, Alexander Woollcott was a grandly notorious figure, widely known for his brilliant and caustic wit (he could have driven almost anyone to tears); but also, with his wide girth, he was one of the most physically recognizable literary persons of his time. You loved him if he praised your play, or hated him if he panned it. But he never wrote puff pieces: his integrity as a critic was unquestioned.

He was one of the original members of the legendary Round Table at the Algonquin Hotel in Manhattan, which began as a meeting of literary friends in 1919,[1] where if an innocent soul happened to sit down with such wits as Woollcott, humorist Robert Benchley, sports writer Heywood Brown, playwrights Marc Connelly and George S. Kauffman, actress Tallulah Bankhead, Dorothy Parker (who lived in the Algonquin),[2] and Harpo Marx (with whom Woollcott was especially close and joined on vacations[3]), he might be chewed up and spat out. Yet it was more than a gaggle of wits. According to David Wallace, "Seeing each other on a more or less regular basis created a kind of creative synergism between regular members of the Round Table" as ideas, as well as gossip and jokes, were tossed back and forth.[4]

In 1915, while he was theater critic for the *New York Times*, Woollcott was banned from all theaters owned by the Shubert company, owing to his acerbic reviews. So, he and *Times* publisher Adolph Ochs sued for discrimination. Following a court injunction, he was allowed tickets again,

1. Wallace, *Capitol of the World*, chapter 14.
2. Wallace, chapter 14.
3. Adams, A. *Woollcott*, 157.
4. Wallace, chapter 14.

but he ultimately lost in the New York State Supreme Court which ruled for the Shuberts, stating that only race, creed, or color constituted unlawful discrimination.[5]

He had another side: a man kind and generous to friends, his purse always open to struggling actors and writers. He used his celebrity to raise support for training dogs to guide the blind and to provide eyeglasses for the poor.[6] But his caustic wit was also his social amenity. At the height of his career, it was said that he could eat dinner at a different home in New York every night of the year, so much were people entertained by him, so avidly was he in demand by smart hosts. In 1933 he began a new career as a radio commentator for CBS, and his renown grew exponentially. Despite his social currency, he remained single, probably because while still a young man a brutal bout with mumps left him impotent.[7] He was nothing if not a restless and lonely man.

Moss Hart and George S. Kauffman tried to capture his personality in their comedy play, *The Man Who Came to Dinner*. It became a hilarious movie, with Monty Woolley playing the part of the Woollcottian character Sheridan Whiteside. He was an obvious inspiration for the fastidious, wisecracking, syndicated columnist/radio commentator Waldo Lydeker played by Clifton Webb in the classic detective film *Laura* (1944), except that Woollcott never possessed that character's malice. But few writers have held such celebrity.

His biographer Edwin P. Hoyt makes clear that the brilliant vinegar that made him famous was, toward the end, a front. By his forties he was playing a caricature of Alexander Woollcott, and there seemed no way to publicly take a bow and step out of that role. He became more restless, traveling back and forth over the ocean, changing addresses, overeating, drinking too much, and smoking. His health began to suffer.[8] He had a heart attack in 1940 in San Francisco; in 1942 he was hospitalized in

5. Klee, "Woollcott vs. Shubert," 264–67.
6. "Woollcott Dies after Heart Attack," 54.
7. Adams, 56.
8. Hoyt, *Alexander Woollcott*, 306ff, 315–36.

Syracuse with heart trouble; and on the evening of January 23, 1943, at the age of fifty-six, he suffered a heart attack while on the air for a panel discussion on the tenth year of Hitler's rule in Germany, and died later that night in the hospital.[9]

He was born in 1887 in New Jersey to parents who were adherents to Fourierism, a radical back-to-the-land communal society that lived in agrarian homesteads called phalanxes. Woollcott was raised for a time in one near Red Bank, which was, for its time, a radical mix of agnostics and free thinkers who recognized only civil marriages, outright abolishing religious unions. It was not, however, a free love colony as many people assumed.[10] His father was a restless businessman who moved his family around the country, but somehow they always returned to the phalanx. If the commune was limiting, there was a local library, and he pulled wagonloads of books home with him, the literary light already burning in his brain.[11] And later, there was Hamilton College in Clinton, New York, a place he loved dearly, where he edited the *Hamilton Literary Monthly*[12] and where he graduated with the class of 1909. Not that he got on well with fellow students there who viewed him as eccentric and socially inept, and Sigma Phi gave him the black ball, although later Theta Delta Chi, who were fewer in numbers, gave him the thumbs-up.[13]

Some claim that Woollcott was a Fortean, an adherent to the occult and anomalous phenomena ideas of Charles Hoy Fort,[14] which also included Ben Hecht, John Cowper Powys, Sherwood Anderson, Clarence Darrow, and Booth Tarkington. After all, like Fort, he was a compulsive contrarian.

He liked Hamilton and Upstate so much that when he was a student, rather than returning home to the phalanx, he spent his summers working

9. "Woollcott Dies after Heart Attack," 1, 54.

10. Adams, 21–24.

11. Adams, 37–39.

12. Spartacus Educational, "Alexander Woollcott."

13. Adams, 45.

14. See East, chapter 1, Albany.

Upstate, first at the Roycroft Colony, the cultural center and spa in East Aurora,[15] and thereafter at the Chautauqua Institute.[16] In 1924, Hamilton College awarded him the honorary degree of Doctor of Humane Letters. Whenever possible, he attended Hamilton's commencement ceremonies, one of the few of the alumni who did.

His writing output was voluminous. The earliest books are collected theater reviews, which now, I suppose, would only interest someone studying the history of American theater. But he also wrote the first biography of Irving Berlin. His later works, such as *While Rome Burns* and *Long, Long Ago*, are collections of much broader commentaries on places, events, and personalities, and they are brilliant. In addition, he edited *The Woollcott Reader* and *Woollcott's Second Reader,* anthologies of works by writers that he thought deserved a wider audience. While it is unlikely that you will ever see a production of the play that he wrote with George S. Kauffman, *The Dark Tower,* the DVD of the 1934 film version, *The Man with Two Faces,* starring Edward G. Robinson and Mary Astor, is available.

Edwin P. Hoyt's biography, *Alexander Woollcott: The Man Who Came to Dinner,* is lively and sympathetic to Woollcott, and defends him against harsher critics, but also notes Woollcott's responsibility for his own problems and his lifestyle that led to his eventual demise. When he died, his ashes were sent to his alma mater, Hamilton College, for interment in its cemetery, or "the last dormitory," as he called it. However, they were misdirected to nearby Colgate College in the Village of Hamilton, and his urn finally arrived at Hamilton College with 67¢ postage due.[17] Maybe Hamilton, the cozy little community of Clinton, was the closest thing he had ever had to a real home.

Finding the Grave

To reach Clinton, get off the Thruway at Exit 32 for Westmoreland, and drive south on Route 233 for about seven miles to the intersection with

15. Hoyt, 41.
16. Adams, 52.
17. Adams, 370–71.

10.2: The grave of Alexander Woollcott in Clinton.

Route 412. A left turn puts you on College Street into the village. To the right is College Hill Road, which takes you into the Hamilton College campus. Turn right again when you see a small sign for "Skenandoa, Wertimer and Wallace Johnson Houses." That road ends at the Sydney and Eleanor Wertimer House, a dormitory for first-year students. I am told that if you arrive on a weekend or during the summer, parking is open. When classes are in session you need a permit.[18] To get to this point via GPS, key in: 198 College Hill Rd., Clinton, NY, 13323.

But let's assume that it's a Saturday, sunny and mild, and there are only a few cars in the student lot at Wertimer House. Directly up the slope from that lot is the Hamilton College Cemetery, and you can see it through the trees. A path will take you to the left around the trees and in the side of the cemetery. It is a small cemetery, and Alexander Woollcott's grave is easy to find. He is four rows down from the high end of the

18. Call Campus Safety at 315-859-4141.

slope, a modest block stone. For a landmark, look for a prominent stone for Shepard. Woollcott is just a few paces in front of that stone.

While you are there, visit Elihu Root and family, with Ulysses S. Grant III under flat stones at the bottom of the slope. In this small cemetery you will also find Oneida Chief Skenandoa, and the missionary to (and advocate for) the Oneidas, Samuel Kirkland, for whom the town is named, and who was the college's principal founder.

Sources

Adams, Samuel Hopkins. A. Woollcott: His Life and His World. New York: Reynal and Hitchcock, 1945.

"Alexander Woollcott." Spartacus Educational (1997, 2020). https://spartacus-educational.com/Jwoollcott.htm.

"Alexander Woollcott Improves." New York Times, March 12, 1942.

Hoyt, Edwin P. Alexander Woollcott: The Man Who Came to Dinner. New York: Abelard-Schuman, 1968.

"Just the Facts." Hamilton College. April 18, 2023. www.hamilton.edu/about/just-the-facts.

Klee, Bruce B. "Woollcott vs. Shubert: Dramatic Criticism on Trial." Educational Theatre Journal 13, no. 4 (1961): 264–68. https://doi.org/10.2307/3204347.

Wallace, David. Capitol of the World: A Portrait of New York City in the Roaring Twenties. Guilford, CT: Lyons Press, 2011. Kindle.

"Woollcott Dies after Heart Attack in Radio Studio during Broadcast." New York Times, January 24, 1943.

11 Elmira

Mark Twain

Elmira's original name was Newtown, and it is near the site of the Battle of Newtown, August 29, 1779, one of the major skirmishes of the Revolutionary War. It is another of many places in the state where the villages of Iroquois tribes were destroyed by Gen. John Sullivan and his Continental troops for aiding the British. It was the beginning of the end of Iroquois rule, and twelve years later, on July 26, 1791, representative whites and Native Americans met here and signed the Treaty of Painted Post, one of several such treaties in the decade between 1784 and 1797 in which Iroquois ceded vast tracts of their land to white settlers, the process that would end with Natives disinherited and living on tiny reservations.

The Erie Railroad reached town in 1849, after which it became a railway hub. Its position on the Chemung River made it a port on the Chemung Canal, another of several Upstate canals—such as the Susquehanna and Genesee Valley Canals—that lost out in competition with railroads. It was the home of the Gleason Sanitarium, where two illustrious husband-and-wife doctors, Silas and Rachel Gleason, practiced hydrotherapy, or the Gleason's Water Cure, for chronic pain. Among their patients were such luminaries as Clara Barton, Harriet Beecher Stowe, and Susan B. Anthony.

Here too was a notorious Civil War prison camp where some 12,000 Confederate prisoners of war were held, beginning in May 1864 (the same year Elmira was chartered as a city) through the end of the war, and where 2,994 soldiers died, mostly from disease including smallpox and diarrhea that spread through the camp. Of that number, 2,973 were buried in Woodlawn National Cemetery on Davis Street in Elmira by a sexton of

11.1: Mark Twain. Library of Congress, Prints and Photographs Division, LC-USZ62-5513.

the Baptist Church, John W. Jones, who ironically was a runaway enslaved person. It is a sobering sight, those thousands of white stones for men buried hundreds of miles from home. Union soldiers are buried here too in the same section; stones with pointed tops are Confederate, those with round tops are Union. Jones, who had fled north in 1844 via the Underground Railroad, was active in the effort to smuggle enslaved people to freedom, and his home in Elmira was an Underground Railroad station. It is now the John W. Jones Museum, open weekends in the summer.

For a city of its size (29,200 in the last census) Elmira has given the world quite a variety of notables. Elmiran Ross Gilmore Marvin, uncle of actor Lee Marvin, was a member of Admiral Robert Peary's polar expeditions: on the second trip north he disappeared, with evidence pointing to his murder by two Inuit cousins. Ernie Davis, the first African American to win the Heisman Trophy, lived here as a teenager and was a local football star. Film producer and director Hal Roach, founder of Hal Roach Studios, who produced Laurel and Hardy, Charley Chase, Our Gang (aka The Little Rascals), and many more early film comedians, was born in Elmira, made his fortune in Hollywood, died at age one hundred, and is buried in Woodlawn, where another celebrity, Samuel Clemens, no doubt Elmira's most famous resident living or dead, is also buried.

Samuel Langhorne Clemens (1835–1910): Our Mark Twain

He was America's greatest storyteller. If there is any such thing as the Great American Novel, I'll vote for *The Adventures of Huckleberry Finn* over *Moby Dick*, although it is also a great novel. It's the book that catches America in the act of being itself: brutish, sweet, and frighteningly vast. It was the first major novel to use the rough vernacular that was spoken in the backwaters of America; in fact, as Huck's raft floats south down the Mississippi, dialects of the people he meets change little by little. Clemens knew those dialects. He had been a riverboat pilot with big ears.

Certainly there is more critical writing on Mark Twain, and on *Huckleberry Finn*, than on almost any other American writer, on almost any other American book. There is something of Clemens in all of us who work as writers. We know we need more than talent and hard work: we need luck. And he was famous for his luck, although he had bad luck too, pretty much in equal proportions.

Even Twain's lesser books hold up, such as *Pudd'n Head Wilson* and *A Connecticut Yankee in King Arthur's Court*. His *Letters from the Earth*, lampooning Christianity among other things, was withheld from publication by Twain himself, fearing it would cause scandal for his family; but his daughter Clara, after withholding it herself, allowed its publication in 1960. He is endlessly absorbing. People who dismiss *Huckleberry Finn* as racist have a point, but I suspect they have not given it a fair read or given it credit for the contribution it has made to our national conscience.

But why is this world-renowned, hugely influential writer buried in Elmira, New York? In 1868, Twain was a journalist on a boat to the Holy Land, to write about the trip for the Alta California newspaper. On board he met a young man named Charles Langdon, the son of a wealthy family in Elmira. They became friends and after the voyage, Langdon introduced Twain to his sister Olivia. For Twain it was love, or at least infatuation, at first sight. They were married in Elmira in 1870, and moved to Buffalo where Twain went to work as an editor on the *Buffalo Express*, later called the *Courier-Express*. They later settled in Connecticut, but summered at the Langdon's Quarry Farm in Elmira, at the home of Olivia's sister Susan and her husband Theodore Crane. The Cranes had an octagonal study built for him near their house; it proved the perfect place for him to write, where *Huckleberry Finn* and many of his other books were written. The study was moved to the Elmira College campus in 1952, where it is open to visitors weekdays during the summer months.

Twain and his family were travelers. He was often on speaking tours in the United States and in Europe and Asia. The house they loved best was in Hartford. But when they died, they went to the Langdon family plot in Woodlawn Cemetery in Elmira. There the great writer rests with his wife and their children.

Finding the Grave

The best approach to Woodlawn Cemetery is from I-86, the Southern Tier Expressway. Get off at Elmira Church Street, and take Church Street

11.2: Mark Twain's grave in Elmira.

to Walnut Street and turn right. Or key 1200 Walnut St. into your GPS. Cemetery maps are available in the office if you need one. When you enter the gate, drive straight to where the path forks, go left, and circle to the top of the hill. The Mark Twain and Langdon family plot is quite distinctive and visible: a short obelisk with two rows of footstones, including Twain's. The obelisk puzzles some visitors: it is in memory of Mark Twain and Ossip Gabrilowitsch who was a renowned pianist and husband of Twain's daughter Clara.

Sources

"Quarry Farm." The Center for Mark Twain Studies. Accessed April 18, 2023. http://marktwainstudies.com/quarry-farm/.
"Twain in Elmira." The Center for Mark Twain Studies. Accessed April 18, 2023. http://marktwainstudies.com/mark-twain-in-elmira/.

12   Fayetteville

Matilda Joslyn Gage

The village of Fayetteville is on Route 5, a few miles southeast of Syracuse in Onondaga County. The traffic on its main drag is heavy enough to give the traveler the impression that many more people live within the village limits than the actual population of just over four thousand, but its quiet side streets give it a more small-town feel. Like many Upstate communities, it made a grab at history by name-association, Fayetteville being a twist on the name of the Revolutionary War hero Marquis de Lafayette. A neighboring town already had dibs on the name Lafayette.

Unlike many municipalities, it did not let developers tear down its best old architecture: grand Victorian, Greek Revival, and Italianate houses are plentiful here. The Stickley Museum is worth seeing, located on Orchard Street, next door to the Fayetteville Free Library, in the furniture company's original building. President Grover Cleveland's boyhood home is on Academy Street.

And there is the home of Matilda Joslyn Gage, the famed suffragist, abolitionist, and author, now called the Gage Home, or the Gage Center, which houses the Matilda Joslyn Gage Foundation, its stated mission dedicated to "educating current and future generations about Gage's work and its power to drive contemporary social change,"[1] with a variety of tours and programs, and scholarly presentations. Its director, Sally Roesch Wagner, is one of the first women in the United States to receive a PhD in Women's Studies.

1. Matilda Joslyn Gage Foundation, "Our Mission."

12.1: Matilda Joselyn Gage. Courtesy of The Matilda Joslyn Gage Center, Fayetteville, New York.

Matilda Joslyn Gage (1826–1898):
Stalwart Reformer and Author

Matilda was born in Cicero, New York, a few miles north of Fayetteville where she would later settle with her husband Henry Hill Gage and where she would live most of her adult life. Her family were staunch abolitionists and supporters of the Underground Railroad, and their home was a haven for religious and political radicals.[2] Matilda Joslyn Gage championed the abolitionist cause, as well as advocating for Native American rights, for which she became an honorary member of the Wolf Clan of the Mohawk tribe who named her Karonienhawi.[3]

But it is for her work in the Woman Suffrage Movement that she is most remembered: becoming a founding member of the National Woman Suffrage Association, serving as its president (1875–76), and publishing their newspaper, the *National Citizen and Ballot Box*. She authored with Susan B. Anthony and Elizabeth Cady Stanton the first three of the six-volume *History of Woman Suffrage*. She was coauthor, with Stanton, of the "Declaration of the Rights of the Women of the United States" for the 1876 Philadelphia Centennial Exposition. She made her first of many public speeches to the National Women's Rights Convention in Syracuse in 1852.[4]

Her tour de force, however, was her book *Woman, Church and State* (1893) in which she takes Judeo-Christian religion to task for perpetuating and codifying women's subservience to men, beginning with the concept of God as male, and the Genesis story that a woman brought original sin into the human family. She asserted that society *and* religion needed fundamental reforms for women to gain control over their own lives. This upset her companions in the suffrage movement, who were not about to do battle with the canons of religion and, according to historians Bruce Elliot Johansen and Barbara Alice Mann, "she was 'read out' of the movement."[5]

---

2. Derr, "Our Struggle Is for All Life."
3. Johansen and Mann, *Encyclopedia of the Haudenosaunee,* 102.
4. Matilda Joslyn Gage Foundation, "Who Was Matilda Joslyn Gage?"
5. Johansen and Mann, 101.

12.2: The grave of Matilda Joselyn Gage in Fayetteville.

She was, however, religious—a Theosophist. Among their beliefs, according to Mary Crane Derr, are "the presence of life and consciousness in all matter; the evolution of spirit and intelligence as well as matter; the possibility of conscious participation in evolution; the power of thought to affect one's self and surroundings; the duty of altruism, a concern for the welfare of others."[6] Partly through her influence, her daughter Maud and Maud's husband L. Frank Baum,[7] author of *The Wonderful Wizard of Oz*, also became Theosophists.[8] Much has been written about the possible influence of Theosophy on the *Oz* books.

6. Derr.
7. Baum was born in nearby Chittenango.
8. Alegro, "Theosophical Wizard of Oz."

According to John Alegro, Gage was "a passionately devoted Theosophist," who had found "a kindred spirit" in Madam Blavatsky, the Russian occultist and founder of the Theosophical Society.[9]

Matilda Joslyn Gage died in Chicago in 1898 at the Baums' home. She was cremated there, and Maud brought her ashes back to Fayetteville Cemetery for burial beside her husband who had died in 1884.

Finding the Grave

To get to Fayetteville from the east, take the Thruway to Exit 34A, then follow I-481 South to Route 5, where you will turn east. From the west, get off the Thruway at the I-690 exit, and follow it through the city of Syracuse to I-481, and down to Route 5. From the north or south, I-81 will get you to I-481 or I-690.

Route 5 East will take you through Manlius's plaza district (Fayetteville is in the town of Manlius). Shortly after you pass the sign welcoming you to Fayetteville, the Gage House will be on the right side. In the center of the village, turn south on South Manlius Street. Fayetteville Cemetery is a short distance on the left. To get to this point via GPS, key in: 307 Spring St., Fayetteville, NY, 13066.

There are three entrances to Fayetteville Cemetery. Take the second entrance. You will be on a paved car path. There are some unpaved paths; take the first such path you see on the left, which is an almost immediate turn. The first large rough-hewn gravestone on the right is Matilda Joslyn Gage. Her husband's name and dates are on the other side. In most cemeteries, the rough style of her stone would be distinctive, but there are dozens of similar stones in this cemetery.

Sources

Alegro, John. "The Theosophical Wizard of Oz." *Theosophy Forward*, August 15, 2009. www.theosophyforward.com.

9. Alegro.

Derr, Mary Crane. "'Our Struggle Is for All Life': The Theosophist/Unitarian Feminist Pioneer Matilda Joslyn Gage (1826–1898 CE)." https://www.the freelibrary.com/%22Our+Struggle+is+for+all+Life%22%3A+The+Theosophist %2FUnitarian+Feminist . . . -a095764450.

Johansen, Bruce Elliot, and Barbara Alice Mann. *Encyclopedia of the Haudeno-saunee (Iroquois Confederacy)*. Westport, CT: Greenwood Press, 2000.

"Our Mission." Matilda Joslyn Gage Foundation. Accessed April 18, 2023. https://matildajoslyngage.org/about-the-foundation.

Wagner, Dr. Sally Roesch. "Oz—Dorothy Gage and Dorothy Gale." *The Theo-sophical Society in America*. Posted from the *Baum Bugle*, Autumn 1984. www.theosophical.org/publications/quest-magazine/1580.

"Who Was Matilda Joslyn Gage?" Matilda Joslyn Gage Foundation. Accessed April 18, 2023. https://matildajoslyngage.org/.

13 Geneva

Sarah Hopkins Bradford

Geneva is a beautiful little city on the northern shore of Seneca Lake. Its hilly streets are lined with old, well-preserved architecture. Good lunch spots, good bars. Fishing enthusiasts call it the Lake Trout Capital of the World. Once it was a prominent Seneca tribal village, and a meeting place of the Iroquois Council of Six Nations, until it was destroyed in Sullivan's invasion in 1779, similar to the fate of the Seneca villages at present-day Canandaigua and Elmira. It is the home of the now-combined Hobart and William Smith Colleges, formerly the Geneva Academy, founded in 1797. Elizabeth Blackwell, native of Bristol, England, studied there, and in 1849 she was the first woman awarded a medical degree in the United States.

Belhurst Castle, built in the 1880s by the eccentric Carrie Harron Collins as a lavish private residence, and run as a supper club and speakeasy by her grandson during Prohibition, is now, under its current owners, a hotel and a tourist attraction and a place to hold a storybook wedding. It is on the National Register of Historic Places.

Geneva's contributions to the arts are well out of proportion to its size. Arthur Garfield Dove (1880–1946), reputedly America's first abstract painter, long associated with Alfred Stieglitz and Georgia O'Keefe, born in Canandaigua, grew up here and went to Hobart College; he maintained a studio in town in the 1930s. Geneva is the birthplace of Marshall Pinkney Wilder (1859–1915), a little person who worked as a vaudevillian comic, professional clairvoyant, and author; unfortunately, he is buried elsewhere, in New Jersey. Michael Muhammad Knight

(b. 1977), author of the novel *The Taqwacores*, known as the Hunter S. Thompson of Islamic literature, grew up in Geneva. And there was Sarah Hopkins Bradford.

Sarah Hopkins Bradford (1818–1912): First Biographer of Harriet Tubman

Born in Moscow, New York, and raised in Mount Morris, Sarah Hopkins moved to Geneva in 1839 when she married lawyer John Bradford, a local politician. However, in 1857 he abandoned her and their six children to form a law practice in Chicago.[1] He died of consumption four years later in 1861. An obituary in a local newspaper blamed his troubles on drink.[2] What went around came around.

Thereafter, she wrote books to support her family, and was one of America's earliest writers to specialize in books for children. They include *Tales for Little Convalescents*; *The Linton Family, or the Fashions of This World*; *Amy, the Glass Blower's Daughter: A True Narrative*; and the six-volume Silver Lake Series *The Budget*; *The Jumble*; *The Old Portfolio*; *Ups and Downs*; *The Green Satchel*; and *Aunt Patty's Mirror*. She also started a school for girls in her Geneva home. Bradford is sometimes compared to Louisa May Alcott for authoring early series of books for girls, although she actually preceded Alcott by a few years.

She probably did not imagine that the books she would be most remembered for would be her biographies of the heroic icon of the Underground Railroad, Harriet Tubman. *Scenes from the Life of Harriet Tubman*, which she published in 1869, was intended to raise funds to prevent Tubman from losing her house in Auburn;[3] and *Harriet Tubman: Moses of Her People*, much the same material retold, was published in 1881 to raise more funds for Tubman's house, which was then a nursing home established by Tubman for African Americans.[4]

1. Lippincott, "The Louisa May Alcott of Geneva."
2. Pierce, "*And Who Was She Anyhow?*" 12–13.
3. Lippincott.
4. Pierce, 27–28.

Occasionally I have seen the two books listed online with Tubman as author in a seller's description. While Bradford is the author, they are Tubman's story *as told to* Bradford in numerous interviews, redacted and rendered into a heroic narrative. However, it was Tubman herself who approached Frederick Douglass for advance comment on the first book.

He wrote back to her from Rochester, August 29, 1868: "Dear Harriet: I am glad to know that the story of your eventful life has been written by a kind lady, and that the same is soon to be published." But he said that he needed commendation from her more than she needed it from him.

> Most that I have done and suffered in the service of our cause has been in public, and I have received much encouragement at every step of the way. You on the other hand have labored in a private way. . . . Most you have done has been witnessed by a few trembling, scarred, and foot-sore bondmen and women whom you have led out of the house of bondage, and whose heartfelt "God bless you" has been your only reward.[5]

The narrative style in the first book falters in places, though less so in the second book, and one gets the sense that she was taking another crack at it. Most contemporary readers would be offended at Bradford's attempts to approximate southern African American dialect, and at a racist narrative tone which, as Preston E. Pierce points out, was common at that time even in books sympathetic to the plight of African Americans.[6] Yet she was in earnest with these books (the first one raised $1,200 for Tubman), and the stories that she relates are riveting, heartbreaking, and inspiring. That Tubman did so much, against such odds, and triumphed, is astounding. Moreover, *Scenes from the Life* was the first biography of Tubman and helped elevate her to fame. Bradford never claimed to be a professional historian, and Pierce notes that, unfortunately, she did not keep her notes from her interviews with Tubman, as a professional historian certainly would.[7]

5. Harriet Tubman Historical Society, "Letter from Douglass."
6. Pierce, 21.
7. Pierce, 21.

Bradford had a personal stake in the Civil War that slavery ignited. She lost her two eldest sons: Charles died of tuberculosis at Chattanooga, Tennessee, July 22, 1865, some months after the war ended, and just as his Union army unit was mustering out of that area; and William, a US Navy master's mate on board the *Bark Roebuck*, died of yellow fever July 29, 1864, at Tampa Bay.[8] Both are buried a few feet from her in Geneva's Washington Street Cemetery, as is a third son, John M. Bradford Jr., a veteran of the Spanish-American War. Although blessed with a longer life than his brothers, he died in Sailors' Snug Harbor, a charity home for seamen on Staten Island where he had lived for twenty-nine years.[9] One of her daughters was Mary Bradford Crowninshield, another author of series-novels for children, such as her three-volume Lighthouse Children series.

But the Hopkins family that she was born into was also illustrious. Sarah's father, Samuel Miles Hopkins (1772–1837), was a US congressman, later a New York State Assemblyman, and circuit court judge,[10] also buried at Washington Street; her brother, Samuel Miles Hopkins II (1813–1901), was a Presbyterian minister and author of *Manual of Church Polity* (1878) and *A Short History of American Presbyterianism* (1903), buried at Fort Hill Cemetery in Auburn.[11] Her great-nephew was Samuel Hopkins Adams (1871–1958),[12] a famous investigative reporter whose series of articles in *Colliers* in 1905, "The Great American Fraud," exposed deceptive claims by drug companies that manufactured some of the most widely used drugs at the time. In the furor that followed, the Pure Food and Drugs Act of 1906 became law (also influenced by Upton Sinclair's *The Jungle*). He was also a fiction writer whose short story "Night Bus" was adapted into the Frank Capra movie *It Happened One Night* (1934), with Clark Gable and Claudette Colbert. His books *Canal Town* and *Grandfather Tales* are still read avidly by Erie Canal enthusiasts; they were among Sen. Daniel Patrick Moynihan's favorite books, and he recommended them to me for

8. Pierce, 14.
9. Kerry Lippincott, historian, email message to the author, August 9, 2018.
10. Geni, "Honorable Samuel Miles Hopkins.".
11. Log College Press, "Samuel Miles Hopkins II."
12. Lippincott, email.

13.1: The grave of Sarah Hopkins Bradford in Geneva.

background when I was a reporter writing about the canal. Adams was cremated and his ashes scattered.

Sarah Hopkins Bradford died in Rochester in 1912, at the age of ninety-three, one year before Harriet Tubman. In her time, it was unusual to live past ninety; but then, she was an extraordinary woman. The house where Bradford raised her family and held her school is now called Bradford House, and is part of Hobart-William Smith Colleges.

Finding the Grave

Take the Thruway to Exit 42, and take Route 14 West, five miles into Geneva. In the middle of the business district, Route 14 turns right, then goes up a hill where it turns left at the second light. After two lights you'll see a sign on the right for Park Place (one way) which loops around a green but leads to Washington Street, where you'll turn right. Go three blocks and turn left on Monroe Street. You can park on the cemetery side of the street. To reach this point with your GPS, key in: 239 Washington St., Geneva, NY, 14456.

There is no vehicle entrance to the cemetery; the gate in the front on Washington Street is just for looks. You'll find a large sign by the sidewalk on Monroe for the Founders Square neighborhood: walk a little to the right of that sign, up the hill into the cemetery until you see a family plot for Armstrong, easily spotted for its dilapidated wrought iron enclosure. A little to the right of that plot is an imposing monument for the Hopkins family. And some fifty feet to the right of that monument is the grave of Sarah Hopkins Bradford, next to the grave of her son, John M. Bradford Jr., and a few feet behind William and Charles.

Unfortunately, I found her stone broken in half. There appears to have been an attempt to repair it with mortar, which did not hold. Being in two pieces, it is somewhat difficult to read.

Sources

Balin, Rabbi Carole B. "Harriet Tubman and Sarah Hopkins Bradford: Women of Moral Courage from Auburn's Past." Auburn Seminary. Accessed April 18, 2023. https://auburnseminary.org/voices/harriet-tubman-and-sarah-hopkins-bradford/.

Faber, Harold. "The World Capital of Whatever." *New York Times*, December 9, 1993.

"Honorable Samuel Miles Hopkins," Geni. Accessed April 18, 2023. https://www.geni.com/people/Hon-Samuel-Hopkins/6000000017866003192.

Lippincott, Kerry. "The Louisa May Alcott of Geneva: Sarah Hopkins Bradford." Geneva Historical Society, Geneva, NY. Accessed April 18, 2023. https://historicgeneva.org/people/the-louisa-may-alcott-of-geneva-sarah-h-bradford/.

"Letter from Frederick Douglass to Harriet Tubman, 1868." Harriet Tubman Historical Society. Accessed April 18, 2023. http://www.harriet-tubman.org /letter-from-frederick-douglass/.

Pierce, Preston E. *"And Who Was She Anyhow?": Sarah Hopkins Bradford, Biographer of Harriet Tubman,* Canandaigua, NY: Ontario County Historical Society, 2009.

"Samuel Hopkins Adams." Spartacus Educational, 2020. Accessed April 18, 2023. https://spartacus-educational.com/USAadamsS.htm.

"Samuel Miles Hopkins II." Log College Press. Accessed April 18, 2023. https:// www.logcollegepress.com/samuel-miles-hopkins-ii-18131901/.

14 Hamilton

Walter R. Brooks

Farmers began plowing the fields around Hamilton in Central New York in the decades following the Revolutionary War. The village of Hamilton, which shares its name with the surrounding town, has well-preserved nineteenth-century architecture that has been on the National Register of Historic Places since 1984. Colgate University now sits on some of the earliest plowed land.

As the focus of the venerable college's curriculum evolved, its original name, the Baptist Education Society, changed to the Hamilton Theological and Literary Institution, then Madison University, and finally its current incarnation as a liberal arts college. But it was a boys-only school (with a few exceptions) until the fall semester, 1970, when it began officially admitting women students.

That is why it has such a bewhiskered list of noted alumni: Oswald Avery, who discovered the relation between DNA and genetic traits, studied here at what is now called the Old Biology Building; journalist and *60 Minutes* commentator Andy Rooney; US Supreme Court Chief Justice Charles Evans Hughes; Ben Cohen of Ben and Jerry's; Charles Addams, famous cartoonist and creator of *The Addams Family*; poet Paul Mariani; and novelist Frederick Busch.

The author who rests in the village's Woodlawn Cemetery is not an alumnus, but he is one of America's most original and celebrated children's authors.

Walter R. Brooks (1886–1958): Master of Talking Beasts

The man who would introduce Freddy the Pig and his talking animal friends to the world, and write the series of stories that inspired the TV show *Mr. Ed*, was born in Rome, New York, in 1886. An orphan by his teens, he was sent to a military academy, studied at the University of Rochester, then took a swing at medical school in New York City before starting a career in advertising.[1] In the early 1930s he wrote "Talk of the Town" pieces for the *New Yorker*.[2]

For the world of Freddy, Walter Rollin Brooks gave us the Centerboro, New York, farm of Mr. and Mrs. Bean, and their menagerie of animals: Hank the Horse, Mrs. Wiggins the cow, Charles the rooster, a gaggle of talking ducks, Fritz the Cat, and the central character Freddy the Pig who lives in a cozy pen complete with a study and a typewriter. He is usually benevolent, sometimes curmudgeonly, a good ten IQ points above most of the sapiens he interacts with. He is the one who runs a little bank for the other beasts, prints a newspaper, and plays detective to solve whatever mysterious trouble comes up. He is unquestionably the farm's first citizen.

The first Freddy book, *To and Again* (1927) drew a *shush* from a few librarians and other critics for its use of common tongue and colloquial brays and oinks in a time when children's books were generally dressed in more formal language. One would think that they would have been more open-minded half a century after *Huckleberry Finn* ran the gauntlet on the same charge. But a successful series of twenty-six books can't be wrong.

Besides, what sort of formality would one expect from titles such as *Freddy and the Popinjay*, *Freddy and the Ignoramus*, *Freddy Rides Again*, *Freddy Goes to the North Pole*, and *Freddy and the Spaceship*? Anthropomorphism has a long tradition in literature—think of Apuleius's *The Golden Ass* or the pigs on Circe's island in *The Odyssey*; think of Beatrix

---

1. Young, "Walter R. Brooks."
2. Young.

Potter, Lewis Carroll, and A. A. Milne, all of whom were the highly imaginative inheritors of the *otherness* and *innerness* of animal folk tales.

So, what makes the Freddy books stand out? For one, Brooks was a superb storyteller, and this encompasses all the usual elements that make good fiction: a solid, unpredictable storyline; tantalizing subplots; dialogue that sounds like real speech; and especially character development—his characters have flesh and blood and emotions. Brooks is never silly, but he's funny; sometimes heartbreakingly funny, which is funny on a higher level.

Susannah Pearce, in an issue of the *Imaginative Conservative*, wrote, "If you put P. G. Wodehouse, Kenneth Graham, and Mark Twain into a Martini shaker, the cocktail you'd pour out would be Walter R. Brooks."[3] And Pearce is right on the mark with "It is really a mournful state of affairs that these masterpieces of delightful American humor have been so long neglected."[4]

Neglected? Well, yes, fewer readers nowadays are acquainted with Freddy. But today there is another kind of otherness: farming accounts for only 1.3 percent of the American labor force,[5] down from 30.2 percent in the 1920s[6] when Freddy first came waddling into American literature, so fewer kids hear the sound of a cowbell.

Mr. Ed became one of the most popular TV comedy series of its era, 1961–66. But Walter Brooks's beloved talking horse stories went through some alterations to suit the CBS-TV studio executives, not the least of which was switching the original location from Mount Kisco, a village in Westchester County, New York, to Southern California. Mr. Ed's owner and interlocutor also experienced a metamorphosis from an often tipsy Wilbur Pope to a more staid Wilbur Post, and his intemperate horse was made likewise more discreet.[7] It is doubtful that Brooks, who sold the TV rights in 1958 just before his death, would have approved of Hollywood's

---

3. Pearce, "The Forgotten 'Freddy the Pig.'"
4. Pearce.
5. Leply, "9 Mind-Blowing Facts about Farming."
6. "Farm Population Lowest since 1850s," 12.
7. Patten, "Review: 'Mr. Ed.'"

14.1: The grave of Walter R. Brooks in Hamilton.

cleanup job since, when the *Saturday Evening Post* editors groused about the booze, Brooks simply moved the story series to *Argosy*, where the editors had a more robust sense of humor.[8]

He was living in Roxbury, New York (the little town where poet and naturalist John Burroughs lived),[9] with his wife Dorothy when he died from a heart attack.[10] But he is unlikely to be forgotten. Some of his readers have organized the International Friends of Freddy, which promotes Brooks's memory, and all things Freddy.

You may well ask, what was Brooks's connection to Hamilton? His namesake-grandfather, Dr. Walter Rollin Brooks, was a Baptist clergyman

8. Patten.
9. See East, chapter 6, Roxbury.
10. "Brooks, Author, Dies at 72," 12.

in Hamilton who taught at Colgate when it was still called Madison University.[11] He established a family plot at Woodlawn in Hamilton, where the ashes of grandson Walter came to rest.

Finding the Grave

From the center of the village, take Lebanon Street south out of the residential area and turn right on Cemetery Road, which will take you directly into the front gates of Woodlawn Cemetery. You can reach this point with your GPS by keying in: Lebanon Street, Hamilton, NY, 13346. Once inside turn right and stay on the outermost car path, which can be rugged in places, around to the back. Find the equipment shed by the back fence and park. From that point, look west-south into the cemetery at the knoll (pictured).

Walter Brooks's gravestone is distinctive, but there are others like it in the cemetery, so you can't go on looks alone.

Sources

Cart, Michael. "Walter R. Brooks." Friends of Freddy (2023). Accessed April 18, 2023. http://freddythepig.com/?page_id=35.

"Farm Population Lowest since 1850s." *New York Times,* July 20, 1988.

Leply, Sara. "9 Mind-Blowing Facts about the US Farming Industry." *Business Insider,* December 20, 2019. https://markets.businessinsider.com/news/stocks /farming-industry-facts-us-2019-5-1028242678.

Patten, Fred. "Review: 'The Original Mr. Ed,' by Walter Brooks." *Flayrah,* October 22, 2012. www.flayrah.com/4381/review-original-mr-ed-walter-brooks.

Pearce, Susannah. "The Forgotten 'Freddy the Pig.'" *Imaginative Conservative,* August 7, 2020. https://theimaginativeconservative.org/2020/08/forgotten-freddy -the-pig-walter-r-brooks-susannah-pearce.html.

"Walter Brooks, Author, Dies at 72; Wrote Freddy the Pig Children's Books." *New York Times,* August 19, 1958.

Young, Sue. "Walter R. Brooks 1886–1958." *Sue Young Histories.* November 30, 2008. www.sueyounghistories.com/2008-11-30-walter-r-brooks-1886-1958.

11. Cart, "Walter R. Brooks," paragraph 1.

15 Interlaken

Rod Serling

Interlaken is a tiny village originally called Farmerville, and other variations of that name, until incorporation in 1904 when the name Interlaken was borrowed from the Swiss town of the same name, giving it a bit more refinement. It's one of a string of small burgs on Route 96 which connects Rochester with Waterloo, the Central New York wine country, Trumansburg, and Ithaca, ending at Route 17. It has the Lively Run Goat Dairy, one of the longest running goatmilk dairies in the Northeast. While it may seem an unlikely place for such an esteemed presence, Rod Serling, the famous writer and TV producer, had a summer cottage in the area when he taught at Ithaca College, and his resting place is in a cemetery on the edge of town.

Rod Serling (1924–1975): Maestro of the Imagination

With three Emmy wins already, Rod Serling sat for a televised interview with Mike Wallace. It was 1959, and Serling talked about his new show *The Twilight Zone*, destined of course to be become classic TV. But much of the interview concerned "pre-censorship," or the TV writer's unspoken knowledge of controversial subjects that one has to avoid, such as race. Serling was also producer of the new show, and he knew well the parameters he had to work in, however much the restrictions rankled him. "As long as you're not ashamed of anything you write," he said, the work could go on. Even more optimistic, he stated, "I stay in the

124

medium because I happen to like the medium," and added, "I think it has promise, Mike."[1]

Serling was more than an important writer. He was a visionary. For me, a kid growing up in the 1950s and '60s, *The Twilight Zone* was highly stimulating entertainment, and a good excuse to stay up a half-hour later than my normal bedtime. There had been nothing like it before on television, and maybe nothing better. Every kid I knew watched it and discussed its episodes on the school bus the next day. But also, it turned on a light in my ten-year-old brain, one that stayed lit, that illuminated the possibility that storytelling could depart from the strict confines of realism. Yes, I already knew that science fiction worked that way, as did Aesop's fables and Jules Verne and so on. But many of these half-hour scripts, about seventy percent of them written by Serling himself, extrapolated from our own world, our time and place. In fact, he said as much in a 1970 interview with science fiction writer James Gunn: "I like to know what happens Thursday, not in the next century."[2] Maybe a lot of them are better called fantasy than sci-fi. But if it works, why should category matter?

Serling's distinctive voice in the introduction to each show foreshadowed that something not only unexpected, but truly weird, was coming in the next half-hour: "There is a fifth dimension, beyond that which is known to man; it is a dimension as vast as space and as timeless as infinity . . . a dimension not only of sight and sound but of mind. . . ." An alternate dimension? Something oddly different than straight-laced 1950s America? I wanted more. I went to the library looking for books with loony-genius twists.

When they rolled the credits at the end of each show, Serling's Cayuga Productions company escaped my notice. But Upstate New York associations were at work. He and his family had a summer home on Cayuga Lake, one of the longest of the Finger Lakes, running from near Seneca Falls all the way down to Ithaca.

1. Wallace, "Interview Featuring Rod Serling."
2. Gunn, "Interview with Rod Serling."

Before *The Twilight Zone*, which ran from 1959–64, Serling was probably best known as the author of *Requiem for a Heavyweight*, a story of a boxer's bad fortunes, first presented on TV in 1956 in the CBS *Playhouse 90* series, and judged by some as one of the best plays to grace that series. Serling, a physically small man, had been a boxer in the Army during World War II, had his nose broken in three places, and knew what he was writing about. It was produced again for the big screen in 1962 with Anthony Quinn, Mickey Rooney, and Jackie Gleason, with both productions directed by Ralph Nelson, later the director of *Lilies of the Field*. A prize fighter with the moniker of Mountain comes to the natural end of his career: he's been knocked out too many times, and he gets pushed out the door into a world where he now has to fight to maintain his dignity as an old palooka. If Mike Lane as Toro Moreno in *The Harder They Fall* broke your heart, then Jack Palance in the TV production of *Requiem*, or Anthony Quinn in the screen version, will bust it to pieces. *Requiem* won five Emmy Awards, including one for Serling. He also won for an earlier play, *Patterns*, and another for *The Comedian*. With Paddy Chayefsky, Reginald Rose, and a few others, he was one of the geniuses of the early golden age of television.[3]

His teleplay *In the Presence of Mine Enemies* (1960), starring Charles Laughton and a young Robert Redford, was one of the first shows to deal with the Holocaust on television, taking place in the Warsaw Ghetto. It was produced in 1960 for *Playhouse 90*. In fact, it was the last such play because CBS was cutting out sophisticated live drama in favor of more sitcoms. I remember watching it when I was a kid. I did not know that Serling had written it. But the play was a shocking eye-opener for me.

For the big screen he cowrote the screenplay for *Planet of the Apes* (1968), adapted from Pierre Boulle's novel; the screenplay adaptation for *Seven Days in May* (1964) from the novel by Fletcher Knebel and Charles W. Bailey II; and the screenplay for *The Yellow Canary* (1963) from the novel *Evil Come, Evil Go* by Whit Masterson. He hosted and wrote for the TV series *Night Gallery* which began airing in 1970.

3. Albarella, "Cowboy with a Conscience."

Not that the *Twilight Zone* was just good clean fun. He found he could say things in a fantasy script that he couldn't get away with in the realism of his teleplays, such as social prejudice. Years before, he had written a play, *Noon on Doomsday*, about the murder of Emmett Till, and the men who got away with it. The studio heads, worried about losing sponsorship from southern companies, chopped it up, set it in another time and place, and rendered it in numerous other ways unrecognizable.[4] But if he put controversial material in the dialogue of a fantasy, the half-hour shows became small morality plays. The public ate it up, and the heads of CBS let it fly.[5] *Twilight Zone* episodes tapped into the insecurities of our modern age, including shows addressing the threat of nuclear war and its imagined aftermath. Other stories pushed the buttons on our inner insecurities, such as a traveler who arrives in a town and finds no one there; a man suddenly realizes that no one knows him, all evidence of himself having been erased; a man finds that he can read the thoughts of people he encounters, and wishes he couldn't. According to Bruce Bawer, "The anxieties reflected in these storylines are relatively unambiguous. Perhaps everything is not as we think it is. Perhaps we are not who we think we are."[6]

Rodman Serling was born to a Jewish family in Syracuse, New York, on Christmas Day, 1924, and was raised in Binghamton. He served in World War II as an Army paratrooper. The GI Bill paid his way to Antioch College where he began working on local radio stations and wrote his first scripts.[7]

He crammed a lot of writing into his abbreviated life. He must have gone through typewriter ribbons like tissues. Some people thought he had a tortured soul, probably because that is a common romanticized notion of artists. But the picture we see in his daughter Anne's memoir, *As I Knew Him: My Dad, Rod Serling*, is a loving and playful family man. No,

4. Metress, "Submitted for Their Approval," 143–45.
5. Wallace.
6. Bawer, "The Other Sixties."
7. Hudson, "Serling of 'Twilight Zone' Dies."

15.1: The grave of Rod Serling in Interlaken.

nothing particularly strange about him. He simply had an extraordinary imagination, and saw the possibilities of the new medium of TV better than most.

In the spring of 1975 Serling had a couple of heart attacks, and after two weeks in Thompkins Memorial Hospital in Ithaca, he went by ambulance to Strong Memorial Hospital in Rochester for open-heart surgery, which was still a risky procedure then. He was a serious smoker, and he even convinced the paramedics to stop along the way so that he could get out and have a cigarette.[8] On June 28, he died of complications following surgery, aged fifty, leaving his wife Carol, and daughters Jodi and Anne.[9]

8. Serling, *As I Knew Him*, 236.
9. Hudson.

Finding the Grave

Rod Serling is buried in Lake View Cemetery in Interlaken, in Seneca County. From the Thruway, take Route 96 South, approximately 67 miles. Look for County Road 150, about three-quarters of a mile north of the Interlaken village. You'll turn east. Or key into your GPS: 3675 County Road 150, Interlaken, NY, 14847. When you turn into Lake View Cemetery, you'll see a chapel to your left, on the rear of which is a list of plots and a map. Serling is in Section 6, Plot 1044, and the map may come in handy, since the cemetery is a maze of winding dirt paths. Make your first right on the car path and keep making right turns until the path circles around to the left on the east end of the cemetery. At about the point where you're heading west again, pull over and park. Serling's place is atop the knoll to your right, in the shade of a large maple.

As with many writers, he has a humble marker, but one of the most decorated by visitors that I've found; in fact, it is rivaled only by Carl Sagan's marker. When I visited, the stone was a bit crowded by a lamb's ear planting, dozens of small coins, a skeleton key, and a small stone on which was written, "Miss you Dad." I left a chip of sea glass. Tucked between the lamb's ear and the stone was a full pack of Marlboros. So, we know what brand he smoked. Same brand as me, when I still smoked.

Sources

Albarella, Tony. "Cowboy with a Conscience." Rod Serling Memorial Foundation. December 10, 2003. https://rodserling.com/cowboy-with-a-conscience-2/.

Bawer, Bruce. "The Other Sixties." *Wilson Quarterly (1976–)* 28, no. 2 (2004): 64–84. http://www.jstor.org/stable/40261250.

Gunn, James. "Interview with Rod Serling (*The Twilight Zone, Night Gallery*)." Center for the Study of Science Fiction at the University of Kansas. 1970. https://www.youtube.com/watch?v=_U_sWVKUnHQandt=391s.

Hudson, Edward. "Rod Serling of 'Twilight Zone' and 'Night Gallery' on TV Dies." *New York Times, December 29, 1975*.

Metress, Christopher. "Submitted for Their Approval: Rod Serling and the Lynching of Emmett Till." *Mississippi Quarterly* 61, nos. 1/2 (2008): 143–72. http://www.jstor.org/stable/26476645.

Serling, Anne. *As I Knew Him: My Dad, Rod Serling*. New York: Citadel Press, 2013.

Wallace, Mike. "The Interview featuring Rod Serling." Harry Ransom Center, University of Texas at Austin. 1959. Accessed April 18, 2023. https://archive .org/details/The_Mike_Wallace_Interview___Rod_Serling.

16　Ithaca

Carl Sagan, Deborah Tall,
A. R. Ammons, William Strunk Jr.

The city of Ithaca is nestled between wooded hills at the southern foot of Cayuga Lake. It has the distinct atmosphere of a college town—home to both Ithaca College and the Ivy League Cornell University. Ithaca was a destination for me long before I became concerned about who is buried there. I'm a foodie (and, truth be told, a drinkie), and some of the restaurants and cafes there are true destinations. My favorite used bookstore Autumn Leaves is on the Commons in the center of the city. There are lecture series and Botanical Gardens on campus. It's a great town to stay out late, stay overnight, and hit the State Street Diner in the morning.

There is a web of roads connecting Ithaca to the outside world: Routes 34, 89, 79, 13, 96, 366, the map resembling an illustrated circulatory system. I'm probably leaving out one or two roads. You can drive north on Route 13 from Elmira, or if you are coming from the Thruway, you can get off at Exit 34A at Canastota, and take Route 13 South. Or Route 96 South from Exit 42. Or, just hand off the job to your GPS. Keep in mind that none of New York's big highways, not the Thruway, not US 81, 390, 690, 17, or 86, lead to Ithaca. Yet the determined traveler finds a charming small city, and the feeling of being nestled in a warm valley.

Lake View Cemetery

Four authors of note are buried in the outskirts of Ithaca. Two, Carl Sagan and Deborah Tall, are in Lake View Cemetery, and two, A. R. Ammons and William Strunk Jr., are in Pleasant Grove. Geographically, the cemeteries are near neighbors. But I'll begin with Lake View, the one closer to town.

Carl Sagan (1934–1996): Citizen of the Cosmos

There have been certain people in our culture who have inspired public interest in things that it might otherwise have avoided or ignored. I think of Leonard Bernstein who, in his narrations in televised concerts, patiently explained or illuminated classical music for millions of us who, thanks to him, were no longer skeptical of buying a ticket to the philharmonic or of spending our money on a recording of Jascha Heifetz. Julia Child took the fear and trembling out of French cooking. And astronomer Carl Sagan brought us the galaxies in his PBS series *Cosmos* and in his twenty books, telling us what science knew about the universe in language that nonscientists could understand.

But he did more than that; he was equally comfortable talking about geology, oceanography, and microbiology. On *Cosmos*, he imitated the voice of a whale. And beyond that, he could talk convincingly about the sacredness of life. In his *Varieties of Scientific Experience*, an obvious allusion to William James's famous *Varieties of Religious Experience*, he makes a case for a spirituality of a cosmic consciousness fully cognizant of new science.

I wonder that such a man had time to teach, but he was a professor of astronomy and space sciences at Cornell for twenty-nine years and directed their Laboratory for Planetary Studies. He was also on the NASA imaging team for the Mars probe, Mariner 9, the first spacecraft to orbit another planet; for Viking 1 and 2, the first successful Mars landings, he helped select the landing sites.[1]

He was also a public voice for peace, for the environment, for nuclear disarmament, for sanity. He died of pneumonia, a complication of the

---

1. Dicke, "Carl Sagan Dead at 62," 1, 26.

16.1: The grave of Carl Sagan in Ithaca.

cancer he was being treated for, on December 20, 1996. He was only sixty-two.[2] Do we miss him? You bet we do.

Finding the Grave

From the city, head north on Route 13. It looks like an expressway for a few miles. Look for the exit for Route 34 North, from which you will actually turn south. Just before the exit, you will see Ithaca High School and its athletic fields on the right side. After you take the exit, turn right, drive slowly, and keep your eyes sharp. In about a quarter mile you will see a

2. Dicke, 26.

pedestrian crossing for the high school; a small sign on the left marks the entrance of Lake View Cemetery.

The narrow path looks more like someone's driveway than a cemetery entrance. It will take you around a curve and through a barrier of trees before the vista of the cemetery opens before you. The path remains narrow, so be cautious and ready to squeeze right if you meet a vehicle. You are now at the lower end of Lake View. The path dips into a valley before taking you uphill. Or set your GPS for 605 Eastshore Dr., Ithaca, NY, 14850.

When you reach the top there will be a small area to pull off. Walk a short distance back down the slope. You will see a low, dark, single-chain fence on your right. Carl Edward Sagan, the great astronomer, is buried on the slope just beyond the fence and adjacent the path, next to his parents. His is a flat, modest stone.

As with Rod Serling's grave, visitors often leave a variety of memorabilia. The first time I visited his site in 2016, it had its share of tokens. The second time, in August of 2017, some of the debris had to be moved aside to read the inscription. A man obscured by adulation.

Deborah Tall (1951–2006): Lyrics of Memory and Passion

In the chapter on Brockport I talk about the Writers Forum Summer Workshops that used to be held at the college there, and what an exciting time it was in the 1980s. I worked in the Lift Bridge Book Shop and two days a week as an amanuensis (sort of) at BOA Editions, also in Brockport. For anyone in town who loved writing; anyone who wanted to be a writer, devoured books, read poetry on their coffee breaks, read in the bathtub, argued about books in bars (some of us do)—that week in June was almost too exciting to bear, whether or not you actually came up with the $200 to participate in one of the morning workshop classes. There would a visiting poet, novelist, and nonfiction writer in town; there were readings at night and parties off campus. Two hundred dollars was a stiff bill for me then, with two minimum wage jobs, and in the summer of '85 I couldn't scrape it together. But I went to the afternoon and evening events just to hang out and listen.

The Island of the White Cow by Deborah Tall had recently been published; it was getting glowing reviews, there was a feature on her in the *Rochester Times-Union*, and she came to the Writers Forum to teach nonfiction. I'd already read it and loved it. It is a rich story, a journal actually, of a young woman who leaves America with her Irish professor to live in a remote community on the island of Inishbofin (Gaelic for Island of the White Cow) off the west coast of Ireland.

Since then, in her home country, she published five collections of poetry, including *Come Wind, Come Weather*; *Summons*; and *Afterings* (published posthumously); and two more volumes of nonfiction, including *From Where We Stand: Recovering a Sense of Place* and *A Family of Strangers*. She died of cancer in 2006, leaving a husband, poet David Weiss, and two daughters.

At Hobart, Tall was an editor of the *Seneca Review*, one of the little journals that every poet wants to be in because of its stellar reputation. Under the editorship of Tall and John D'Agata, the *Review* was first to define, in the Fall 1997 issue, the parameters of the "lyric essay":

> These "poetic essays" or "essayistic poems" give primacy to artfulness over the conveying of information. They forsake narrative line, discursive logic, and the art of persuasion in favor of idiosyncratic meditation. . . . The lyric essay partakes of the poem in its density and shapeliness, its distillation of ideas and musicality of language. It partakes of the essay in its weight, in its overt desire to engage with facts, melding its allegiance to the actual with its passion for imaginative form.[3]

Today the lyric essay is a widely practiced form under the pen of such notable authors as Mary Ruefle, Claudia Rankine, Anne Carson, the late David Foster Wallace, and numberless others. An extraordinary contribution to American letters.

Her book *A Family of Strangers* is one of the most unusual books I have read in recent years. In a series of brief lyric, autobiographical vignettes, she tells the story of her upbringing in Levittown in the 1950s,

3. Tall and D'Agata, "The Lyric Essay."

the daughter of Jewish parents who have effectively divorced themselves
from their families' past, her father an engineer for the US Nuclear Early
Warning System. Secrecy is paramount; to ask about her ancestors ver-
boten. She wonders, does it have something to do with the Holocaust, or
with her father's security clearance? After his death, she is contacted by an
uncle in Florida whom she did not know. With the information he provides, and her own genealogical research and travels to Ladyzin, Ukraine,
other relatives appear out of the past, there is a recreation of memory, and
a deeper story opens.

But to my mind she has been first and foremost a poet. In her last collection, *Afterings*, she faces her approaching death squarely. I do not like
the word "fearless." Is anyone ever truly fearless? I prefer "brave," which is
a quality we actually find in the book. Mary Ruefle says in her comment
from the back of the book, "These astonishingly beautiful poems, these
'afterings,' have as their guide an edgy intelligence that is clear, bright,
memorable, and brave."[4]

Here is a poem from *Afterings*:

Your Absence Has Already Begun
Say a calling knocks you out of sleep
draws blood
is accessible only by water.

Say you believe you pilot your life
but you have looked away
and your absence had already begun.

You grapple out, patched together
by medication
and makeup, scale the broken

cadence, the first frost-heaved lanes
walking papers
clenched to your chest.

4. Ruefle, liner notes, in *Afterings*.

16.2: The grave of Deborah Tall in Ithaca.

It's late in the season. You forget
what lured you:
Icarus still tumbling through the stunned stars

his fingerprints
all over your heart.[5]

From a Levittown childhood of silence to a college-age woman who
defies the expectations of the norm and runs off to Ireland to live with an
older man in an isolated place, to the accomplished poet, groundbreaking
essayist, editor, teacher, and family woman, she is an example of a life of

5. Tall, *Afterings*, 17.

artistry fully lived. Her poems, said Irish poet Eavan Boland, "have the power of the gaze that doesn't fail to notice and never turns away."[6]

Finding the Grave

From Ithaca, head north on Route 13 to the exit for Route 34 North. After the exit, turn right, drive slowly, and keep your eyes sharp. In about a quarter mile you will see a pedestrian crossing for the high school; a small sign on the left marks the entrance of Lake View Cemetery. Or set your GPS for 605 Eastshore Dr., Ithaca, NY, 14850.

The narrow path dips into a valley before taking you uphill. When you reach the top there will be a small area to pull off. To find Deborah Tall's grave, walk the path toward the back gate. About a hundred feet before the gate, find on the left side the prominent stone for Darling, and walk back seven rows. I found many small stones on Deborah Tall's grave from other visitors.

Pleasant Grove

Pleasant Grove Cemetery has a Nobel Laureate, Peter Debye (1884–1966), a theoretical physicist born in the Netherlands. As the Nobel Prize website (https://www.nobelprize.org/prizes/chemistry/1936/debye/facts/) notes, he received the Nobel Prize in 1936 for "his contributions to our knowledge of molecular structure through his investigations on dipole moments and on the diffraction of x-rays and electrons in gases." He taught at Cornell, as did another interment, Thomas Gold (1920–2004), an Austrian-born astronomer and geoscientist who advanced a theory of new matter constantly occurring and expanding rather than the "Big Bang Theory." It was he who originally coaxed Carl Sagan to join the faculty at Cornell.

Here also are two extraordinary literary men, poet A. R. Ammons, and literary critic and author William Strunk Jr.

---

6. Boland, liner notes, in *Afterings.*

Finding the Grave

Take Route 13 from Ithaca to the exit for North Triphammer Road. After exiting, turn right. The sprawling Triphammer Plaza will be on your left. Proceed about three-quarters of a mile, where you'll come to a rather difficult intersection where several roads cross. Fortunately, it's not a busy intersection, usually. Stay on North Triphammer Road and keep an eye out for Pleasant Grove Road on your right which will come up quickly. Make the turn, and you'll find Pleasant Grove Cemetery about an eighth of a mile on your right. To get to this point using GPS, key in: 184 Pleasant Grove Rd., Ithaca, NY, 14850.

There are three entrances. Take the center one through the wrought-iron arch. Just as you near the top of the hill, you'll see a prominent stone for Luce on your left. Stop there and walk to the right for about seventy-five feet. A. R. Ammons's grave is under a fir tree. His inscription reads "This is just a place," which is from his poem "In Memoriam Mae Noblitt." Sit with Archie for a bit. It is just a place, peaceful, fragrant with pine.

William Strunk Jr. (1869–1946): Man of the Elements

When you were in college you probably did not give much thought to the two authors of a little book titled *The Elements of Style* when it appeared on your syllabus, but you went dutifully to the college bookstore and bought a copy for use in a writing class. Or you may have been aware that one of them, E. B. White, was the author of *Charlotte's Web*, which your aunt gave you for Christmas when you were nine or ten. You may even have known that White had once been on the staff of the *New Yorker* and was the author of *One Man's Meat*.

Okay. But who was this Strunk guy? You imagined two men sitting in a book-lined office making up the rules of writing, all the *do-this* and *don't-do-that* stuff, taking an occasional sip of vinegar. Actually, White was Strunk's student at Cornell, and only in later years did he revise his revered teacher's book and add a few of his own rules and regs.

In his introduction, White wrote of his old mentor,

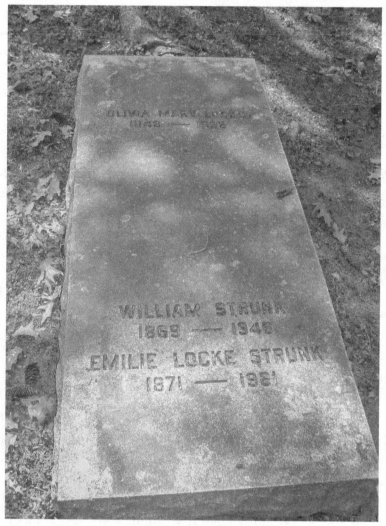

16.4: The grave of William Strunk Jr. in Ithaca.

Professor Strunk was a positive man. His book contains rules of grammar phrased as direct orders. In the main I have not tried to soften his commands, or modify his pronouncements, or remove the special objects of his scorn. I have tried, instead, to preserve the flavor of his discontent while slightly enlarging the scope of the discussion.[13]

13. White, "Introduction," xiv.

William Strunk Jr. was a noted literary scholar, author of *The Impor-
tance of the Ghost in Hamlet,* of a critical edition of James Fenimore
Cooper's *The Last of the Mohicans,* and of a study of poetic forms, *English
Metres.* He was the father of musicologist Oliver Strunk. But he'll always
be best known for his contributions to the table manners of writing. All of
us who call ourselves writers are indebted to him.

His peremptory "Omit needless words" and "Use the active voice"
were taken quite seriously by White, who wrote, "Under the remembered
sting of his kindly lash, I have been trying to omit needless words since
1919."[14]

Finding the Grave

Take Route 13 to the exit for North Triphammer Road. After exiting, turn
right. Stay on North Triphammer Road and keep an eye out for Pleasant
Grove Road on your right which will come up quickly. Make the turn,
and you'll find Pleasant Grove Cemetery about an eighth of a mile on
your right. To get to this point using GPS, key in: 184 Pleasant Grove Rd.,
Ithaca, NY, 14850.

There are three entrances. Take the center one through the wrought-
iron arch, then drive or walk to the end of the road and turn left, and go
all the way to the end of that road. A caretaker's shed is on your left. To
your right is a prominent stone for Sheldon. Walk beyond it about fifty
feet and you will find a flat stone for William Strunk (1869–1946), the plot
he shares with his wife Emilie Locke Strunk (1871–1961) and her mother
Olivia Mary Locke (1848–1932).

Sources

Carl Sagan

Dicke, William. "Carl Sagan, an Astronomer Who Excelled at Popularizing Science, Is Dead at 62." *New York Times,* December 21, 1996.

14. White, xv.

Deborah Tall

Boland, Eavan. Liner notes. In *Afterings*, by Deborah Tall. Introduction by David Weiss. Geneva, NY: Hobart and William Smith Colleges Press, 2016.

Ruefle, Mary. Liner notes. In *Afterings*, by Deborah Tall. Introduction by David Weiss. Geneva, NY: Hobart and William Smith Colleges Press, 2016.

Tall, Deborah. *Afterings*. Introduction by David Weiss. Geneva, NY: Hobart and William Smith Colleges Press, 2016.

Tall, Deborah, and John D'Agata. "The Lyric Essay." Website of Hobart and William Smith Colleges. Accessed April 18, 2023. https://www.hws.edu/offices/senecareview/lyric-essay.aspx.

A. R. Ammons

Ammons, A. R. *Collected Poems 1951–1971*. New York: W. W. Norton, 1972.

Chiasson, Dan. "The Great American Poet of Daily Chores." *New Yorker*, December 4, 2017. https://www.newyorker.com/magazine/2017/12/04/the-great-american-poet-of-daily-chores.

Poulin Jr., A. *Contemporary American Poetry*. 5th ed. Boston: Houghton-Mifflin Co., 1991.

Wilson, Emily Herring. "The A. R. Ammons I Knew." *Wake Forest Magazine*, January 20, 2011. https://magazine.wfu.edu/2011/01/20/the-a-r-ammons-i-knew/.

William Strunk Jr.

White, E. B. "Introduction." In *Elements of Style*, 4th ed., by William Strunk Jr. and E. B. White. Boston: 2000.

17   Lakemont

Paul Bowles

If you are going to Lakemont in New York's Finger Lakes to visit Paul Bowles, you should also celebrate and take in the wineries. This is wine country. In good weather most of them have a tasting room open. Get a designated driver and make a day of it. The nearest to Lakemont Cemetery would be Hickory Hollow Winery in the hamlet of Glenora where the kindly people gave me directions. No, they'd never heard of Bowles, but they knew where to find the cemetery.

One of the things I find interesting about the countryside of Central New York is the variety of cottage industry. Many homes have a sign on the lawn: "Small Engine Repair," "Autobody Paint and Restore," "Fudge," "Eggs," "Quilts," and so on—much enterprising energy. Diners, small business, wineries, a lovely rolling landscape, and the Finger Lakes themselves: the good country.

Paul Bowles (1910–1999): A Lion in Stillness

If any one of my trips to the graves of writers could be called, unequivocally, a pilgrimage, it would certainly be to Paul Bowles's grave. He was an extraordinary man and adventurer. No, he did not go big-game hunting or deep-sea fishing like Ernest Hemingway; he didn't go to war like Thucydides or James Jones. But, before settling in Tangier in Morocco, he followed a profound wanderlust, sometimes with little or no money, through Europe, North Africa, and South America, though it often meant rugged conditions, illness, and cheap hotels. These travels of course gave

145

him the rarified experience and narrative authority to write *The Sheltering Sky*, which became a film by director Bernardo Bertolucci.

He was a fine novelist, yes, but also a master of the short story and a superb composer. As a young man he traveled with Aaron Copeland, who became his tutor in music.[1] In Paris, he befriended Gertrude Stein, Christopher Isherwood, Jean Cocteau, and Andre Gide, and Christopher Isherwood in Berlin.[2] According to his obituary in the *New York Times*, which called him an "icon of individualism," he was best known for his fiction, but also "for his songs, concertos, incidental music and operas; for his marriage to Jane Bowles [a novelist and playwright who died in 1973]; and, simply, for being Paul Bowles." The obit goes on, "He put a stamp of sui generis on whatever he chose to do, or not to do. In many ways, his career was one of avoidance."[3] Copeland was also an avid reader of Bowles's books, according to his biographer Howard Pollack, "and was struck by how strangely dark his fiction was compared to his music, whose freshness and charm he had long admired."[4]

But writing would eventually predominate. About *The Sheltering Sky*, Jane Bowles commented in a letter, "I know it did him a great moral good to be at last a lion which he has deserved for many years and had somehow never gotten in music."[5]

His childhood began in New York City with parents who kept him locked indoors, and he never met another child until he was six years old.[6] His father, according to family legend, tried to kill him in his infancy by putting him naked in a basket on a windowsill during a snowstorm until his grandmother came to his rescue.[7] That was apparently the last attempt on his life, at least at home. Adulthood arrived with not only a career in music, but with a stint as a music critic for the *New York*

1. Green, *Dream at the End of the World*, 4–5.
2. Gussow, "Bowles Dies at 88," B–4.
3. Gussow, B–4.
4. Pollack, *Aaron Copeland*, 185.
5. Green, 73.
6. Bischoff, *Paul Bowles Photographs*, 250.
7. Gussow, B–4.

Herald Tribune,[8] and restless abrupt travel so frequent and peripatetically mad that one wonders how he kept track of it all, which he details in his autobiography *Without Stopping*.

Finally, he did stop. He settled in Tangier in 1947, which became his final mise-en-scene, where he lived out the next fifty-two years as a writer and translator. In a sense, the desert in *Sheltering Sky* is a metaphor for the desert of his lifelong detachment. He has written, "Immediately when you arrive in the Sahara, for the first or the tenth time, you notice the stillness. An incredible, absolute silence prevails. . . ."[9]

He was a member of no movement in literature, only his own, although he became a kind of inadvertent host to Beat writers such as Jack Kerouac, Allen Ginsberg, and William S. Burroughs who all made a path to his house in Tangier. Yet he claimed to feel no real connection to the Beats, that they were merely contemporaries.[10]

His marriage to Jane is also hard to fathom for its detachment; they remained married and somehow devoted to each other, though they seldom lived together and both took other lovers. "We played everything by ear," Bowles told writer Michael Mewshaw. "Each one did what he pleased."[11]

The Sheltering Sky made his reputation; but *Up Above the World* and *The Spider's House* are fine novels too. There are also his translations of oral-tradition storytellers in Morocco. Michael Mewshaw met two of them in Bowles's apartment in Tangier. Mohammed Mrabet, the best known of them, was in an apparent snit with the other who sat silent and glaring. Mewshaw said, "It was a rare example of literary rivalry between illiterates."[12]

Some of his other books are *Let It Come Down*; several collections of short stories; five collections of poems including *Next to Nothing: Collected Poems 1926–1977*; thirty-one volumes of translations including *The Chest*

8. Gussow, B–4.

9. Bowles, *Their Heads Are Green*, 12.

10. Mewshaw, *Do I Owe You Something*, 125.

11. Mewshaw, 113.

12. Mewshaw, 116.

and *The Storyteller and the Fisherman* by Mrabet, and *For Bread Alone* by Mohamed Choukri; and nine volumes of travel and autobiography.

The discography of his music is vast. You can sample some of it in the CBS-TV production of Tennessee Williams's *The Glass Menagerie*, available on YouTube. It is haunting and mysterious, befitting the play. Try his "Baptism of Solitude" and "Night Waltz," and "Heavenly Grass," also on YouTube.

Most of us who work as writers can do only one thing truly well: write. Sure, many of us can also teach, pay the bills, be a spouse. Maybe ride a unicycle or make a risotto. But a man who could write such influential fiction and also compose stunning music, and still gain a reputation for avoidance—that is a meeting of remarkable genes.

But what was his connection to Upstate New York?

Bowles died in 1999 of a heart attack in a hospital in Tangier where he had been a patient for more than a week.[13] He is buried in rural Lakemont, near Seneca Lake, in the Bowles family plot in Lakemont Cemetery. His grandfather, or "Daddypapa," owned a cabin and boathouse in nearby Glenora on Seneca Lake where his uncle Charles also owned property, and where Bowles as a boy spent formative weeks and months in the summers.[14] Viewed from that perspective, it is not so strange that a man who spent the final fifty-two years of his life in North Africa should be buried here. He wasn't a sentimental man. But we all have a homing instinct, more pronounced in some than in others. He insisted that Jane's name be also inscribed on the stone, although she is buried in Spain where she died many years earlier. Which is par for their course: connected by name and by love, but forever at a distance.

Finding the Grave

From the Thruway, take Exit 42 for Geneva. Take a right turn after the tollbooths and take Route 14 South. Be careful not to get on Route 96—easy to do, I've done it myself. You want Route 14, to go to the west side of

13. Gussow, B–4.
14. Bowles, *Without Stopping*, 19ff.

17.1: The grave of Paul Bowles in Lakemont.

Seneca Lake (Route 96 will take you to Cayuga). Stay on Route 14, which will take you through Geneva. Once you are out of town you will be heading due south.

In about twenty-six miles you will make a right turn onto Lakemont Himrod Road, which is Yates County Highway 01. Some miles before, there is a Himrod Road, but don't be fooled, you want *Lakemont Himrod*. As you near the turnoff, you will pass the Railroad Crossing Diner on your left, and Hickory Hollow Winery. A yellow barn looms on the right side, just before your turn—at least as of this writing it is yellow. Slow down and get ready to make a very sharp right. Take Lakemont Himrod Road for just over a half mile, then make a left onto Hayes Road. This is lovely countryside, grape fields everywhere. Lakemont Cemetery will be about one-half mile on your left. Or you can key into your GPS: 390 Hayes Rd., Lakemont, NY, 14857.

The entrance is on the far side. Follow that entrance path for a couple hundred feet until you see a sign that reads "Section C." Bowles is right next to the sign under a cluster of arborvitae trees, on the cemetery's west edge, one of three low stones facing away from you toward the east. He is buried next to his parents, Claude and Rena, and a few steps from Frederick T. and Ida Willa Bowles, his grandparents.

Sources

Bischoff, Simon, ed. *Paul Bowles Photographs: "How Could I Send a Picture into the Desert?"* New York: Scalo Publishers, 1994.

Bowles, Paul. *Their Heads Are Green and Their Hands Are Blue: Scenes from the Non-Christian World.* New York: Ecco Press, 1957, 1963.

Bowles, Paul. *Without Stopping: An Autobiography.* New York: Ecco Press, 1972.

Green, Michelle. *The Dream at the End of the World: Paul Bowles and the Literary Renegades in Tangier.* New York: HarperCollins, 1991.

Gussow, Mel. "Paul Bowles, Elusive Composer and Author Known for 'Sheltering Sky' Dies at 88." *New York Times*, November 19, 1999.

Mewshaw, Michael. *Do I Owe You Something? A Memoir of the Literary Life.* Baton Rouge: Louisiana State Univ. Press, 2003.

Pollack, Howard. *Aaron Copeland: The Life and Work of an Uncommon Man.* New York: Henry Holt, 1999.

18   Newark

Charles R. Jackson

Newark is a village in the town of Arcadia on the Erie Canal, about half-way between Rochester and Syracuse. An area on its east side was once known as Lockville, where a cluster of three canal locks operated, and which have been preserved for a historical park. Like most villages on the canal, it owes its early prosperity to Erie traffic; the presence of even one lock was good for local business, general stores and taverns particularly, simply because boats were delayed there and canallers availed themselves of whatever was at hand.

Famous dancer and choreographer Sybil Shearer (1912–2005), born in Toronto, grew up here. Journalist Harriet Van Horne (1920–98) graduated from Newark High School. Songwriter, singer, and animator Peter Hannan is from Newark. And, although few in Newark now remember him personally, there was author Charles Reginald Jackson.

Charles R. Jackson (1903–1968):
Weekends Lost and Regained, and Lost

Charles Jackson was a kid addicted to books, who spent his weekend afternoons in the Newark village library instead of on the ballfield. In fact, that is where he was on November 12, 1916, when a call came for him to come directly home. Bad news was waiting. His older sister Thelma, sixteen, and four-year-old brother Richard, had been riding in a car that was hit by a passenger train at a nearby railroad crossing. Both were killed, along with one other.[1] Besides paralyzing the family, the tragedy traumatized the entire community.

At the funeral, the two siblings were laid out together in one casket, Thelma on her side as if napping, with Richard's head on her arm and holding her hand.[2] Not long after, the father, Fred, who had found work in Manhattan, wrote to say that he wouldn't be coming home again.[3] Thereafter, Charles grew very close to his mother, although their relationship was rocky.

The youths of many writers seem grounded in tragedy. Among Upstate authors, John Gardner[4] caused a farming accident that killed his younger brother Gilbert; Adelaide Crapsey[5] was devastated by her father being defrocked from the priesthood by the Episcopal Diocese; Mark Twain's brother died in a riverboat fire. How much those traumas fired their creative drive is a matter for speculation, more things than can be dreamt of in our philosophy.

Charles Jackson—short and slight of build—was a closeted bisexual, which in those times was a scandalous complication, and may have been a driving force behind his later alcoholism, although Jackson hung the responsibility for both on his mother.[6] He enrolled in Syracuse University in 1921, but left after a dustup over a fling with another fraternity member.[7] Four years later in 1925, he left Newark on a train for Chicago and worked in bookstores and as a newspaper editor there, and later moved to New York City.

But in 1928 he began coughing up blood, and by 1929, living in Newark again, he went to Rochester General Hospital where they collapsed his right lung as a treatment for tuberculosis. Since antibiotics for the disease

1. Bailey, *Farther and Wilder*, 7–9.
2. Bailey, 21.
3. Bailey, 11.
4. See West, chapter 27, Batavia.
5. See West, chapter 36, Rochester.
6. Bailey, 24.
7. *Prabook*, "Charles Reginald Jackson."

did not arrive until 1946, this was the only practical medical intervention, allowing tuberculous damage to heal. Finally, he and his brother Fred, who also suffered from the disease, went to a renowned sanitorium in Switzerland for treatment, which included rest and clean air, and sleeping in frigid temperatures. The bill was paid by Bronson Winthrop, a wealthy lawyer that Charles had befriended a few years before.[8]

Unlike Rochester poet Adelaide Crapsey[9], Jackson regained his health after his bout with tuberculosis.

Jackson was a hard-working writer. While still in his teens he was local editor of the Newark *Courier-Gazette*, writing much of what passed for news in the small town. His first novel, *The Lost Weekend* (1944), a story of five days and nights in the life of an alcoholic writer on a binge, which years later he admitted was largely autobiographical, made him famous, and while none of his other novels quite came up to it in critical acclaim or in sales, he remained a highly respected writer and a well-paid lecturer. *Lost Weekend* was translated into fourteen languages and, according to Jackson biographer Blake Bailey, aroused the jealousy of British poet and novelist Malcom Lowry who was hard at work on his own "alcoholic masterpiece," *Under the Volcano*.[10] Thomas Mann compared it to Knut Hamsun's *Hunger*.[11]

Focusing on a writer's dipsomania—intriguing to some readers—is often a diversion from what truly matters about the works. But, as with Frederick Exley,[12] it is inescapable with Jackson. *Lost Weekend* was one of the big publishing events of 1944. Philip Wylie, in a review in the *New York Times*, said,

> Charles Jackson has made the most compelling gift to the literature of addiction since De Quincey. . . . [He] makes plain the psychic states

8. Bailey, 61–64.
9. See West, chapter 36, Rochester.
10. Bailey, 128.
11. Breit, "Talk with Charles Jackson," 20.
12. See Central, chapter 24, Watertown.

which give rise to the morbid eloquence of Poe, on one hand, and to such phenomena, on the other, as the late F. Scott Fitzgerald's identification of glamor with literal intoxication.[13]

The book was destined for classic status.

Director Billy Wilder made it into a 1945 movie, which the New York Times's Bosley Crowther called "an illustration of a drunkard's misery that ranks with the best and most disturbing character studies ever put on the screen."[14] It won the Oscar for Best Picture, Best Actor for Ray Milland, and a Best Adapted Screenplay for Wilder and Charles Brackett.[15]

But novelists are rarely happy with their film treatments. Hemingway didn't like any of his movies. And Jackson, while initially thrilled with the script, wrangled with the Wilder-Brackett team when they tacked on an upbeat ending that they knew would be more palatable to the public and less apt to rile the Hays motion picture production censors. He felt cheated, but finally gave in,[16] although he became a nagging thorn in Brackett's side, who wrote in his diary January 4, 1945, "Charles Jackson's letter arrived (a five-page agony of hatred of the final sequence). It sounded so repetitious it was like a loop. . . ."[17] One day the following August a phone call from Jackson got Brackett out of the bathtub. Peevishly, he wrapped a towel around himself and went to answer it. "I said, 'I don't want to hear your voice. I don't want to hear your name. I am just God-damned bored!' With that I hung up."[18]

Jackson tried to be a devoted husband to his wife Rhoda, and was a doting father to his daughters. For long stretches of time he remained sober, even traveling as a national spokesman for Alcoholics Anonymous. It is worth listening to one of his talks, "Charles R. Jackson—Alcoholics Anonymous Speech (1959)," which is available on YouTube. He mentions

13. Wylie, "Wingding," 50.
14. Crowther, "The Lost Week-End," 28.
15. See East, chapter 7, Saratoga.
16. Bailey, 183–85.
17. Brackett, *It's the Pictures That Got Small*, 259.
18. Brackett, 273.

there that he did not actually begin drinking to excess until age twenty-six, unlike most big drinkers he had known who were more precocious. However, even while traveling for AA, he had trouble staying out of the sauce. Near the end of his life, he deserted his family as had his father before him. He died in 1968 from an intentional overdose of barbiturates at Saint Vincent's Hospital in Manhattan[19] (where Dylan Thomas had died from inebriation fifteen years before). Jackson was sixty-five.

And yet, all considered, his life was a triumph, not just over tragedy, tuberculosis, and stretches of time lost to alcohol, but over the self-doubt that plagues every writer. Inside of this small man was a core of strength and genius. Robert Markel, his editor at Macmillan, stated, "Mr. Jackson felt life as deeply as anyone I've known, and this comes out in his work."[20]

His books that followed *Lost Weekend* were *The Fall of Valor* (1946), *The Outer Edges* (1948), *The Sunnier Side: Twelve Arcadian Tales* (1950), *Earthly Creatures* (1953), and *A Second-Hand Life* (1967).

Finding the Grave

No freeway goes to Newark, but trusty Route 31 runs through it, the road that more than any other runs parallel to the Erie Canal in that part of the state. Coming from the east on the Thruway, get off at Exit 42 for Geneva and Lyons; take Route 14 north several miles to Lyons, and turn west on Route 31. From the west, take Exit 41 for Palmyra and travel east on Route 31. In the center of the village, turn south on Main Street, then left (east) on East Maple Avenue, which, in about a mile, will intersect with Vienna Street, where you will turn right. Or set your GPS for Vienna Street, Newark, NY, 14513. The cemetery seems not to have a published street number.

The main road into the cemetery is called Pine Street. Take this road, passing a wooden shed on the right. You will see Aspen Street on the left, but Aspen is actually a loop. Go to the second intersection with Aspen.

19. Bailey, 419–20.
20. "Jackson, Author of *Lost Weekend*, Dies," 88.

18.1: The grave of Charles Jackson in Newark.

The Jackson family plot is on the corner, and Charles Jackson is nearest to the corner. Next to him is the grave of Thelma and Richard. Their mother Sarah and brother Fred are nearby.

Sources

Bailey, Blake. *Farther and Wilder: The Lost Weekends and Literary Dreams of Charles Jackson*. New York: Alfred A. Knopf, 2013.

Brackett, Charles. *"It's the Pictures That Got Small": Charles Brackett on Billy Wilder and Hollywood's Golden Age*. Edited by Anthony Slide. Foreword by Jim Moore. New York: Columbia Univ. Press, 2015.

Breit, Harvey. "Talk with Charles Jackson." *New York Times*, April 30, 1950.

"Charles Jackson, Author of *Lost Weekend*, Dies." *New York Times*, September 22, 1968.

"Charles Reginald Jackson." Prabook. Accessed April 18, 2023. https://prabook
.com/web/charles.jackson/8174.

Crowther, Bosley. "The Lost Week-End, in Which Ray Milland Presents a Study
in Dipsomania, Makes Its Appearance at the Rivoli." Movie review. *New
York Times*, December 3, 1945.

Jackson, Charles R. Alcoholics Anonymous Speech. 1959. Accessed April 18,
2023. https://www.youtube.com/watch?v=QoiP5xsJzvs.

Wilder, Billy, director. *The Lost Weekend*. Paramount, 1945. 1:41.

Wylie, Philip. "Wingding: The Lost Week-End." *New York Times Book Review*,
January 30, 1944.

19   Ontario / Furnaceville

Jane Roberts

An early settler on the shore of Lake Ontario found ore while digging a well. While it wasn't gold ore, it set off a local industry of open mining and forging, and by 1816 a small furnace in what would become the town of Furnaceville was producing a whopping four hundred pounds of pig iron per day. But then came the investors to stoke bigger furnaces. The Ontario Iron Company in 1870 built a giant facility with anthracite blast ovens. Furnaceville and its environs became a region of pits where men mined ore and hauled it by wagon to barges on Bear Creek. The night sky over the town was a dull orange, as was the soil by day.

Business began to slack off by the late 1880s, caused by competition from newer mines in the Mesabi Range of Minnesota. The last of the iron production ended in 1922, and the fires of Furnaceville, now part of the town of Ontario, went out—*poof.* That is the history of industrial America: a little thing becomes a big deal, and later becomes no deal at all.

Today there are no obvious traces of the old industry, save for historical landmark signs noting the location of the open mining pits and a blast furnace. Furnaceville is reforested and sleepy, with charming lakefront residences, but without welcoming amenities. That is, there is no downtown. Schoolhouses and a grocery store are long gone. A man at a yard sale there told me that all that's left is the cemetery and the Rod and Gun Club.

In that cemetery, however, is Jane Roberts, whose spiritual self-help books developed an international following.

Jane Roberts (1929–1984): Power in the Present Moment

Jane was born in Albany, New York, and grew up in Saratoga Springs, tending to her invalid mother. She went to Catholic school and to Skidmore College on a poetry scholarship. She didn't finish but eloped with a boyfriend to California—a brief marriage. Back home again, she met and married a young illustrator named Robert Butts.[1] They left Saratoga for Elmira where she and Robert planned to work part-time jobs while pursuing writing careers. Not an auspicious beginning for a woman who would soon draw so many seekers into her circle.

It was in Elmira in 1963, in their upstairs apartment on Water Street, that their lives took a sudden and interesting turn. Jane discovered that she had the gifts of a psychic-medium when her life was suddenly and mysteriously imposed upon by a spirit named Seth; she began "channeling" Seth who, speaking through Jane, held court with wisdom from the beyond,[2] which sounded a lot like what was later called New Age.

Robert Butts transcribed the Seth sessions, which became ten popular books, among them *The Nature of the Psyche: Its Human Expression; Seth Speaks: The Eternal Validity of the Soul;* and *Value Fulfillment.* Their books sold millions of copies as she developed an international following.

Today, so much material on Jane Roberts and Seth can be found on the internet and in print that it can be confusing and difficult to sift through it all. (Her papers, by the way, were acquired by Yale.) But Rich Kendall's book *The Road to Elmira*, his memoir of attending Jane's group sessions in her apartment in the early 1970s, gives a vivid picture of what those occasions were like, to encounter the spirit of Seth—who seemed to know intuitively everything about anyone who walked in the door. Even if Jane was not channeling a spirit, her psychic, or at least intuitive, powers must have been profound.

Whether or not you believe in spirits, let alone one that seems all-wise, it is nevertheless significant that almost forty years after her death in 1984

1. Kestenbaum, "Till Seth Do Us Part," 55.
2. *California Seth Conference*, "Brief History of Jane."

(from rheumatoid arthritis)[3] she has retained a large following. While she was alive she counted among her enthusiasts motivational author Louise Hay; New-Age self-help author Deepak Chopra; Richard Bach, author of *Jonathan Livingston Seagull*; spiritual writer Wayne Dyer;[4] and puppeteer and animator Jim Henson.[5] Seth or no Seth, the advice gained from her sessions and books has resonated.

Christian writers have claimed that Jane was actually channeling a demon intent on luring people away from God. And, you may well ask, was she the center of a personality cult? No, according to Kendall, "Her purpose as a teacher was not to magnify her own persona at the expense of her students but to lead each of us back to our own sense of power; to inspire within each of us the confidence to look for our own answers; and to trust the authority of our own psyche."[6] Some demon.

According to the *Seth Worx* website,

> The essence of the Seth Material can be contained within the phrase, "We each create our own personal reality and the point of power is the present moment." However, understanding the full implications of this deceptively simple phrase requires a complete reassessment of our world, our lives, and what we truly are.[7]

After Jane's death, Robert Butts remarried. He kept Jane's ashes, and when he died in 2008, his widow had them buried together, next to Robert's brother in Furnaceville Rural Cemetery.[8]

Finding the Grave

From the Thruway, take Exit 45, then drive north on I-390. Near Rochester, take the right side exit to I-590, until you see signs for Route 104.

---

3. Kestenbaum, 55.
4. "Brief History of Jane."
5. Kestenbaum, 55.
6. Kendall, "Number 2 Must Try Harder," in *The Road to Elmira*.
7. Seth Worx, home page, paragraph 2.
8. Mary Dillman, Ontario town historian, email message to the author regarding burial of Jane Roberts Butts and Robert Butts, May 12, 2018.

19.1: The grave of Jane Roberts and Robert Butts in Furnaceville.

Take the exit for 104 East, cross the Irondequoit Bay Bridge, and drive approximately twelve more miles until you see a sign reading "Furnace Road 800 Feet." Turn left (north) at the traffic light. Drive approximately two miles to the intersection with Trimble Road, where you will turn right. Furnaceville Rural Cemetery will be a tenth of a mile on your right, across from Anderson's Christmas Tree Farm. Or for GPS directions, key in: 2280 Trimble Rd., Ontario, NY, 14519.

Take the second, easternmost entrance (the original wrought-iron arch is still there, but it is no longer an entrance, it's just ornamental) onto a paved drive. When you come to a crossing, turn left onto a short gravel drive and park at the end. You will be facing a pine woods and the last row of graves on the eastern side. From that point, walk to the right along that row. On the seventh plot is the stone for Jane Roberts Butts and her husband Robert Fabian Butts. An inscription reads "The Seth Book Authors."

When I visited in July 2017, it was a well-tended grave with artificial flowers, some live plantings, and an American flag.

Sources

"A Brief History of Jane Roberts, Robert Butts, and Seth." *California Seth Conference.* Accessed April 18, 2023. www.californiasethconference.com/2021
-conference.html.

Kendall, Richard. *The Road to Elmira*. Rich Kendall Books. New Haven, 2011. Kindle.

Kestenbaum, Sam. "Till Seth Do Us Part." *New York Times*, February 29, 2019.

Seth Worx. October 29, 2019. http://sethworx.com/index.htm.

20   Port Byron

Clara Barrus

As its name suggests, the village of Port Byron was a docking place on the Erie Canal when the inland waterway was in its prime. For many years the canal brought it prosperity and culture. A former village historian once told me that Lord Byron was the port's namesake, although I understand that that claim has been disputed. Its population of around 1,200 has remained remarkably constant since the late nineteenth century.

For the canal enthusiast, a remnant of the old Erie, from the era (1836–62) when it was widened from its original 40-foot span to 70, but not its current 120-foot, is in Rudolf J. Schasel Park on the edge of the village; and a couple miles out on Route 31 is Centreport Aqueduct Park, where you can see remnants of an 1854 aqueduct over Cold Spring Brook. A little west of Port Byron on the Thruway, you can see the restored Lock 52, which is now Erie Canal Heritage Park.

Brigham Young arrived in 1825, a few years before joining the Mormon faith, and rented a house on the corner of Pine Street and South with the first of his fifty-five wives and the first of his fifty-eight children. He would become the leader of the Mormon Church after the death of Joseph Smith. The house still stands, although it is empty, in dilapidated condition. Isaac Singer, an actor and inventor whose later practical improvements to the sewing machine would make him fabulously wealthy, lived briefly in Port Byron in the 1830s, as did Henry Wells, then an Erie Canal agent, before moving to Aurora, New York, founding Wells Fargo and Wells College. It missed by a hair becoming a solid industrial port: a physician named Henry Julian Allen founded the first mincemeat

163

factory here, but it was short-lived. His brand, which once filled countless American holiday pies, was Imperial Mincemeat.

It may seem remarkable that such a tiny village contained, in its early years, several of history's world-shakers. But the old Erie lured through its locks an extraordinary migration of fortune seekers, inventors, gamblers, pilgrims, hucksters, evangelists, geniuses, dandies, prostitutes, poets, circuses, and criminals. The towns like Port Byron that grew up around its locks and drydocks were exciting, rough-and-tumble places, yearning to become the big cities of America's future. Amid all these elements, the story of Clara Barrus, a writer and pioneering physician, goes almost unnoticed.

Clara Barrus (1864–1931): Physician and Author

Clara Barrus met John Burroughs in 1902, and helped nurse his wife in her final illness. And she became the philosopher-naturalist's late-life assistant when he needed care himself.[1]

Barrus herself was also an extraordinary person. She graduated with a medical degree in 1888 from Boston College, a time when few women attained that goal in a male-dominated profession. She practiced privately in Utica, and at the Middletown State Homeopathic Hospital for the Insane, one of two such hospitals in New York, the other being in Gowanda.[2] Homeopathy was a widely accepted treatment for mental illness at that time. She wrote two books on the subject, *Nursing the Insane* and *Insanity in Young Women*. Later she was professor of psychiatry at Women's Medical College of New York City. She briefly operated a private sanitarium in Pelham.[3]

She would produce several books about Burroughs: *Our Friend, John Burroughs*; *Whitman and Burroughs, Comrades* about his friendship with the poet; the two-volume *The Life and Letters of John Burroughs*; and *John Burroughs: Boy and Man*; and edited his posthumous works for

1. See East, chapter 6, Roxbury.
2. Homeopathe International, "Dr. Clara Barrus (1864–1931)."
3. "Dr. Clara Barrus, Physician, Is Dead," 26.

20.1: Barrus family plot in Port Byron. Clara Barrus marker is in foreground.

publication. She died in 1931, aged sixty-six, shortly after approving the proofs for *Whitman and Burroughs*.[4]

Finding the Grave

For the best route to Port Byron, take the Thruway to Exit 40 for Weedsport, a little west of Syracuse, then turn east on Route 31, and travel about four miles into Port Byron. To get to Mount Pleasant Cemetery, take South Main Street to Park Street, just a short distance from the center of the village, where you will make a left turn (east). Then veer right onto McClellan Street, then right onto Park Street, which will take you directly

4. "Dr. Clara Barrus, Physician, Is Dead," 26.

through the cemetery gates. Or set your GPS to Park Street, Port Byron, NY, 13140. The cemetery does not have a street number. But the village is tiny and you cannot get lost.

Once inside the gates, make the first right onto the ominously named Vault Avenue. Drive to the top of the hill. You will come to two intersections. Stop at the second. To your left will be a cinder path, to your right a grassy lane between sections of the cemetery. Walk that lane for about a hundred yards, with large shady pines to your left. The second from the last spire on the left is the Barrus family plot. The names of her father John and mother Sarah are on the spire. Clara has a modest stone nearby.

Sources

"Dr. Clara Barrus (1864–1931).", Homeopathe International, 2004. http://homeo int.org/photo/b2/barrusc.htm.

"Dr. Clara Barrus, Physician, Is Dead." *New York Times*, April 5, 1931, 26.

21   Syracuse

Mary Raymond Shipman Andrews,
Edward Noyes Westcott

The GPS was invented for cities like Syracuse—the downtown part any-way, where, once you get off the expressway you can become completely lost in the tangle of streets. I know, I lost my way there many times before I got one of those marvelous devices. But it is one of many underappreciated communities in Upstate New York. In the beginning of the movie *Tootsie*, Dustin Hoffman plays a struggling actor on stage in Syracuse, which is meant to convey that his career is not going very well because he's not in the big city. Today when people say "Syracuse" (that is, people who do not live in Syracuse), they are generally referring to the Syracuse University Orange basketball team, or to Syracuse University itself. But all Upstate cities suffer from being knee-high to New York City.

Syracuse has a fascinating history, older than settlements in Rochester by at least a hundred and fifty years if you count the Jesuit mission Sainte Marie among the Iroquois in 1656. It was a major port on the Erie Canal near the junction of lateral waterways, the Seneca and Black River canals, as well as a crossing for railroads and highways. It was once a center of the salt industry, near salt springs. At one time the most common dining ware in schools, hospitals, cafeterias, and modest hotels was Syracuse China, immediately recognizable for its cream color and its heft—built to with-stand almost perennial use. And this city still hosts the annual New York State Fair.

Many well-known people are *from* Syracuse, most outside the scope of this book. But two writers, Mary Raymond Shipman Andrews and Edward

Noyes Westcott, both nearly forgotten, are buried in the massive Oakwood Cemetery on the south end of the city, just off of I-81.

Mary Raymond Shipman Andrews (1860–1936): Romantic Mythmaker

Mary was an avid big-game hunter, and her experiences on the trail of moose and bear in Canada informed the romantic novels she wrote for boys who dreamed of adventure. She wrote more than twenty books, some of which are fueled by the theme of patriotism.[1] Without doubt, she is best remembered for her book about Lincoln and the Gettysburg Address, *A Perfect Tribute*, a bestseller in its time (1906). Historian Kent Gramm has pointed out that her story of Lincoln writing the address in one draft with a broken pencil while on route by train to Gettysburg is anything but accurate history. Moreover, he says that she romanticized the scene of its delivery, and that her version of events following in which, on his return to Washington, he visits a dying Confederate soldier in a hospital, are entirely and shamelessly fiction.[2]

On the other hand, Lincoln is probably the most mythologized president in our nation's history, and Andrews is hardly more guilty—or less well-intentioned—than John Ford (a mythmaker if one ever lived) for his 1939 film *Young Mr. Lincoln*, generally considered classic cinema. In fact, Hollywood took two cracks at Andrews's story, a short film in 1930 and a 1991 made-for-TV movie starring the 5-foot-8-inch Jason Robards as the 6-foot-4-inch Lincoln.

Some of her other books include *A Good Samaritan*; *Joy in the Morning*; and *A Lost Commander*. Two others hit the silver screen in the silent era: *The Courage of the Common Place* (1917) and *Three Things*, retitled *Unbeliever* (1918).[3]

She lived on an estate called Wolf Hollow, a little west of Syracuse, with her husband William Shankland Andrews, an associate justice on

1. Onondaga Historical Association, "Mary Shipman Andrews."
2. Gramm, "A More Perfect Tribute," 52, 54–55.
3. "Mary Shipman Andrews."

21.1: The Andrews family plot in Syracuse. Mary Raymond Shipman Andrews's marker is in the foreground.

the New York State Court of Appeals. Their son Paul Shipman Andrews was once dean of the Syracuse University College of Law.[4]

Finding the Grave

To get to Oakwood Cemetery from the west, take the Thruway to Exit 39 for Route 690. In 9.6 miles, take the exit for Route 81 South; from east, take Thruway Exit 36 for Route 81 South. From Route 81, take Exit 17 and turn right on South State Street. After a third of a mile, turn right on East Colvin Street. Take this to Comstock Ave. and turn left. Once on Comstock you cannot miss the cemetery. However, you will fare better with your GPS: 940 Comstock Ave., Syracuse, NY, 13210.

4. "Mary Shipman Andrews."

I strongly recommend that you stop in the office and ask for directions and a map. It is not that Oakwood is so large—although it is, indeed, very expansive—but the roads and paths wind so circuitously that one can quickly lose sense of direction, and thus my poor abilities to guide you must bow to the authority of the folks in the office, which is open weekdays during normal business hours and on Saturdays. I found the staff to be very helpful, by the way.

But let's say that you have been given directions to section 48, where Mary Raymond Shipman Andrews is buried, and you have located that section. It slopes downhill to a crossing of two paths; and at that point, at the corner facing that crossroads, is a monument for the Andrews family plot. You will find a number of footstones for family members, and the author's stone is near a granite stairway.

Edward Noyes Westcott (1946–1998): The Triumph of the (Posthumous) Last Chance Novelist

Edward Noyes Westcott was a rejection-slip collector, like most writers. But in 1896, while in bed with tuberculosis, he gave it another go, and wrote a novel. Westcott's illness, which he knew to be fatal, was only his most recent turn of bad luck. His wife had died of pneumonia; his father, Dr. Amos Westcott, a prominent dentist and former mayor of Syracuse, committed suicide. While performing with a Syracuse militia on stage at a local opera house, Edward fell into the orchestra pit and sustained a head injury from which he never quite recovered. Westcott's own banking and brokerage business had gone belly-up.[5]

When tuberculosis struck, he traveled to Naples, Italy, for a short convalescence, then returned to his home on James Street in Syracuse where illness confined him to his upstairs bedroom. There he completed *David Harum: A Story of American Life*. After rejection by six publishers, it was accepted by Appleton and Co. late in 1897.[6]

---

5. O'Shea, *Westcott's Tale*, 1.
6. Case, "The Westcotts and David Harum," 7–8.

21.2: The grave of Edward Noyes Westcott in Syracuse.

When it was published in the fall of 1898, six months after Westcott's death, it soared to the top of the sales charts, reaching a million-and-a-half copies by 1911, making his heirs, his daughter and two sons, individually wealthy.[7] Who would have guessed? Certainly not Westcott himself, who had claimed he expected his bad luck to prevail into the hereafter.

David Harum, now considered a classic American novel, is a humorous story of an Upstate New York banker who trades horses on the side. The setting, Homeville, may have been a veiled representation of Homer, New York, a small town south of Syracuse, and David himself may have been modeled on a man in Homer who was a friend of Edward's father—at least the people in Homer thought so. But all that is much disputed.

Westcott's novel is written in the country vernacular of Central New York, or at least as it was spoken in the nineteenth century, rich in allegory

7. Case, 3.

and metaphor that makes it a colorful read. It became a stage play, then a silent film in 1915, and at last a sound film in 1934, starring none other than Will Rogers as David Harum.

Finding the Grave

From the west, take the Thruway to Exit 39 for Route 690, then take the exit for Route 81 South. From the east, take the Thruway to Exit 36 for Route 81 South. From Route 81, take Exit 17 and turn right on South State Street. After a third of a mile, turn right on East Colvin Street. Take this to Comstock Ave. and turn left. Once on Comstock you cannot miss the cemetery.

Edward Noyes Westcott is buried in section 13. Again, you'll need a map and directions from office staff. But section 13 is in one of the older sections, on the far side of the cemetery from the office. I suggest taking the route past sections 25 and 24. Just past the chapel in section 15, you will make a right turn; section 13 is just past 14. Park and walk up the small hill. You will find a flat stone, about two feet square, marking the Westcott family plot, and two rows of footstones, among which is Edward Westcott's.

When you leave, go back the way you came, since the roads up the hill to the north are very rugged.

Sources

Mary Raymond Shipman Andrews

Gramm, Kent. "A More Perfect Tribute." *Journal of the Abraham Lincoln Association* 25, no. 2 (2004): 50–58. http://www.jstor.org/stable/20149063.
"Monday Ms. Stories: Mary Shipman Andrews." Onondaga Historical Association. Accessed April 18, 2023. www.cnyhistory.org/2015/11/monday-miss-stories-mary-shipman-andrews/.

Edward Noyes Westcott

Case, Richard G. "The Westcotts and David Harum." *Courier* X, no. 2. Winter (1973): 3–14.

"Edward Noyes Westcott (1846–1998), Author of David Harum." SSWDA. Accessed April 18, 2023. www.sswda.org/archive/edward-noyes-westcott-1846 -1898-author-of-david-harum.

O'Shea, Jane C. *Westcott's Tale: Revisiting 19th Century Central New York*. Self-published, 2014.

22 Pulaski

Claude Bragdon

Pulaski, on the Salmon River, is a homey village named for the Polish general Count Casimir Pulaski who fought heroically in the Continental Army in the American Revolution. It is part of the town of Richland and is the site of the Selkirk Lighthouse on Lake Ontario at the mouth of the Salmon River, now a hotel and on the National Register of Historic Places. A fire in 1883 destroyed the business district, and a good part of what is there now is the rebuilt Pulaski, although part of the village is also on the Historic Places register. It is a charming place to walk around.

It is directly downwind of Lake Ontario, and thus takes the brunt of lake-effect snowstorms that come walloping off the water, and in fact lies near the Tug Hill Plateau region so famous for heavy snowfall.

Buried here is one of the most unusual writers and innovative artists that America ever produced.

Claude Bragdon (1866–1946): Architect, Mystic, and Author

He was born in Oberlin, Ohio, and raised in several Upstate New York towns, including Oswego, Utica, Dansville, Watertown, and finally Rochester, as the family followed his father's itinerant career as a reporter and news editor. His mother wrote articles for women's magazines to help feed the family whose income was often disrupted in the process of his father changing jobs. Claude Fayette Bragdon was the great-grandson of Samuel Bragdon, aide de camp to George Washington in the Revolution, and the grandson of a Congregationalist minister and fiery abolitionist. The

174

family's farm in Troy had been a regular stop on the Underground Railroad where runaway enslaved people were fed and rested before being smuggled off to stations in Syracuse, Auburn, and Rochester.[1]

Wherever the family landed, his father stocked the bookshelves with reading that clearly fed the soul and imagination of the Theosophist that Bragdon would become. While still a teen, Bragdon was deep in Emerson and Thoreau as well as the Hindu Vedas and the *Bhagavad Gita*, and he devoured books by Madam Blavatsky and Mabel Collins. He became so utterly absorbed in Emerson's *Conduct of Life* that he lost all sense of time as he moved through its pages, finally refusing one Sunday to accompany his parents to church so that he could remain with Emerson. "I date my conversion to Theosophy from that hour," he wrote, "for Emerson's essays are so largely a distillation of the Ancient Wisdom through the consciousness of a New England Brahmin."[2] He would never again be the same.

The family moved to Rochester in 1884, where his father went to work as an editorial news writer for the *Union and Advertiser.* Claude, a skilled artist and draftsman, was briefly a political cartoonist for a Rochester comic paper until one of his drawings lampooned D. W. Powers, a mighty local businessman, whose namesake Powers Building still stands. Powers threatened legal action and, in an attempt to defuse the situation, the paper's editor fired the upstart cartoonist.[3]

He now saw his future in architecture. But at age thirty, dissatisfied with apprenticeships with Rochester firms, some of which paid him peanuts while others paid nothing, he went to Europe and studied architecture by touring the grand cathedrals. He spent a month drawing in London, and then went on to Paris, Turin, Siena, Rome, and Vienna. And he began to paint. Returning to Rochester in 1896, he founded the architectural firm Bragdon and Hillman. One of their first commissions was the Livingston County Courthouse in Geneseo. He also designed advertisements and book covers, and wrote articles for architectural magazines.[4]

1. Costa, "Claude F. Bragdon," 2.
2. Taylor, "Claude Bragdon," 2.
3. Costa, 4.
4. Costa, 7–9.

His first marriage was to Charlotte Coffyn Wilkinson of Syracuse, a socially connected woman whose gregarious personality drew him into upper society in Rochester and resulted in numerous commissions.[5]

The Beautiful Necessity, maybe his best-known book, is a Theosophical approach to architecture: the yoking of beauty and the sciences, as an expression of the soul. In *A Primer of Higher Space*, he elaborates his theory of a fourth dimension:

> The idea that space may have more than three dimensions may seem highly revolutionary, but it is no more so than that the world is spherical instead of flat, or that the earth revolves around the sun instead of the sun around the earth. These familiar truths contradict the evidence of the senses, and therefor they were received with incredulity until the proof of them became overwhelming.[6]

In his autobiography, *More Lives Than One*, he affirms his belief in reincarnation. Bragdon used Theosophy in mathematical expressions in his design of Rochester's New York Central Railroad Station. Until it was torn down in the urban renewal madness of the 1960s, it stood as one of the city's most distinctive structures. His idea of projected ornament, using geometric patterns in architecture, can be seen in Rochester's First Universalist Church. His Bevier Memorial Building in Rochester also still stands.

When Charlotte died in childbirth with their second child, he took on the role of a single parent. In doing so, according to Erville Costa, he developed a sympathy and understanding of "the problems, needs, and special psychology of women."[7] He became drawn to women with psychic powers, whom he called "the Delphic Sisterhood."[8] His second wife Eugenie, whom he married in 1912, was a spiritualist, and he believed

5. Costa, 9.
6. Bragdon, *Primer of Higher Space*, 4.
7. Costa, 14.
8. Cannon, "Builders of the Future," 6.

unquestionably in her psychic powers and ability to contact spirits through automatic writing.[9]

He started his own publishing company, the Mana Press, and published the Russian philosopher Peter Ouspensky's famous second book *Tertium Organum* (which he also helped translate from Russian); *Confessions of Two Brothers* by the Welsh writers John Cowper Powys and Llewelyn Powys; and *Verse*, the first and only book of poems by Rochester poet Adelaide Crapsey who had died of tuberculosis some months before.[10]

Then in 1915 he did something even more extraordinary. He began staging public "Festivals of Song and Light" in Rochester's Highland Park, with choruses and architecturally designed electric light shows. It was truly innovating—no one had ever used electric light so enthrallingly before. He traveled to other cities recreating the Highland Park show, and held a grand finale in Madison Square Garden.[11] Rochester's literary center Writers & Books held a recreation of the light shows on University Avenue in Rochester, a hundred years after the first exhibition. (Writers & Books, by the way, is in a former police precinct station designed by Bragdon.) The Highland Park show was the mother of the art light shows that followed, like the psychedelic light shows in the 1960s and the phantasmagorical shows that are held today in Europe. I suppose that even German film director Leni Riefenstahl, with her "Cathedral of Ice" lighting in *Triumph of the Will*, owed a debt to Claude Bragdon.

He closed his architectural business, ostensibly after a dust-up with George Eastman over the design of the Rochester Chamber of Commerce Building.[12] He moved to New York City, and put his skill in architecture, design, and lighting to more lucrative use in theater as a stage designer. He died there in 1946.

In addition to the above list, he wrote and published *The Golden Person in the Heart* (his first, in 1898) and *An Introduction to Yoga*, and, from

9. Cannon, 3.

10. See West, chapter 36, Rochester.

11. Taylor, 10.

12. Taylor, 3.

22.1: The Bragdon family plot, with Claude Bragdon's grave in Pulaski.

his Manas Press, *The Small Old Path*; *Episodes from an Unwritten History*; *Theosophy and the Theosophical Society*; *Projective Ornament*; *Four-Dimensional Vistas*; *Old Lamps for New: Ancient Wisdom in the Modern World*; and several more.

Finding the Grave

Claude Bragdon is buried with his parents, sister May, and son Chandler in the Bragdon family plot in Pulaski, not far from where they once lived in Watertown. His first wife Charlotte is buried in Oakwood Cemetery in Syracuse. Bragdon's own stone is oddly askew; perhaps not a fitting memorial, considering that he was an architect.

Take Exit 36 from the Thruway and head north on Route 81. If you're coming from points north, such as Watertown or the North Pole, Route 81 is still your best bet. The exit for Pulaski is coincidentally also No. 36, which will bring you to Route 13. Turn left toward Pulaski, and turn north on Route 11, which will take you through the village. The Pulaski Village Cemetery is just outside the village limits on your right, in the town of Richland. Or on your GPS, key in 2667 Richland Rd., Pulaski, NY, 13142. There is no parking allowed on the grass, and the roads through the cemetery are narrow, but Bragdon is fairly close to the road and if you are concerned about blocking cemetery traffic, you can park along the shoulder of Route 11 and walk. Take the last, fourth, entrance. About 150 feet in you will see a prominent stone for Davis on the left, and a monument for Trumbull on the right. Start at one row beyond Trumbull, and walk straight down the row for several paces and you will find the Bragdon family plot.

Sources

Bragdon, Claude. A *Primer of Higher Space*. Rochester, NY: Manas Press, 1913.

Cannon, Anna V. *"Builders of the Future: Claude Fayette Bragdon and Mikhail Matyushin in Search of the Cosmic Brotherhood."* Academia.edu. Accessed April 18, 2023. www.academia.edu/36550817/Builders_of_the_Future_Claude _Fayette_Bragdon_and_Mikhail_Matyushin_in_Search_of_the_Cosmic _Brotherhood.

Costa, Erville. "Claude F. Bragdon, Architect, Stage Designer, and Mystic." In *Rochester History*, edited by Blake McKelvey, Vol. XXIX, no. 4 (1967): 1–7.

Taylor, Karen. "Claude Bragdon." Senior thesis, University of Rochester, Rare Books and Special Collections. 1998. Accessed April 18, 2023. https://rbscp .lib.rochester.edu/3514.

23 Utica

Harold Frederic

The city of Utica is thought to be the model location for Harold Frederic's Octavius, the town in which a late-nineteenth-century Methodist minister meets his spiritual demise in the novel *The Damnation of Theron Ware*. Not that anything you see there, if you have read the novel, will strike a gong of recognition, although there are fine structures in the city from the nineteenth century. Unlike many municipalities in the Mohawk Valley which owe their founding to the Erie Canal, Utica was founded decades earlier (the British built Fort Schuyler here in 1758, and settlers began arriving soon after); but the population almost tripled when the canal opened, and it was chartered as a city in 1832. Abolitionists gathered here in 1835 to form the New York Anti-Slavery Society. Watertown residents and stalwarts insist that their native son Frank Woolworth dreamed up his five-and-dime store scheme while still at home there with his dog and his fishing pole, which may well be true, but he actually founded his first store in Utica in 1879. It failed, but he was undeterred.

I've made a few trips to Utica to see friends and hit a few restaurants. It is still a good place to get an Italian dinner. If you find Utica Greens on a menu, go for it. It is a dish of blanched escarole with red cherry peppers, prosciutto, garlic, and parmesan, and when it is made with care it is worth a drive across the state to get it. They hold a Utica Greens Fest in the fall.

Utica had the wisdom to preserve the architecture of its train station—to the envy of many other towns on the Amtrak line. And when I went searching for Harold Frederic's grave, I was in for another happy surprise.

23.1: Harold Frederic. Courtesy Oneida County History Center, Utica, NY.

Forest Hills Cemetery is one of the loveliest garden-style burial grounds I have seen on the American continent; wooded and well maintained.

Harold Frederic (1856–1898): An Author and His Fast Life

Harold Frederic was born in Utica in 1856, and before he was out of his teens he was working for the *Utica Observer*. George Chandler Bragdon, father of Claude Bragdon[1] was once an editor there. Frederic was what we would call a whiz-kid today. He was soon editor of the *Observer* himself, then editor of the *Albany Evening Journal*. At age twenty-eight, before his chair at the *Journal* was quite warm, he was off to England to work as London correspondent for the *New York Times*, where he distinguished himself as a correspondent and news analyst. Except for a couple of visits to New York, England was home for the rest of his life,[2] although he traveled Europe reporting on outbreaks of cholera in Italy and France, and Russia where he wrote about the persecution of Jews.[3] Meteoric rises are a very American thing. For example, take Grover Cleveland: he was district attorney of Erie County at twenty-nine, then sheriff at thirty-four, soon mayor of Buffalo, then right up the ladder to governor of New York and on into the White House. He had to stop there, I guess.

In England, Frederic also began writing his novels, the first being *Seth's Brother's Wife* (1887). Among his friends there was George Bernard Shaw, who, according to Susan Albertine, took a strong interest in Frederic. "The two men shared a remarkable number of social concerns. . . . More to the point, the playwright appreciated the American writer's cleverness, his courage, and his politics."[4]

The Damnation of Theron Ware, Frederic's best-known novel, was seen at the time as "an attack on the clergy,"[5] which it is decidedly not. The protagonist, Reverend Ware, is a young minister assigned to a church in little

---

1. See Central, chapter 22, Pulaski.
2. Woodward, "Harold Frederic," 248.
3. Legimi, "Essential Novelists."
4. Albertine, "Shaw's Interest in Frederic," 69.
5. Woodward, 248.

out-of-the-way Octavius, New York. There he and his wife become dart-boards for hostile and catty members of the congregation who bear down on them for a perceived lack of piety. But Ware is also undergoing a profound inner change. Starved for intellectual communion, he comes under the friendly influence of the village's Catholic priest, a scholarly man who talks to Ware about his doubts concerning holy scriptures, shaking the very foundations of Ware's faith. Meanwhile, he becomes infatuated with Celia Madden, the priest's beautiful and alluring organist. Before long, Ware, his marriage, and his job—indeed, his career and his life—are teetering. I'm not giving away the whole plot; there is much more to follow.

Frederic's rise came with some infamy attached. He had brought his wife to London with him, and they had five children. But there he separated from his wife and took a mistress, and thus took on the expense of two households. Society in the 1890s, whether in Britain or the United States, chafed at creative domestic arrangements, and the bad publicity stalked him. He soon lost most of his friends. The weight of the expense, along with constant work, together with his refusal to heed medical advice, took its toll in August of 1898 when he suffered a severe stroke. Unfortunately, he was at the house of his mistress Kate Lyon when he fell ill, and she was a Christian Scientist—rather than seek medical help she tried faith healing, and he died. For this error in judgment, she was brought up on manslaughter charges, along with a faith healer named Mrs. Athalie Mills, but both were acquitted in a sensational trial.[6] After all, she *meant well*.

His reputation went dormant for a time, but a revival of academic interest in his work began in the 1950s.[7] In all he wrote ten novels and seven story collections, plus a biography of William II of Germany and *The New Exodus: A Study of Israel in Russia*, an impressive output for a man who only made it to age fifty-nine and spent a lot of energy—and money—on his love life. None quite rose to the quality of *Theron Ware*—certainly a classic—but *The Market Place* is considered a very fine novel. My friend Bill Kauffman wrote the screenplay for *Copperhead*—Frederic's

6. Bigsby, "The 'Christian Science Case,'" 77–80.
7. O'Donnell, "Harold Frederic (1856–1898)," 39.

23.2: The grave of Harold Frederic in Utica.

story of Upstate New Yorkers who resisted conscription and support for the Union cause in the Civil War—and it became a very good film directed by Ron Maxwell, released in 2013, starring François Arnaud, Lucy Boynton, Casey Thomas Brown, and Peter Fonda.

When he died, the wanderer's remains were returned to his old hometown.

Finding the Grave

To get to Utica, and to Forest Hills Cemetery, take the Thruway to Exit 31. Following the signs, take Genesee Street about two miles over the Mohawk River, through the city's business section; at the traffic circle take Oneida Street, heading southwest. Drive about two more miles. On your left you will see New Forest Cemetery. Immediately after you pass this cemetery, you will see the grand gates of Forest Hills Cemetery, also on your left. Or key into your GPS: 2201 Oneida St., Utica, NY, 13501.

Forest Hills is a showcase of history. In its ground are twelve congressmen, some going back to the early days of the republic; also Sen. Roscoe Conkling; Supreme Court Justice Ward Hunt; John Warren Butterfield, founder and namesake of Butterfield Overland Express which carried passengers and mail by stagecoach in the American West from 1857 to 1861; Horatio Seymour, governor of New York who ran for president as a Democrat in 1868; Irving Baxter, who won two gold and three silver medals in the 1900 Olympic games in Paris; Ellis Henry Roberts, the twentieth treasurer of the United States; Col. Benjamin Walker, aide to General Washington; Dr. John Cochran, surgeon general in the Continental Army; and Samuel Dove, an enslaved person brought from Richmond, Virginia, to Utica, where he was freed and became one of the nation's first African-American firefighters.

The cemetery's website does not mention Harold Frederic among its other "Famous Residents."

As you enter the gate, you will see a covered sign containing a map of the cemetery with lot numbers. From the gate, turn left and follow the road with the iron fence on your left (it separates Forest Hills from New Forest). You will come to a roundabout, planted with hedges. Turn left there, again keeping the fence on your left. Soon you will see a marker on a corner for lot 32. Turn right and follow that short road to the end. Turn left and park. Frederic is about 150 feet ahead on the left, in the outer perimeter of lot 39.

Sources

Albertine, Susan. "Shaw's Interest in Harold Frederic." *Shaw* 6 (1986): 69–76. http://www.jstor.org/stable/40681171.

Bigsby, C. W. E. "The 'Christian Science Case': An Account of the Death of Harold Frederic and the Subsequent Inquest and Court Proceedings." *American Literary Realism, 1870–1910* 1, no. 2 (1968): 77–83. http://www.jstor.org/stable/27747580.

"Essential Novelists: Harold Frederic." Legimi. Accessed April 18, 2023. www.legimi.pl/ebook-essential-novelists-harold-frederic-harold-frederic,b797899.html.

O'Donnell, Thomas F. "Harold Frederic (1856–1898)." *American Literary Realism, 1870–1910* 1, no. 1 (1967): 39–44; http://www.jstor.org/stable/27747560.

Woodward, Robert H. "Harold Frederic: A Bibliography." *Studies in Bibliography* 13 (1960): 247–57. http://www.jstor.org/stable/40371290.

24   Watertown

Frederick Exley

Not far from where it empties into Lake Ontario, the Black River powered Watertown's early mills, hence the city's name. For a city of its size (population about 27,000), and a rather out-of-the-way location in New York's snowy north, it has an impressive list of notables: Allen Welsh Dulles, one-time director of the CIA, and John Foster Dulles, his brother and secretary of state, who lived here as youths; Robert Lansing, another secretary of state and the Dulles boys' uncle; Roswell P. Flower, the thirtieth governor of New York; Allen and Joe Bouchard, members of the Blue Oyster Cult rock group; and Frank Winfield Woolworth, the department store tycoon. And let's not forget Arthur Shawcross who moved to Rochester and there became one of the country's most notorious serial killers.

Claude Bragdon,[1] architect, author, and mystic, was a child in Watertown when it was a papermill burg and his father wrote for the local newspaper. In a fate similar to nearby Pulaski, the town's center was destroyed by fire in the mid-nineteenth century. And like Pulaski, the citizens rebuilt.

When I visited Watertown in 2019, no one I talked to, including in the Roswell P. Flower Memorial Library, was aware that a famous novelist had once lived in their midst. This was hardly a surprise. It is what I have found in numerous communities around the state who also had a deified writer. But when I told them about Frederick Exley it aroused their curiosity, as it should. That library, named for the hometown boy who made it to

---

1. See Central, chapter 22, Pulaski.

the governor's mansion, is a magnificent building that would be famous if it were in Manhattan, with its stunning dome murals by Frederick Lamb depicting figures from classical mythology and the Bible, and representative figures from all major genres of literature and branches of science.

Frederick Exley (1929–1992): His Destiny to Be a Fan

It must have been around 1995 or '96 when I was in New York City and I wandered into the Lion's Head bar with a friend. After we ordered our drinks I said, "I think this is where Fred Exley hung out." The bartender overheard me and said, "Yes, and that's where he always sat, over there," pointing to a stool a few feet away from us.

Probably no one talks extensively about Exley without slipping, quite naturally, into a discussion of his alcoholism, nor does it distort our understanding of his books since his protagonist is himself. Once, in a conversation with T. C. Boyle, he shook his head and said to me, "Poor Fred Exley had to live every book he wrote." Yes, poor Fred, because the wonder is that he made it to age sixty-two.

It was *A Fan's Notes*, his first book, which raised Exley to prominence in the literary world. Far fewer people opened *Pages from a Cold Island*, and even fewer finished it; ditto for his third and final book, *Last Notes from Home*. In the view of most readers and critics, Exley's best book was *A Fan's Notes*. Yet it's remarkable that one novel still earns him generations of new fans. In one respect, the book belongs to the lineage of bawdy novels in which a brilliant misfit is pitted against a dour, proper society, such as J. P. Donleavy's *The Ginger Man* or Joyce Cary's *The Horse's Mouth*, except, more to the point, Exley's vision of the world is a sharp recognition of the malaise that afflicted the American male in post-war America—or even now, for that matter—particularly one who felt the pangs of failure in the land of opportunity, to be consigned to the bleachers with other mediocre men, in awe of a hero on the field. Perhaps it's best summed by a line from *Fan's Notes*, which is also the epigraph on his gravestone: "It was my fate, my destiny, my end, to be a fan."

Yet he was a success as a writer, even if it was a bumpy trip, even though his reputation rests only on one book—which, by the way, won the William Faulkner Award for the Best First Novel. And who would have believed that a football hero, in this case Frank Gifford, whom he so admired, could be so metaphorically central to a literary novel?

Exley was born in 1929 in Watertown when its economy still ran on industrial jobs. He lived there and in nearby Alexandria Bay, except for relatively short stints in New York City and Los Angeles and Hawaii.[2] His father, a power company lineman, was a high school star football player, a hard drinker but kindly man who developed lung cancer and died when Fred was a teen.[3] Fred might have followed in his footsteps, but he proved himself a bungler in football and instead became, simply, a hard-drinking writer. But the game was still deep in the intelligence of his heart, and so the admiration that he might have had for his father, or the vision that he might have had for himself as an athlete, was transferred to another idol. In fact, Gifford was charmed by the attention he got in the novel, and even threw a party for Exley in New York in 1988.[4] According to Thad Weitz, "Though Exley never explicitly makes the connection, the parallels between his father and Gifford are clear."[5]

If Exley was a one-book wonder, it's still, in the estimation of his biographer Jonathan Yardley, "one of the few monuments of postwar American fiction. It stands, in its unique and inimitable way, with the best work of Ralph Ellison, Eudora Welty, Peter Taylor, Bernard Malamud, Saul Bellow, Flannery O'Connor, John Cheever—all the other writers of the best books of our age."[6]

Finding the Grave

Frederick Exley's ashes are buried in Brookside Cemetery in the outskirts south of the city next to his parents Earl and Charlotte, and his twin sister and her husband.

2. Cantwell, "Hungriest Writer."
3. Yardley, *Misfit*, 11–23.
4. Cantwell, 30.
5. Weitz, "In Praise of Frederick Exley."
6. Yardley, prologue, XX.

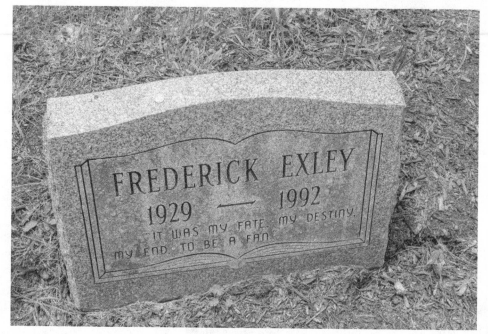

24.1: The grave of Frederick Exley in Watertown.

Unless you are a local person, you will probably approach Water-town from Route 81 North. Take Exit 45 for Arsenal Street (so named because Fort Drum is nearby), turn east and drive about two miles to Public Square. You'll see a monument to Governor Flower by American Renaissance sculptor Augustus Saint-Gaudens. Turn right at the Square onto South Washington Street. Continue driving south for three miles and turn left onto Watertown Center Loop (marked by a road sign with tiny writing, so be watchful). When you reach the first stop sign, the main gates of Brookside Cemetery will be staring you in the face. Or, using your GPS, key in 19000 County Road 165, Watertown, NY, 13601.

The cemetery is lovely and well managed, and it has a staffed office where you can get directions if you need them.

After you enter the gates, drive straight, down the hill, past the flag-pole, and uphill again all the way to where you will see a black border fence. Turn left and follow the meandering path, keeping the fence on your immediate right, until you see the maintenance buildings, in the far, rear corner. The last section of graves on your right is section 11. Exley and his family are in lot 26, about fifty feet from the back fence and about forty feet from the big trees to your left as you face the fence. His stone bears the afore-mentioned epitaph: "It was my fate, my destiny. . . ."

Sources

Cantwell, Mary. "The Hungriest Writer: One Fan's Notes on Frederick Exley." *New York Times*, September 13, 1992.

Weitz, Thad. "In Praise of Frederick Exley." *Shea Magazine, March 28, 2013.*

Yardley, *Jonathan. Misfit: The Strange Life of Frederick Exley.* New York: Random House, 1997.

West

25　Allegany / Olean

　Robert Lax

Maj. Adam Hoops, the Revolutionary War officer who originally pur-chased the property on the Allegheny River from the Holland Land Com-pany in 1804, called the settlement Olean, a name that he had twisted from the Latin word oleum, meaning oil. It must have seemed an odd association at the time, but it was prescient, since New York's Southern Tier would become, in the age before big oil tycoons, petroleum states, and OPEC, the largest producer of oil in the world. It all dried up, so to speak, in the mid-twentieth century when bigger oil fields in Texas and Oklahoma and the Middle East began disgorging crude.

Olean was the southern terminus of the Genesee Valley Canal, the waterway that opened in 1840 to connect the Erie Canal at Rochester to the Allegheny River, hence to the Ohio. Unfortunately, it was obsolete almost from the start. Its dimensions were forty feet wide by four feet deep, the same as the Erie when it was first built, but the Erie had already begun construction projects to widen and deepen it to accommodate the larger barges that were making up most of the traffic. Moreover, railroads were already crisscrossing the area. Olean remained an industrial hub, but the canal went bust and closed in 1878. The state of New York kept the Erie Canal open in order to keep railroad cargo prices down.

St. Bonaventure University is usually associated with Olean, although it is actually in the neighboring town of Allegany (the town name is spelled differently from the river). Thomas Merton taught there briefly. In the summer before the United States entered World War II, before he

25.1: Robert Lax. Photo by Jack Kelly.

became a monk, Merton lived in a cabin in the hills above town with his friend Robert Lax, an Olean native who would become a poet and exile.

Robert Lax (1915–2000): The Contemplative in the World

Robert Lax, who may be the most idiosyncratic American poet of the twentieth century, lived much of his life on a remote Greek island. He was also an engine of invention. His poems range from highly experimental concrete poems where a noun or an adjective is repeated with small variations, to imagistic narrative, to circus fabulism. His journals, many detailing only his solitude, his diurnal doings, and his interactions with people in the Greek islands, are nevertheless deeply fascinating and transporting—a reader can slip very easily into a sense of his solitude.

Yet, although he produced about fifty books in his life, he was little known in his native country—a little better known in Europe—and even that small reputation owes much to his well-known friendship with Thomas Merton who has much to say about their friendship in his classic spiritual autobiography, *The Seven Storey Mountain.*

Lax was born in Olean in 1915, the son of a Jewish tailor and a community-minded mother. He went to Columbia University where he met Merton (as well as the poet John Berryman, and where he studied under poet Mark Van Doren), and they became lifelong friends and voluminous correspondents. After college, Merton began graduate studies, and both men converted to Roman Catholicism.[1] Merton took monastic vows while Lax tried his hand at journalism. He joined the staff of the *New Yorker* for a time, then worked as a clown with the Cristiani Circus in Canada,[2] before leaving the United States for the Mediterranean in 1962, making a home on Patmos (according to church tradition, the island to which Saint John was exiled and where he had his apocalyptic visions) and Kalymnos, returning only four times in the next three decades. He made a final journey home to Olean in 2000 when he realized that he was going to die. It has been suggested that he lived as a hermit in the islands, but

1. Keiderling, "Bard of God's Circus."
2. Hirschfield, "A Life Slowly Lived."

it is not quite true. Whatever solitude he found in his simple quarters on Patmos, he still liked people, and he mixed easily with the islanders during his daily walks.

Merton wrote, "he was a kind of combination of Hamlet and Elias. A potential prophet but without rage. . . . the secret of his constant solidity I think has always been a kind of natural, instinctive spirituality, a kind of inborn direction to the living God."[3] Jack Kerouac called him "one of the great original voices of our times."[4]

Paul Spaeth, head of libraries at St. Bonaventure College near Olean where Merton once taught and curator of Lax's papers, affirms that he was better known in Europe, where many of his books were published. Some of his books published in the United States include *33 Poems* (New Directions 1988), *Love Had a Compass* (Grove 1996), *A Thing That Is* (Overlook 1997), *Circus Days and Nights* (Overlook 2000), and *The Hermit's Guide to Home Economics* (New Directions 2015).

I was lucky in my search for Robert Lax. A friend, the writer Bill Kauffman, gave me contact information for two Lax enthusiasts, Sally and Lou Ventura, high school English teachers in Olean who agreed to show me the gravesite. They also introduced me to Spaeth. We visited the site, and spent a wonderful afternoon in the archive amid the banker boxes of Lax's manuscripts, correspondence, photos, etc. The man was a tireless, probably compulsive, writer.

"To sum it up," Merton wrote, "even the people who always thought he was 'too impractical' have always tended to venerate him—in the way people who value material security unconsciously venerate people who do not fear insecurity."[5]

Finding the Grave

The best way to get to Saint Bonaventure Cemetery is via Route NY 17 / US 86. Take Exit 24 for Allegany and St. Bonaventure. Turn south from

3. Merton, *The Seven Storey Mountain*, 198.
4. Hirschfield.
5. Merton, 198.

25.2: The grave of Robert Lax in Allegany.

the exit and left onto Route 417. You will pass the college in two miles. The entrance to the cemetery is on the left, immediately before the sign for the St. Bonaventure Clubhouse, and a short distance before the bridge over the railroad.

Once in the gate, drive all the way to the top, and turn left. You will see a sign for "Section a" (lower case) ahead. Turn left there and stop. Between two prominent stones, one for McGuinn and one for Boyle, you will find a small angel and a flat stone for Robert Lax. His poem inscribed on the stone reads:

slow
boat
calm
riv
er

qui
et
land
ing

Sources

Hirschfield, Robert. "A Life Slowly Lived." *Beshara Magazine*, 12 (2019). https://besharamagazine.org/arts-literature/robert-lax-a-life-slowly-lived/.

Keiderling, Timothy J. "Bard of God's Circus: In Search of Robert Lax." *Plough Quarterly*, no. 7. February 9, 2016. www.plough.com/en/topics/justice/sustainable-living/bard-of-gods-circus.

Merton, Thomas. *The Seven Storey Mountain: An Autobiography of Faith.* New York: Harcourt Brace and Co., 1948.

Spaeth, Paul. "Robert Lax Archives St. Bonaventure University" Accessed April 18, 2023. http://web.sbu.edu/friedsam/laxweb/.

26 Arcade

Fran Striker

Before the New York State Thruway and other major freeways were built, it was an advantage for a town to be at the crossing of two or more well-traveled roads. Nowadays, if a crossroads town seems somewhat out of the way, it's good to remember that old travel routes once gave it an edge. The village of Arcade, where Routes 98 and 39 converge, is part of the town of Arcade in the southwest corner of rural Wyoming County, about forty miles southeast of Buffalo. As with Ithaca and Rushford, and a few other towns in this book, there is no quick freeway-route. But the rolling hills make some of the loveliest farm country in the state, now dotted by enormous windmills that in recent years have popped up like mushrooms, dutifully grinding out electric power, so common now that one hardly notices them.

It's home to the Arcade and Attica Railroad, an antique rail line that offers train excursions pulled by an old-fashioned steam locomotive, although it doesn't go to Attica now, but to North Java, about halfway. Arcade was once also the home of Fran Striker. He was one of the most successful creators of modern adventure heroes.

Fran Striker (1903–1962): A Genius of Hero Tales

My deeper relationship with the Lone Ranger, that is, beyond the level on which many boys of my era admired and identified with him, began one long Columbus Day weekend in the mid-1960s when I was sent to Bible camp. Young people, all teenagers, converged there from a number of

201

area churches. The camp was at a small farm near Arcade, which, I found out after I arrived, had been the home of a writer named Fran Striker who was the original creator of the Lone Ranger, Sergeant Preston of the Yukon, and the Green Hornet. Striker had died in a car crash near Buffalo in 1962. After his death, his family had turned the farm over to a church organization, and it was now called the Good News Camp.

The large house itself had been converted into meeting rooms for religious programs, complete with a small dining hall. The boys' barracks was in an old barn while girls slept in what may have once been a chicken barn. One of the ministers told me that the girls' dorm—in its previous incarnation—was where Striker's office had been, at the far end where the windows faced a pasture. It was where he wrote, where he dreamed up characters and plots. I do not know where Pastor Salzman got that specific information, but he sounded like he knew what he was saying.

So, one day after lunch, while everyone else was playing ball, another boy and I tried the door of the girls' dorm, found it unlocked, and made for the end where Striker's desk had been. Now, of course, it was all bunkbeds. But I wanted to stand there and breathe, absorb the same light from the same window, the same silence. Like awaiting a Dharma transmission. Had we been caught, we would have been shamed before the entire camp congregation, and no one would have believed that we weren't in there raiding girls' underclothing. But *of course* it was worth the risk. I couldn't understand why everyone was not as drawn to that place as we were. I was beginning to realize that writers live everywhere, not just in New York City, London, or Paris.

The Lone Ranger series was first broadcast in 1933 on the Buffalo radio station WEBR where Striker—who was born in Buffalo—was a scriptwriter and announcer. After Striker moved to WXYZ in Detroit, the station owner George Trendle pressured him to sign over rights to the Lone Ranger character. After that, Trendle was credited as creator on episodes of *The Lone Ranger*.[1] It's hard to imagine why Striker would let go so quicky. Maybe because it was the height of the Great Depression, good

---

1. Fampeople, "Fran Striker: Biography."

paying jobs were hard to come by, and he had a family to support. Or, maybe he didn't realize what a gold mine he possessed. In 1954 Trendle sold the rights to the Wrather Corporation for $3 million.[2]

And yet, Striker still hammered out *Lone Ranger* scripts, more than 150 per year, plus the *Sergeant Preston of the Yukon* series. He wrote a long series of Lone Ranger and Tonto novels under his own name, as well as the Tom Quest series of books for boys, and he wrote numerous segments of *The Green Hornet* for radio.[3] An astonishingly productive writer. When he appeared on a segment of *To Tell the Truth* in 1960, he appeared as *The Lone Ranger's* creator. George Trendle was nowhere to be seen. For anyone who does not remember that popular game show of the '50s and '60s, three people would be invited onto the show, each claiming to be a particular noteworthy person. The panel of contestants (themselves well-known people in show business, as well as Bennett Cerf from Random House) would ask questions of the three and then make their guesses. Interestingly, when the host Bud Collyer said, "Will the real Fran Striker please stand up," none of the panelists had guessed he was the one. He was a short, nondescript fellow, showing his age—not a Lone Ranger by any stretch.

John J. Valadez points out that the Lone Ranger was a whitewashing of the earlier Mexican hero Zorro. "His transformation from swashbuckler to lawman was straightforward. Instead of a sword, Trendle gave him a gun. In place of a black hat and a black horse, his hero would wear a white hat and ride a white horse." He adds that the Lone Ranger made the transition from radio to TV just in time "to shape the values of a righteous nation as it entered the Cold War."[4]

Fair enough, I guess. But *The Lone Ranger* TV series, with Clayton Moore as the masked former Texas Ranger, which debuted in 1949 and ran through 1957, was successful not merely because they were good stories. They also had a certain moral decalogue that the Lone Ranger and

2. Goldstein, "Moore Dies at 85," B8.
3. Fampeople, "Fran Striker: Biography."
4. Valadez, "Lone Ranger Unmasked," 138.

his Native American partner Tonto lived and fought by when they went after bad guys and rescued victims from evil.

The Lone Ranger's Creed
I believe:
1. That to have a friend, a man must be one.
2. That all men are created equal and that everyone has within himself the power to make this a better world.
3. That God put the firewood there, but that every man must gather and light it himself.
4. In being prepared physically, mentally, and morally to fight when necessary for that which is right.
5. That a man should make the most of what equipment he has.
6. That "this government, of the people, by the people, and for the people," shall live always.
7. That men should live by the rule of what is best for the greatest number.
8. That sooner or later . . . somewhere . . . somehow . . . we must settle with the world and make payment for what we have taken.
9. That all things change, but the truth, and the truth alone, lives on forever.
10. I Believe in my Creator, my country, my fellow man.[5]

His work was formulaic, of course, and he was in no danger of winning a Pulitzer Prize. But it has fascinated me that a man could sit at a typewriter with a thermos of coffee and a pack of cigarettes and bang out one story, one script, one book after another. Of all the authors covered in this volume, only Walter B. Gibson,[6] author of The Shadow novels, probably turned out more words.

Just an aside: Jay Silverheels, born Harry J. Smith, who played Tonto in the TV productions of *The Lone Ranger* as well as roles in *Key Largo*; *Broken Arrow*; and *The Man Who Loved Cat Dancing*, was a Native

---

5. Striker, "Lone Ranger's Creed," *Cowboy Way*.
6. See East, chapter 5, Kingston.

26.1: The grave of Fran Striker in Arcade.

American from Ontario, Canada.[7] As a professional lacrosse player in the 1930s, before his Hollywood days, he played on indoor teams in Toronto, Buffalo, Rochester, Atlantic City, and Akron, New York. He was discovered by a movie scout when he played lacrosse in Los Angeles.[8]

Striker gave our culture some iconic phrases. The "silver bullet" nowadays usually pertains to a single thing or ingredient that truly works. And "Who was that masked man?" There was Tonto's affectionate name for his masked sidekick, "Ke-mo-sah-bee." The yell with which the Lone Ranger roused his horse Silver to action: "Hi-yo Silver! Away!" is probably as immortal as Johnny Weissmuller's Tarzan yodel.

7. "Silverheels, Actor, 62, Dead," D19.

8. Klein, "Sidekick's Little-Known Leading Role," SP–13.

Finding the Grave

Fran Striker is buried in Arcade Rural Cemetery. Either of two streets in the center of the business district, Prospect and Park, will take you to the cemetery, situated on a hillside. However, I advise caution: the paths up the hill, if you decide to drive them, are narrow, bordered in places by sobering drop-offs. To reach this point with your GPS, key in: 107 Park St., Arcade, NY, 14009.

The place you are aiming for is the very top of the hill, on the opposite end of the cemetery from the entrances, where the path curves near a neighboring field. Look for a row of four stainless steel crosses a short distance from a maple tree on the corner of the path. They are fairly easy to pick out because they are unlike other markers in the cemetery. The second from the left is Francis Hamilton Striker. More steel crosses nearby include their three sons, one of whom, Fran Striker Jr., finished his father's last novel, *One More River.*

Sources

"Fran Striker: Biography." FamPeople. Accessed April 18, 2023. https://fam people.com/cat-fran-striker.

Goldstein, Richard. "Clayton Moore, Television's Lone Ranger and a Persistent Masked Man, Dies at 85." *New York Times*, December 29, 1999.

"Jay Silverheels, Actor, 62, Dead; Was Tonto in TV Lone Ranger." *New York Times*, March 6, 1980.

Klein, Jeff Z. "A Sidekick's Little-Known Leading Role in Lacrosse. *New York Times*, August 31, 2013.

"The Lone Ranger." *Fandom.* Accessed April 18, 2023. https://loneranger.fandom .com/wiki/Lone_Ranger.

Striker, Fran. "The Lone Ranger's Creed." *Psychiatric Times.* Accessed April 18, 2023. https://www.psychiatrictimes.com/view/the-lone-rangers-creed-remembering -the-masks-we-wear.

Valadez, John J. "The Lone Ranger Unmasked: Zorro and the Whitewashing of the American Superhero. Filmmaker Essay." *Chiricú* 1, no. 1 (2016): 135–51. https://doi.org/10.2979/chiricu.1.1.11.

27 Batavia

John Gardner

Batavia's best-known author before John Gardner was probably William Morgan, sometimes referred to as Capt. William Morgan, a veteran of the War of 1812 who settled in Batavia with an itinerant past in a variety of trades. While in town, he applied for membership in the Masonic Lodge, but was rejected. Incensed, he threatened to write and publish an expose of the secrets of Freemasonry. He disappeared in 1826, apparently kidnapped and probably murdered. None of the several corpses that turned up was ever positively identified as Morgan, although four of his accused abductors spent a brief time in jail. Forensic policework had to wait for another century.

But the incident incited a nationwide scandal, and sentiment flared against the Masons (even among many politicians who were probably Masons themselves). They were accused of being a secret anti-democratic power organization. The Anti-Masonic Party was formed; William H. Seward, later Lincoln's secretary of state, ran for the US Senate in 1830 on the Anti-Masonic ticket, and the party ran a presidential candidate in 1832, former Attorney General William Wirt. The new party lost, of course, after which its flame sputtered out. Morgan's book, *Illustrations of Masonry*, was published after his disappearance anyway, and sold briskly because of the publicity and intrigue the Masons had inadvertently bestowed on it.

Batavia was the seat of the Holland Land Company, a group of Dutch agents who in 1792 and 1793 purchased large tracts of what is now Western New York from Robert Morris, who had originally purchased it from the state of Massachusetts. However, Seneca Indians still held title. This led to the Treaty of Big Tree between the Seneca Nation and the United States, in which the native tribe sold their rights to most of their traditional land in Western New York. The Holland Land Office building still stands on Main Street, and is now a museum of local history, well worth visiting.

I drove taxi in Batavia when I was in my twenties; I loved its quirky mix of city and small-town character. But a large section of downtown now looks like a city that was rebuilt after a great fire. Actually, it was the urban renewal craze that hit American cities in the 1960s and '70s, which took out much of the north side of Batavia's Main Street, leaving several blocks looking like any old plaza in any old city in the United States. The south side retains some of the old architecture, except that there are also some dispiriting developments. The beloved old Mancuso Theater is now a church, or so it says on the marquee. Other old businesses that I knew and loved are gone.

I do not mean to suggest that the city has lost its appeal altogether. Many of the residential areas of the city are lovely streets of Victorian and later craftsman-style houses. And the Richmond Memorial is a very good public library. There is still Batavia Downs, the oldest harness racetrack lighted for night racing in the country (where untold numbers of people have blown their life savings), although it is partly a casino now—keeping up with the times. In case you still have some money left after the race, you can blow it on the slots.

John Gardner (1932–1982): "All he spoke or cast was mysterious and holy"

I should have met John Gardner. My first wife and I lived near his mother and father, Priscilla and John Sr., and we were friends and breakfast partners. He was teaching at Binghamton College at the time, and lived across the border from the college in Northern Pennsylvania. He came back to the old homestead a few miles east of Batavia fairly often, but whenever we were at the farm (a dairy farm, although the family no longer kept cows), he had either just left or was expected some days hence. Yet there were ever signs of him. As his aging father became more infirm, John built a ramp on the side porch for his wheelchair. One late spring day in 1982 when we came to pick up John Sr. and Priscilla and take them to a local diner, I noticed skeins of white rolling across the yard in the wind, and I asked Priscilla what it was. "That's the author's hair," she said. They had cut his famous long locks on the porch the day before. "I wish we'd have cut it back in April," she added, "then the birds could have made their nests out of it."

The following September, he was dead, killed in a motorcycle accident on a rural road, just over the border from Binghamton, in near his home in Pennsylvania. For me, some of the magic went out of Batavia when he died, as it must have drained out of Asheville, North Carolina, when Thomas Wolfe died, or out of Oxford, Mississippi, when William Faulkner passed—although, like Gardner, both were living elsewhere at the time.

A man told me once that while he was eating lunch one day at the counter in the Pok-A-Dot Restaurant in Batavia, expounding to a friend about *Grendel,* Gardner's retelling of the Beowulf saga from the perspective of the monster, an elderly woman tapped him on the shoulder and asked him if he wanted to meet the author. It was Priscilla, of course, and Gardner was sitting a few feet away at a table where they had been eating lunch. John Gardner sightings in Batavia were common; I just was never in the right place, apparently—but if you saw him on the street he would have been hard to miss, a slightly paunchy guy with shoulder-length white hair and a pipe hanging out of his mouth.

He has been gone a long time, and people who knew him are fewer now, but when I lived in the area many people not only knew him, but knew some of the characters in *The Sunlight Dialogues,* a psychological novel set in Batavia. John Sr. and Priscilla were woven into the story themselves, under the name Hodge. In a few cases he did not bother to change the names. Most people I knew in town read his books, and they admired him, not simply because he was one of their own, but because they are good books, with the absorbing depth one expects of literary fiction.

Among his many other books are *October Light, Nickel Mountain, Mickelsson's Ghosts, The Art of Living,* and the *Wreckage of Agathon,* and his translation with John Maier of *The Gilgamesh*, the ancient Sumerian epic; also a biography of Chaucer, and *Dragon, Dragon* for children.

His funeral was in the First Presbyterian Church on Main Street, the location of a pivotal scene in *Sunlight* where chief of police Fred Clumly meets the strange Sunlight Man, an irony which I could not get out of my mind when I attended the service.

On the east end of town, near the turnoff to Route 33, is the Miss Batavia Diner where one Thanksgiving Day I saw John Sr. and Priscilla eating a lunch of cheeseburgers, chili, and French fries. Somewhat more rustic (and cash-only) is the afore-mentioned Pok-A-Dot on the corner of Liberty and Ellicott Streets, outside of which is a permanent bench dedicated to Gardner. Or, if you have extra time, drive south on Route 98 (Walnut Street) about ten miles, where you'll find Twilight Meadows, the diner reputed to be the model for the restaurant in *Nickel Mountain*.

27.1: The grave of John Gardner in Batavia.

Finding the Grave

John Gardner is buried in the family plot in the Grace Lawn section of Grand View Cemetery, which is on Route 33, on the northeast edge of the city. Take the Thruway to Exit 48 at Batavia. From there, drive straight south on Route 98 for a few blocks and turn left on Main Street, Route 5. Continue east through the city until you see Route 5 split with Route 33, and turn left. Grand View Cemetery is a short distance ahead on your right. Or key into your GPS 80 Clinton St., Batavia, NY, 14020.

Pull into the path closest to the highway, and you'll find the collection of Gardner stones about ten paces east of the path, toward the southwest corner where you entered. The author has two markers there, a footstone with his dates, and another without dates but containing the enigmatic inscription: "All he spoke or cast was mysterious and holy." Both of his stones are dwarfed by the stone for his parents John Sr. and Priscilla. Here also is the footstone for Gilbert Day Gardner, the author's younger brother who was fatally crushed under a cultipacker in 1945 while twelve-year-old John was pulling it with a tractor, an incident which tormented the author for the rest of his life and informed his masterful short story, "Redemption."

28　Brockport

A. Poulin Jr., Mary Jane Holmes

It was in a factory in Brockport in 1845 that Cyrus McCormick first mass-produced his McCormick Reaper, which in that century greatly increased crop production while reducing farm labor—more wheat for less sweat and less expense. The Erie Canal in the nineteenth century was essential to the local fruit-growing industry. Some mulberry bushes can still be found in the village, remnants of silk producers in that era.

Brockport, in the Monroe County town of Sweden, is home to a State University of New York college. It's crossed by Route 19, a two-lane north-south road. There is no Thruway exit, but the nearby terminus of the Route 531 expressway connects Brockport to Rochester. Canal traffic is mostly sporty people in pleasure boats who won't stop unless they're thirsty for something they do not happen to have on board. But to pass through they have to wait for two lift bridges. The bridge decks creaking as they rise—and bottling up traffic—is actually one of the village's charms. The happy result is not isolation, but rather a village with a nestled, autonomous feel, where it means something to be a "townie." Live theater on campus during the spring and fall semesters, as well as art exhibits, add to the cultural atmosphere.

It was an exciting place when in 1982, as an aspiring poet, I came to Brockport to work at the Lift Bridge Book Shop. Real poets lived in the village, such as William Heyen, Anthony Piccione, Stan Rubin, Judith Kitchen, and A. Poulin Jr. There were two small literary presses, BOA Editions and State Street Press. And the Brockport Writers Forum on the SUNY College at Brockport campus attracted an astonishing stream of visiting writers: Seamus Heaney, Derek Walcott, May Sarton, William Stafford, Stanley Kunitz, Louis Simpson, Carolyn Forche, Grace Paley, Edward Albee, and many more. There is still a Writers Forum, although the summer workshops that gave people like me the opportunity to learn the widgets of poetry at the feet of a master (in my case Stanley Plumly) are no more. And I should mention that the undergrad program turned out two of America's best contemporary poets, Michael Waters and Li-Young Lee.

Two prominent writers are buried in Brockport, A. Poulin Jr. and Mary Jane Holmes.

A. Poulin Jr. (1938–1996): The Labor of a Vision That Would Change the World

One morning in 1985, I was finishing a late breakfast and drinking a couple extra cups of coffee, killing time before I had to drive ten miles to Brockport to start my afternoon shift at the Lift Bridge Book Shop. When the phone rang, my wife went into the hallway off the kitchen to answer it. She held the phone out to me with a puzzled look, "It's for you . . . it's Al Poulin."

I was surprised—no, astonished. Poulin taught at the college, and came into the bookshop frequently. Thin as a pool cue, with a pince-nez, he wore a knit wrap on his shoulders like a cape. He coughed occasionally—he had emphysema and asthma, I was told, but he carried an intensity one would expect from Rainer Maria Rilke, the German-French poet of whose work Poulin was then the preeminent translator in America. His anthology *Contemporary American Poetry* was the most widely adopted textbook of its genre in college classrooms. He was a poet, and the visionary founder of BOA Editions, Ltd., which in the coming years would become one of America's best-known poetry publishing houses.

I once told him that he was the most broadly successful man I ever knew, and he was a little surprised, and pleased, to hear that. And yet, at this time, in '85, he was an enigma to me. The only words we had exchanged before that phone call were when I'd pull down from the shelf one of his books and ask him to sign it for me—his translation from the

German of *The Duino Elegies and Sonnets to Orpheus*, or one of his volumes of Rilke's French verse—and had it deducted from my meager salary. Each time he signed, he said, "Now, what did you say your name is?"

"Steve," he said on the phone now, "this is Al Poulin. Do you know who I am?"

I almost laughed.

"I'm wondering if you would come to work for me."

He said he had a big problem. One of the books that BOA had published the previous year, *Yin: Poems* by Carolyn Kizer, had won the Pulitzer Prize in Poetry. It was the first time that a "small press" had published a book that had taken the poetry prize (BOA had an annual budget of a mere $25,000 then). But after the shock had worn off and the euphoria receded, he realized that he needed someone to help him with publicity, to plan a big party for Kizer at the George Eastman House (now the George Eastman Museum) in nearby Rochester. And there would be other work for me after that—he needed an amanuensis and, truth be told, a valet. The first person he could think of who might want the job was *what's-his-name* in the bookshop who was always after him to sign a book. He'd called the store and they gave him my personal information.

So now I was a thirty-five-year-old man with two part-time minimum-wage jobs, and I was walking on air, which was a good thing, because whenever I came down to earth there were bills to pay. We had a long friendship and working relationship until his death in 1996, after which I became publisher at BOA, which by then had moved its office to Rochester. But thanks to Al Poulin I was initiated into the company of poets which, with the possible exception of a few mad, wine-drinking monks in the mountains of China, are the best human company.

Poulin was born in Lisbon, Maine, in 1938, to a family of francophone Canadian immigrants. As far as his devout mother was concerned, Al was destined for the priesthood. But he had other ideas. After he took his MFA from the University of Iowa, he taught at various colleges in the United States, Germany, and Greece, finally landing in Brockport with his wife Basilike. And he settled down to write and translate, edit and publish.

In addition to his translations of Rilke, his own collections of poetry include *In Advent*; *Cave Dwellers*; *A Momentary Order*; and *A. Poulin, Jr.:*

Selected Poems (published posthumously). I think he would have written more books of poetry if he had not been so busy publishing other people.

When I first started working with him, he could drink most of a quart of scotch in an afternoon while writing a grant proposal or negotiating a publishing contract or a delicate co-publishing arrangement in English and French, never showing the least signal of intoxication. In his last years his emphysema and congestive heart caught up with him—although he still had a martini in the evening and smoked even with an oxygen tube in his snout. And he still loved a good meal.

But the health issues were always in the room. The steroids that kept his heart pumping bloated him until, with his round face and wide-brim hat, he looked more like Alexander Woollcott than the stick figure that had paced the aisles of the bookshop. Ambulances raced him to Lakeside Hospital with increasing frequency. But he stayed sharp and kept up his work. We were a staff of three by then, including poet Thom Ward. Our relationship was contentious at times, especially when we disagreed about the aesthetics of book design. But we were dear friends, and I cannot think of anyone I have missed more. Ever. He died in June 1996.

Finding the Grave

Alfred Poulin Jr. is buried in section B at Lakeview Cemetery in the town of Sweden, about a mile north of the village of Brockport.

Take Exit 47 from the Thruway onto the 490 Expressway, then take an almost immediate exit for Route 19 North and drive about twelve miles. Along the way it becomes Lake Road. Just as you start downhill into the plaza district of the town of Sweden you will see a sign for Shumway Road on your right, and the Lakeview Cemetery entrance is about one-tenth of a mile farther, also on the right. Or key into your GPS 4988 Lake Rd. South, Brockport, NY, 14420.

The most common cemetery name in Upstate New York that I have encountered is Lakeview, or sometimes Lake View, undoubtedly because New York has so many substantial lakes. But none that I have yet found actually provides a view of a lake. In the case of this cemetery, it might be referring to the big lake in the sky, because it is a good ten miles from

28.1: The grave of A. Poulin Jr. in Brockport.

the nearest one, Lake Ontario. Here the paths meander around hills in a merry fashion, but to find Poulin's grave you need to wend your way to the path on the northside, where the cemetery will be on your left and woods on your right. Park in the small gravel turnaround at the woods' edge.

From there, look directly south. Immediately visible near the path are stones for Hinz and Jurek. Immediately beyond them is Poulin's stone, just outside the dripline of a giant fir tree. As with most writers' stones, his is of modest size. But it is not readable until you stand directly in front of it, because its inscriptions are on an embossed brass plate bolted to the stone, forged by the painter and printmaker Robert Marx, who was one of his close friends. It reads:

> . . . he has labored with
> the patience of a man obsessed
> with meticulous details
> of a vision that would change
> the world.
> —A. Poulin Jr.
> 1938–1996

Its placement here is in keeping with Al's personality. He was indeed a patient man obsessed with detail, and I think he believed that poetry has the potential to change the world, and he'd probably be willing to cross swords with W. H. Auden over that issue. That the inscription is impossible to read from more than about three feet is also pure Al—he didn't do anything the easy way, and he naturally would not make his name and inscription easy to spot if he thought that doing so would compromise the plate's beauty. On the other hand, any curious cemetery wanderer, upon seeing the plate from a distance, would have to stop, gaze, and wonder. It is remarkably singular. But maybe his real monument is the press he founded, BOA Editions, which, long after we parted ways, is still one of America's most respected literary presses.

When I checked findagrave.com for Lakeview Cemetery, it had links to "two famous interments." But he wasn't listed. Certainly our members of Congress, our manufacturers, and our generals deserve recognition. But so do our poets and writers. And our publishers.

Mary Jane Holmes (1828–1907): The Seriousness of Romance

Mary Jane Holmes, nee Hawes, was born in Brookfield, Massachusetts, in 1825, the fifth of nine children. After marrying lawyer David Holmes in 1849 they moved to Kentucky, and both taught there for two years. They moved to Brockport in 1853 where she finished her first novel, *Tempest and Sunshine* (1854). Over the next fifty years she published almost a book each year, of which there are substantial collections in the Seymour Public Library on East Avenue in Brockport and in the Morgan-Manning House, a historic landmark house and museum (which also deserves a visit if you come to Brockport). She was a very popular and financially successful author.[1]

She wrote in the genre of romance, and the temptation might be to dismiss her work on that account. But Prof. Earl Yarington has pointed out that:

> Holmes, who engaged in the class, gender, and race struggles that encompassed nineteenth-century social politics, took her writing very seriously. Through sentimental romances, short stories, and novellas, Holmes created characters who influenced readers toward more equal relations with men and women of all races. . . . Holmes's works bring these struggles into context for the modern reader, shedding light on the social issues that were center stage during the nineteenth century.[2]

Her novels and story collections include *Tempest and Sunshine; Dora Deane, or the East India Uncle; Daisey Thornton; Forest House;* and *Ethelyn's Mistake.* Most of her books are still available online in both print and e-books. Not immortality, perhaps, but a highly honorable perdurance.

1. Urness, "Holmes, Mary Jane Hawes," 208.
2. Yarington, 142–43.

28.2: The grave of Mary Jane Holmes in Brockport.

Finding the Grave

In 1987–88, I lived three blocks from Brockport's High Street Cemetery, but was not aware of it. It is rather secluded. High Street takes you east from the bucolic residential Park Avenue to the industrial edge of the village.

Take Thruway Exit 47, driving north on Route 19. After exiting Lakeview Cemetery, or passing it as the case may be, continue north on Lake Road through the plaza district. Shortly you'll be entering the village of Brockport. At the fourth light (after Lakeview) turn right onto Park Avenue, then make the next right onto High Street. The cemetery is at the end of the street on the right, surrounded by a wrought-iron fence. Or key into your GPS High Street, Brockport, NY.

The second opening in the fence is the entrance. Although the cemetery grounds seem well-kept, the concrete path is rough, so proceed slowly. Drive all the way to the end, where the path turns right; after a couple hundred feet, it turns right again; in about hundred feet more, stop. Looking west (to your left) is a tall spire for Benedict, although most of the names are on the other side facing the fence, including Holmes. Just beyond that spire is a smaller spire with a Celtic cross, which marks the Holmes' plot. On the other side you'll see two footstones for Mary J. and David.

Sources

Mary Jane Holmes

Urness, Carol L. "Holmes, Mary Jane Hawes." In *Notable American Women 1607–1950: A Biographical Dictionary*, Vol II, edited by *Paul Boyer*, Edward T. James, and *Janet Wilson*, 208–9. Cambridge, MA: Belknap Press of Harvard University Press, 1971.

Yarington, Earl. "Mary Jane Holmes (1825–1907)." *Legacy* 25, no. 1 (2008): 142–50. http://www.jstor.org/stable/25679636.

29   Buffalo

*Al Boasberg, Shirley Chisholm,
Leslie Fiedler, Anna Katherine Green,
Edward Caleb Randall, Edward Streeter*

Forest Lawn Cemetery in Buffalo is one of the largest in Upstate New York. For those of us who are familiar with hometown cemeteries the size of a softball field, this one is stunning: 269 partially wooded acres and more than 163,000 interred persons who, if they were up and around today, would make up 61 percent of the city's current population. Like many of the large, urban cemeteries included in this book, it is a microcosm of our nation's history. Red Jacket, the Seneca Indian orator and warrior, and Ely S. Parker, the Seneca man who was adjutant to General Grant, wrote the terms of surrender at Appomattox, and later served in Washington as the first Native American head of the Bureau of Indian Affairs, are buried at the foot of the giant monument to Red Jacket which greets you as you enter the gate.

The cemetery was founded by lawyer and businessman Charles Ezra Clark in 1849, the year that he was elected to Congress as a Whig, although he himself is buried in Brookside Cemetery in Watertown. Here lies President Millard Fillmore; Dr. Frederick Cook, reputed discoverer of the North Pole; William Fargo, cofounder of the American Express Company and Wells Fargo; E. R. Thomas, early car manufacturer whose four-cylinder Thomas Flyer in 1908 won the only around-the-world auto race ever held; Dorothy Goetz Berlin, the first wife of Irving Berlin; and Louise Bethune, the first professional woman architect.

There is a special section for seventeen unidentified victims of the infamous wreck of the New York Express train of the Lake Shore and

Michigan Southern railroad. Bound for Buffalo on the afternoon of December 18, 1867, the last two passenger cars jumped the rail on the bridge over Big Sister Creek in the town of Angola, near Lake Erie, and plunged into the creek, killing forty-nine and injuring forty more. Most of the dead were in the last car which caught fire when the stove spilled, and the unidentified were burned beyond recognition. Known as the Angola Horror, it was one of the worst accidents in US railroad history. The tragedy led to safety reforms—phasing out flammable wooden cars in favor of iron and the standardization of track gauges.

Among the mausoleums is one for Edwin H. Butler, the founder and one-time owner of the *Buffalo Evening News*. It was his carriage that, on September 6, 1901, drove President William McKinley to the Temple of Music at the Pan-American Exposition in Buffalo, where he was shot by Leon Czolgosz. A more recent interment, singer-musician-producer Rick James, is buried here near the Scajaquada Creek; a Buffalo native whose highly successful career and troubled life ended in cardiac arrest at his home in Burbank, California.

And we mustn't forget the contributions of Buffalo dentist Alfred P. Southwick, also buried in Forest Lawn. He was the inventor of the electric chair, first used at Auburn Prison on August 6, 1890. There had been a number of botched hangings around the country in recent years and authorities wanted a humane alternative. The lucky Number One, convicted murderer William Kemmler, also from Buffalo, was dispatched to the stars on the above date, despite his lawyers' efforts to stop it on the grounds of cruel and unusual punishment. Prior to Kemmler's execution, the contraption was tested out on stray dogs by the Humane Society. And, by the way, Czolgosz himself would be executed in that chair in 1901.

You will see many extraordinary monuments in Forest Lawn, but perhaps none as startling, or as spooky, as the monument to a sad bit of history. Nelson Blocher, the only child of wealthy Buffalonians John and Elizabeth Blocher (John was a manufacturer of footwear for the Army, among other enterprises) fell in love with the family's maid Katherine Sullivan. Predictably, Mom and Dad disapproved and put a stop to it by sending Nelson on a business trip to Europe. When he came back and found that Katherine had been dismissed, he went in search of her and when he couldn't find her, he became despondent. His health broke down, and he died in 1885 at age thirty-seven. Now it was Mom and Dad's turn to be brokenhearted, and they built one of the most extraordinary monuments in America for their son, with a hexagonal glassed-in room complete with marble likenesses of John and Elizabeth, and an angel, standing vigil over their son lying on his deathbed, upon his chest the Bible left for him by Katherine. All three family members are buried in a crypt below. Katherine Sullivan, by the way, never reappeared. Who could blame her?

Getting to Forest Lawn

From the New York State Thruway, take the Kensington Expressway (Route 33) west toward the city of Buffalo. Take the exit for the Scajaquada Expressway (Route 198) and follow it to the right-side exit for Delaware Avenue, where you will turn right again. Following Delaware Avenue, you'll see the sloping hills of the cemetery on your left. Stay in the left lane. The cemetery gate is on the corner of Delaware and West Delavan Avenue, on the left. Or, tell your GPS to take you to 1411 Delaware Ave., Buffalo, NY, 14209.

The turn into the gate is tricky in traffic, and you must be cautious. The office is just inside the gate on the left. While I have done my best to give directions to individual graves, this is a large and complex cemetery, and I strongly advise you to get an overview map from the office as well as smaller photocopied maps for individual sections. The staff are happy to look up names and mark locations on the maps. The overview map is essential cartography; you will be lost without it, and my directions here will make regular references to it. It shows all sections, main edifices, mausoleums, and the maze of connecting roads. Some of the roads are marked in combinations of white, blue, or yellow stripes without which you would become quickly disoriented in the rolling, wooded terrain.

Albert Boasberg (1892–1937): Laughing at Death

Alfred "Al" Boasberg, movie screenwriter and director, was the Buffalo-born son of a jewelry merchant who attached himself to vaudeville actors coming through town and developed wisecracks and one-liners for them, even telegraphing jokes to them after they had moved on. He moved to Hollywood in the 1920s where he wrote gags for Buster Keaton's *The General* (1926) and *College* (1927).[1] It was called "punching up" a scene when a gag man wrote the cards. Then came the sound era, which was fertile ground for ambitious, dialogue-savvy screenwriters.

Although Boasberg directed a number of short films, he was mainly known as a comedy screenwriter and a dialogue doctor: when sections of screenplays seemed slow, they could hand it off to Boasberg and in a few hours he'd pass it back with new gags and jokes. He liked to work while sitting in the bathtub rattling off jokes into a Dictaphone. But he also did his research. In 1931 he told a reporter that he traveled twice a year to various cities and towns and gathered his material by striking up conversations with people, getting their life stories, "their habits and peculiarities." Then he filed it all for future use.[2]

He was often uncredited, so no one knows how many jokes he wrote for the movies, much less for vaudeville. But his film list includes *Let 'Em Have It* (1935 additional dialogue), *The Nitwits* (1935 screenplay coauthor), *Make a Wish* (1937 additional dialogue), *Cracked Nuts* (1931 dialogue), *Jailbirds of Paradise* (1934 screenplay sole author), and the Marx Brothers' *A Night at the Opera* (1935 uncredited dialogue, in addition to the famous stateroom scene) and *A Day at the Races* (1937 uncredited).

It is probably a good thing that he was not credited for dialogue for one film, *Freaks* (1932), which was not a comedy at all, but a kind of morality play in which circus "freaks" get brutally even with a trapeze diva and her strongman boyfriend for trying to poison a little man and rob him of his inheritance. It is now considered a classic, but audiences found it so repugnant (because real circus "freaks" were in the cast) that it all but ended the career of director Tod Browning, and it was the first film that MGM pulled from theaters in mid-circulation. According

1. Erickson, "Al Boasberg."
2. "Comedy Author Reveals Secrets," 5.

to the *New York Times*, "The only thing that can be said definitely for 'Freaks' is that it is not for children. Bad dreams lie that way."[3] His lesson was stick to comedy.

Boasberg's death, in June 1937, came as a shock to many. The *New York Times* reported that Boasberg had been stricken while telling a joke to his friends that he was planning to go to a big Hollywood epic that evening in order "to get some sleep." The *Times* obituary headline was "Al Boasberg, Writer of Jokes for Radio," as if he had been a one-medium man. It also reported that he had just signed a contract with Jack Benny for $1,500 per week.[4] Big bucks in those days.

Finding the Grave

From the main entrance, follow the road with the white, yellow, and blue stripes. Where the striped path turns right, go straight, and you will cross a bridge over Scajaquada Creek. Proceed on that path until you round a corner at section X. The next section on your right is FF, which is your destination. Stop where you see a stone for Lewin and walk straight back about five hundred feet. There is an array of stones for the Boasberg family, including a marker for the family plot large enough that you will see it easily. It may be difficult at first to find Al's stone since the family plot seems to go in all directions, but it is there. And along with the stone is a large brass plate in the ground, placed by "the children of his affectionate younger sister Phyllis Boasberg Michaels." The plate contains extraordinary testimonials:

> "Our biggest break was to get Boasberg to write for us. He was a comic genius."
> —Groucho Marx.
> "He lived in a world of laughter."
> —Chico Marx.

3. "Circus Side Show," 6.
4. "Boasberg, Writer of Jokes for Radio," 17.

29.1: The grave of Al Boasberg in Buffalo.

"The greatest gag man who ever lived."
—Jack Benny
And a quote from Boasberg himself: "If I can make people laugh at
their troubles, if I can make them laugh at death, I have reached a
sort of perfection."

Shirley Chisholm (1924–2005): Unbought and Unbossed

She was a fighter in the best sense of the word. A teacher and political organizer in her home base, Brooklyn, Shirley Chisholm served in the New
York State Assembly, starting in 1965, where she quickly gained a reputation for being a scrapper, for not playing political poker with the big guys,
and for being unpredictable. In 1968 she became the first black woman
elected to the US Congress where she served until 1983, and where she
fought for refugees, Native American land rights, legal services for the
poor and the marginalized, and for special education, and was the first
woman to seek the Democratic Party nomination for president.[5] (Margaret Chase Smith, Republican, was the first woman to run for any major
party's presidential nod in 1964.) Her campaign slogan was "Unbought
and Unbossed." The mention of her name was almost always in the con-
text of feminism, peace and justice, racial equality, and sanity.

She did what she thought was right, and damn the torpedoes. She
visited Alabama Gov. George Wallace in the hospital after he was shot in
Maryland while running for president, which brought stinging criticism
down on her head; after all, he was the one who had stood in the door at
Alabama University to resist desegregation. But she felt it was the decent
and compassionate thing to do.[6] He later helped her win the votes she
needed to win minimum wage for black women workers. Being unpredictable pays dividends to the honest. According to his daughter, Peggy
Wallace Kennedy, Chisholm's kindness touched Wallace deeply. "Shirley

5. Trescott, "Chisholm in Season of Transition."
6. Trescott.

29.2: Shirley Chisholm in 1971. Warren K. Leffler, U.S. News and World Report Magazine Photograph Collection, Library of Congress, Prints and Photographs Division, LC-DIG-ppmsca-55919.

29.3: The crypt of Shirley Chisholm in Buffalo.

Chisholm had the courage to believe that even George Wallace could change," she said. "Chisholm planted a seed of new beginnings in my father's heart." They became political allies. And he renounced racism.[7]

Most do not think of her as an author. Yet her autobiography, *Unbought and Unbossed* (1970), was republished in 2010 in a fortieth anniversary edition. It is a strong book, and an eyeopener. She was born in 1924 in New York City to immigrant parents from Barbados. They may have hoped that the United States would be their promised land. But when her father was out of work, she was sent along with her two sisters to their family homestead in Barbados where they were raised by their grandmother until their parents could get on their feet. She credited the British school system on the island for the quality of education that gave her the advantage to take leadership roles in her community and, eventually, in the US Congress, and for her ease at writing.

7. Sommers, "Lessons of a Black Pioneer."

After her retirement from Congress, she moved to the Buffalo suburb of Williamsville. She died on New Years Day 2005 in Florida where she had later moved. But in death she returned to her adopted community of Buffalo.

Finding the Grave

Shirley Chisholm is in the Birchwood Mausoleum. From the main entrance, follow the road with the white, yellow, and blue stripes, which turns to the right before the first bridge over Scajaquada Creek; continue to follow past Mirror Lake and the grand field of classic-style mausoleums and cross the second bridge over the creek, after which follow the yellow route up the hill. Birchwood Mausoleum is No. 6 on the Overview map. She is in the Center Lane, Wall 32, Row 158, Tier F. Walk in the front door. Her crypt is about twelve feet off the floor on the left side, which she shares with her second husband Arthur Hardwick.

Leslie Fiedler (1917–2003): Come Back to the Raft Ag'in

Literary critics become famous far less often than writers of other genres, even poets. There are Lionel Trilling and Susan Sontag. More often, as with T. S. Eliot and Ezra Pound, they're famous for something besides their critical work. Leslie Fiedler was a titan among critics, a provocateur—which, owing to his approach to the American novel that examined its relationship to American culture, made him also a social critic.

The first of his essays that grabbed the attention of the reading world was "Come Back to the Raft Ag'in, Huck Honey!" in the *Partisan Review* in 1948, in which he woke readers up to the love relationships between white heroes and their dark-skinned partners in numerous American novels. Think of it: Huckleberry Finn and Jim the runaway enslaved person; Natty Bumppo and the Mohican Chingachgook; Melville's Ishmael and Queequeg; and yes, the Lone Ranger and Tonto. According to David Meischen,

> Fiedler blasted away the tired old tropes about plot and character and theme, the symbol hunting that passes for life as an English major. He

took the blinders off me and said, *Look, the myths we live by, our secret longings—the great books lay them bare, if only we have the courage to see.*[8]

Fiedler was born in New Jersey in 1917 to Jewish immigrant parents, attended New York University, and took his MA and PhD at the University of Wisconsin after serving in the Navy in World War II as a cryptologist. He was present when the flag was raised by Marines and a Navy medic on Mount Suribachi in Iwo Jima in February 1945. He joined the faculty of the State University of New York at Buffalo in 1964, and was the Samuel Langhorne Clemens Professor of English from 1973 until his death in 2003.[9]

Probably his most famous book was *Love and Death in the American Novel*, which contained the Huck Finn essay. But there were thirty-nine in all, including *Waiting for the End: The American Literary Scene from Hemingway to Baldwin* (1964), *Freaks: Myths and Images of the Secret Self* (1978), *What was Literature?: Class Culture And Mass Society* (1982), and several volumes of fiction. *Being Busted* (1969) is his account of the sudden invasion of his home in 1967 by Buffalo police who found a small quantity of hashish and marijuana (which it turned out had been planted), and the long legal aftermath of the incident. He wrote in the *New York Review of Books*,

> Where did it all begin, I keep asking myself, where did it really start— back beyond the moment those six or eight or ten improbable cops came charging into my house, without having knocked, of course, but screaming as they came (for the record, the first of their endless lies), "We knocked! We knocked!"; and producing only five minutes later, after considerable altercation, the warrant sworn out by a homeless, lost girl on whom my wife and daughter had been wasting concern and advice for over a year.[10]

8. Meischen, "How a Literary Critic Slapped Me Awake."
9. Lehman-Haupt, "Leslie Fiedler Dies at 85," C12.
10. Fiedler, "On Being Busted at Fifty."

29.4: The crypt of Leslie Fiedler in Buffalo.

Though convicted, he fought the case for five years and finally won.[11]

He was provocative and he made his mark. The furor over *Love and Death* took some time to settle, and for his points therein to become generally accepted. Said his biographer Mark Royen Winchell, "Before Fiedler, hardly any literary critics discussed race and sexuality in American literature. Since him, they talk about hardly anything else."[12]

Finding the Grave

Leslie Fiedler is in the Rosewood Mausoleum. From the main entrance, follow the road with the white, yellow, and blue stripes, which turns to

11. Lehman-Haupt.
12. Rourke, "Leslie Fiedler, 85."

the right before the bridge over Scajaquada Creek ; continue to follow past Mirror Lake and the grand field of mausoleums, and cross the second bridge over the creek, after which follow the yellow route up the hill. Rosewood Mausoleum is No. 4 on the overview map. Walk from the front door all the way through to the atrium. From there a door will lead you to an outdoor brick walk. Follow that path around the back of the building to an area bordered by an arborvitae hedge. Dr. Fiedler is there, about six feet up the wall with his second wife Sally.

Anna Katherine Green (1846–1935): The Detective Genre's Mom

Born in Brooklyn, she came to Buffalo in 1884 when she married actor and furniture designer Charles Rohlfs. Anna Katherine Green is called the Mother of the Detective Novel, and her first, *The Leavenworth Case* (1878), is also noted as the first American bestseller, selling three million copies,[13] as well as the first legal thriller.[14] It was also a hit in Europe, unusual then for an American book. It was the beginning of a long career as a popular mystery novelist for Green, with eventually some forty novels to her credit, including the once-famous Amelia Butterworth series, and her series of detective novels featuring the sleuth Ebenezer Gryce.

But the claim of motherhood is more complicated than that, and some explanation is called for here. Edgar Allen Poe holds the laurel for the first detective fiction with "Murders in the Rue Morgue," which is a short story, not a novel. The first detective novel was actually *The Dead Letter* by another American woman named Metta Victoria Fuller, who wrote under the nom de plume Seeley Regester, beating Green to the genre by twelve years.[15] Fuller had other pennames up her sleeve, but Regester is the one most remembered. She was a dime-novel writer— books that were generally brief and considered a cut below the more mainstream fiction such as Green published with G. P. Putnam—and

13. Mallory, "Mother of the American Mystery."
14. Davis, "Murderous Women Writers of Oz," 9.
15. Fuller, "The Dead Letter."

she wasn't married to mysteries but wrote a wide spectrum of popular genre fiction.

If we call Green the mother (and I do), then it is because she gave it a level of sophistication, whetting the public's appetite for sleuths. She helped establish a standard for mysteries, that the dastardly doer is not discovered until the final five percent of the novel—a standard that still holds. Green's characters are drawn with an admirable level of psychological complexity. But unlike a contemporary murder mystery, the perp in *Leavenworth* is brought to justice by dint of cracking under the weight of guilt; it does not end in a bloody shootout, which is what we would expect today. She said once that "the essentials of a good mystery story are first an interesting plot with a new twist—a queer turn that has never before been attempted. . . . Your story should rise in steps from one unfolding to another, reaching a climax that must be a pleasant surprise—never a disappointment."[16]

The claim of the first bestseller is probably an exaggeration, at least in America, where the laurel more likely goes to one of James Fenimore Cooper's Leatherstocking Tales. Two other women, Harriet Beecher Stowe and Mary Jane Holmes[17] wrote books earlier than Green, which were considered bestsellers.

But, really, what does it matter who was first? Green's work drew a steady readership her entire career. An untitled review in the *Chicago Examiner* in 1913 said, "Let it stand that Anna Katherine Green has her place among the leaders of weaving shuddery, and shivery, ghastly plots peopled with baffling human beings." Wilkie Collins and Arthur Conan Doyle were among her fans.[18]

Green was the daughter of a New York lawyer, so she had a reliable consultant for questions of criminal law, and, according to *The National Cyclopedia of American Biography* (1907), *The Leavenworth Case* was assigned to Yale law classes to demonstrate the precariousness of pursuing

16. "Anna K. Green Dies," 23.
17. See West, chapter 28, Brockport.
18. "Green Dies."

29.5: The grave of Anna Katherine Green in Buffalo.

a case on purely circumstantial evidence. Eventually, *Leavenworth* became a movie, though, unfortunately, not a terribly good one.

Finding the Grave

From the main gate, follow the three-color stripes: white, blue, and yellow, turning right before the first Scajaquada Creek bridge. Sections 1 and 23 will be on your right, 24 on your left. After crossing the second bridge, turn right again, following just the blue and white. At the next crossing, turn left to follow the yellow again. Section 27 will be on your right. A short distance before the next crossing you will see a prominent stone on the right, marked "Pray." Stop, walk directly back for about one hundred feet, and look for a prominent stone for the Rohlfs family, among whom is

Anna Katherine Green Rohlfs. Her name is etched somewhat close to the base, and may be partially obscured by grass.

Edward Caleb Randall (1860–1935): Speaking for the Dead

He was born in 1860 in Ripley, New York, a quiet rural town on the shore of Lake Erie, near Fredonia. It's still a rural place. When you drive the New York State Thruway to the very western end, the surrounding fields and woods are Ripley. But Edward Caleb Randall's life was on an upward spiral. Admitted to the bar at twenty-three, he was a trial lawyer with a yen for business, and before he died he was board president of the American Superpower Corporation, the Niagara Terminals Buildings, Inc., Cataract Development Corporation, and two or three other business—all at once. It's a wonder that he had time to get married, but he did, to Maria Howard of Buffalo, where he had migrated after a short stint as a lawyer in Dunkirk.[19]

Make no mistake, he was a serious man, and by accounts an agnostic. According to N. Riley Heagerty, "he had no place in his mind for even a conception of a spiritual existence, or for any agencies in the universe other than matter and force."[20]

Things began to change in 1890 when several people came to him and asked him to investigate a certain Mrs. French of Rochester, who they said was a magician of some sort, and a fraud. Being a sharp trial lawyer, they assumed that he could raise the shade on her tricks. So, he went to 227 Tremont St. in Rochester and knocked on her door. (The house is no longer there.) The woman he met, Emily S. French, was an elderly widow with a bad heart, living with her daughter in a modest home, a spirit medium who refused to accept money for her services.[21] Everyone I have found who wrote about her attested to her civility and refinement, so Randall must have felt a little disarmed. He was probably expecting a charismatic Madam Blavatsky, or an exotic with a crystal ball.

19. Heagerty, *The French Revelation.*
20. Heagerty.
21. Heagerty.

And here's another interesting detail: He says that when he entered her house, he met two other men "of national reputation."[22] He doesn't say who they were, perhaps because he thought it wise not to expose reputable men who visited spirit mediums. One individual who was named as a regular participant in the early sessions was Monroe County Judge William Dean Shuart,[23] who died in April of 1900 and no longer needed protection when Randall wrote his account. But of all the published obituaries that followed Shuart's death, while attesting to his being an upright citizen with many friends and absolutely trustworthy, none made mention of his dabbling in spiritualism. Another participant was A. W. Moore, a former editor of the *Union and Advertiser* newspaper in Rochester, who was then secretary of the Rochester Art Club.[24] Both men were strong defenders of Mrs. French when others voiced disbelief and insinuated that she was a fraud.

Randall was invited to join the evening's session, and with everyone seated, Mrs. French turned out the lights. Disembodied voices began to talk. It was a life-altering experience for Randall. He became a firm believer in life after death and the author of six books on mediumship and the spirit world. In *The Dead Have Never Died* he wrote,

> I have had strange experiences in my psychic investigations during the last twenty years. Refusing to be limited by accepted laws, I have devoted my thought to conditions prevailing beyond what is generally termed the material, and by combining and blending the mental and vital, with the tangible or physical forces, I have been able to have speech with those long thought dead. As a result I have found an unknown country about and beyond this Earth, and I would not go from this world of men without leaving a record of what I have learned.[25]

Over a period of twenty-two years—until her death in 1912—Randall, Mrs. French, and others communed with the voices. All in attendance joined hands in the seances, so it would have been impossible for her to

22. Randall, quoted in Heagerty, Introduction.
23. Moore, letter quoted in Funk, *Psychic Riddle*, 88.
24. Funk, 87–93.
25. Randall, *Dead Have Never Died*, vii.

pull a lever of some kind. Her house was searched for pipes or other appa-
ratus by which some actor could have imposed his voice. Mrs. French was
nearly deaf, and sometimes she would talk while a spirit was speaking, so it
was not likely that she was an accomplished ventriloquist. Moreover, they
held the same sort of sessions with Mrs. French at other people's homes,
with similar results. One regular spirit voice claimed to be the Seneca
Chief Red Jacket, who lamented the state of his soul at the time of his
death, blaming the "fire water" that whites had given him.[26]

In early 1905, Randall wrote to the publisher Isaac Kauffman Funk,
of Funk and Wagnall's, and suggested that he test Mrs. French. He was
the man who had employed more than seven hundred scholars to produce
the *Funk and Wagnall's Standard Dictionary*. Funk, a Lutheran minister,
was also a psychic researcher, but particularly cautious. Shortly thereafter he
received a letter from Moore, also urging his attention to Mrs. French. But,
being wary, and having been fooled before, he declined. Then he was visited
by an unnamed lawyer from Rochester who had been to numerous seances
with Mrs. French, had known her for many years, and attested to her integrity. It seems there was quite a spiritualist movement in Rochester at that
time in the higher circles of society, although very discreet. Funk relented.[27]

He stipulated a number of conditions to avoid any fakery. She was
to travel to New York City alone except for one "lady escort." The sit-
tings were to take place at a home designated by Funk, one that he could
thoroughly check, and that he would not make known to them until after
they arrived. He later wrote that "These terms were accepted cheerfully."[28]
Although in feeble health, Mrs. French was put through the wringer. On
the first of many nights she sat with Funk and others in darkness for about
twenty minutes until voices of various spirits began to speak. Funk could
find no possible way that she could have produced the voices herself. At
his request, she held water in her mouth to rule out ventriloquism, which
skeptics often suspected. Red Jacket, whose voice was again heard, said,
according to Funk in his book, *The Psychic Riddle*:

26. Funk, 89.
27. Funk, 87–95.
28. Funk, 94–95.

We live as real lives, more real—on this side than we did when on earth. . . . In fact, everything here is so real that many who come over—die, as you call it—do not know for a long time that they are dead. A great part of the work to be done here is to instruct the dead in the true science of progress.[29]

Apparently convinced, Funk wrote,

Again, one word to those who mourn. There is no death; there are no dead. Those whom we love and who loved us, in obedience to the great law of evolution, have simply progressed to a new plane of existence. . . . They walk with us, know our trials, help us by their mental suggestions, and comfort us by tender, loving thoughts.[30]

It is fair to ask, what was really going on? Randall logged some seven hundred sessions with Emily French; some with his wife in attendance, some with Moore, some with Judge Shuart, some with Funk, and many with numerous others. Many seances were held in the Randall home in Buffalo. Could all those people have been deluded on every occasion for the twenty-two years until Mrs. French's death?

Emily S. French and her spiritualist associates, although not organized into any brand of faith, could be viewed as an extension of the movement of enthusiastic faiths that, beginning in the early 1800s, swept east to west across New York State along the route of the Erie Canal, which included revivalist denominations; millennialism, such as Millerism; Jemima Wilkerson's cultist Public Universal Friends; Mormonism, which of course is now recognized as a solid denomination; and the Oneida Colony. The nineteenth-century evangelist Charles Finney called it the Burned Over District. But it is also called the Psychic Highway because it included psychic phenomena and mediums, the most famous of which are the Fox sisters of Hydesville, New York. Today, the largest spiritualist community in the western world is Lilydale, in Chautauqua County.

29. Funk, 103–34.
30. Randall, x.

29.6: Edward Caleb Randall and wife are in the second row next to Howard.

Edward Caleb Randall's books are *Life's Progression* (1906); *Future of Man* (1908); *The Dead Have Never Died* (1917), which is his best-known title; *Frontiers of the After Life* (1922); *Told in the After Life* (1925); and *The Living Dead* (1927). There is also a more recent compilation of his work edited by N. Riley Heagerty, titled *The French Revelation: Voice to Voice Conversations With Spirits Through the Mediumship of Emily S. French* (1995, 2015).

Finding the Grave

From the main entrance, follow the road with the white, yellow, and blue stripes and cross the first bridge over Scajaquada Creek, then continue on that road, keeping left, until you reach the north end of the cemetery where the path curves to the east. Section X is on the right, which is your destination. Circle around the section—which will have you leaving the path for a new narrower one—until you see a sign "U/X" marking the border of the sections. You will see a prominent monument for R. L. Howard. To the left of that monument are two small stones for Edward C. Randall and his wife Maria.

And, by the way, Emily S. French is buried in Mount Hope Cemetery in Rochester, in section O. Judge William Dean Shuart is in section 4.

Edward Streeter (1891–1976): Novelist, Satirist, . . . and Banker

It is hard to think of another successful American writer who was also a banker. I'm talking about Edward Streeter who served for twenty-five years as vice president of the Bank of New York. Before that he served for eight years at Bankers Trust. Wallace Stevens comes close: he was vice president of a major insurance company. I've known a few writers who had a lot of money, but a banker? It does not seem that one individual would be able to survive with those very antithetical ambitions.

Edward Streeter was born in Buffalo in 1891 and attended Harvard University. He became a World War I correspondent for the *Buffalo Express*, which later became the *Buffalo Courier Express*. That was the newspaper Mark Twain wrote for when he lived in Buffalo, but he had moved on to fame before Streeter was born. Along the way Streeter married Charlotte Warren, granddaughter of James Dunlap Warren, owner of the *Buffalo Commercial Advertiser* and Republican Party stalwart.

During World War I he had started a regular newspaper column titled "Dere [sic] Mabel," which were endearing letters from a fictitious soldier named Bill with spelling problems to his true love back home. The column was very popular during the war, and after the conflict ended they were compiled in a book, *Dere Mabel* (1918) and it was a bestseller, followed by *That's Me All Over, Mabel* (1919).[31]

He hit it bigger in 1949 with the novel *Father of the Bride*, a satire of a man's paroxysms of love and anxiety as his daughter gets ready to march down the aisle. This one elevated him to the higher offices of fame, not only because it was a bestseller, but the following year it became a movie

---

31. "Edward Streeter, Humorist, Dies at 84."

with Spencer Tracy, Joan Bennett, and Elizabeth Taylor as the bride. Now he was on a roll. Next came *Mr. Hobbs' Vacation* (1954), which also became a movie in 1962 with James Stewart and Maureen O'Hara. *Merry Christmas, Mr. Baxter* (1956), was adapted for NBC's *The Alcoa Hour*, starring Dennis King, Patricia Benoit, and Margaret Hamilton. He was retired now, and he could spend all the time he wanted writing books; he produced four more, though they did not pack the wallop that his earlier books did. *Father of the Bride* was also a TV series from 1961–62.

His novels are known for dry wit and insight into the modern human condition. Streeter's "genial thesis," said the *New York Times* review of the film version of *Mr. Hobbs' Vacation*, is that "the family unit is perhaps the most anomalous and irritating social arrangement ever devised by so-called civilized man." The family unit survives Hobbs's holiday, said the reviewer, but "Mr. Streeter has still got in some nice, sharp, accurate digs."[32]

Edward Streeter holds a deserved place in American pop culture. His books may not be classics, but the movie version of *Father of the Bride* (1950) certainly is. The 1991 remake does not come close to it. If you see Peter Bogdanovich's *The Last Picture Show* you'll see a short clip of the original being shown in one of the movie theater scenes. Even those few seconds have enough gravitas to send you to the library for the DVD. Or the novel itself—it's in the stacks somewhere. It is, after all, a good story.

Finding the Grave

Streeter's funeral was held at St. Bartholomew's Episcopal Church on East 56th Street in New York City. But for his burial, it was time to come home to Buffalo. He is buried in section 9 at Forest Lawn, and he is easy to find. From the main entrance, follow the road with the white, yellow, and blue stripes. On your left you will pass sections 11 and 8. Streeter is in the next section, 9. There is a triangular roundabout there with a spreading fern tree, and just to the left of a Rose of Sharon tree is a monument to James D. Warren. Around it are twenty-three smaller markers for individual members of

---

32. Crowther, "Mr. Hobbs Takes a Vacation."

29.7: Warren family plot in Buffalo. Streeter is second from the right.

his family, and Edward Streeter is one of them, three markers to the right of the monument. Since he married into James D.'s family, they kindly made room for him in the family plot. His stone has not weathered well these forty-plus years, so you must look closely to read his name.

Sources

Al Boasberg

"Al Boasberg, Writer of Jokes for Radio." *New York Times*, June 19, 1937.
"Circus Side Show." Movie review of *Freaks. New York Times*, July 9, 1932.
"Comedy Author Reveals Secrets of His Writing." *Brainard Daily Dispatch* (Brainard, MN). July 26, 1931.

Erickson, Hal. "Al Boasberg." All Movie Guide. Accessed April 18, 2023. www
.allmovie.com/artist/al-boasberg-p158592.

"Freaks." Accessed April 18, 2023. https://www.tcm.com/tcmdb/title/163/freaks
/#overview.

"Hollywood's Ace Gag Writer Dies." Associated Press. *Joplin Globe* (Joplin, MO).
June 19, 1937.

"Mr. Hope and Others." *New York Times*, May 13, 1932.

Wilk, Max. *Schmucks with Underwoods: Conversations with Hollywood's Classic
Screenwriter.* New York: Applause Theater and Cinema Books, 2004.

Wilk, Max. *The Wit and Wisdom of Hollywood.* New York: Atheneum, 1971.

Shirley Chisholm

Chisholm, Shirley. *Unbought and Unbossed.* Washington, DC: Take Root
Media, 2010.

Sommers, Christina Hoff. "Lessons of a Black Pioneer," *Persuasion*, Dec. 14,
2020. https://www.persuasion.community/p/lessons-of-a-black-pioneer.

Trescott, Jacqueline. "Shirley Chisholm in Her Season of Transition." *Washington Post*, June 6, 1982.

Williams, Vanessa. "'Unbought and Unbossed': Shirley Chisholm's Feminist
Mantra Is Still Relevant 50 Years Later." *Washington Post*, January 26, 2018.

Leslie Fiedler

Fiedler, Leslie. "On Being Busted at Fifty." *New York Review of Books*, July 13,
1967.

Lehman-Haupt, Christopher. "Leslie Fiedler Dies at 85; Provocative Literary
Critic," *New York Times*, July 13, 1967. https://www.nybooks.com/articles
/1967/07/13/on-being-busted-at-fifty/.

"Leslie Fiedler, Celebrity Critic Who Liked to Provoke." *Independent* (UK), February 3, 2003. www.independent.co.uk/news/obituaries/leslie-fiedler-36224
.html.

Meischen, David. "How a Literary Critic Slapped Me Awake: My Favorite
Critic." *Talking Writing*. February 14, 2014. https://talkingwriting.com/how
-literary-critic-slapped-me-awake.

Rourke, Mary. "Leslie Fiedler, 85; Critic and Scholar Explored Roles of Sex and Race in American Storytelling," *Los Angeles Times*, Feb. 1, 2003. https://www.latimes.com/archives/la-xpm-2003-feb-01-me-fiedler1-story.html.

Anna Katherine Green

"Anna K. Green Dies; Noted Author, 88," *New York Times*.

Davis, J. Madison. "The Murderous Women Writers of Oz," *World Literature Today*, 80, No. 1 (Jan.–Feb. 2006), 9–11. https://www.jstor.org/stable/4015901 5?origin=crossref.

Fuller, Metta Victoria (Seeley Regester). "The Dead Letter," *Beadle's Monthly*, 1 (Jan.–June 1866). Internet Archive. Accessed April 18, 2023. https://archive .org/details/1866thedeadletterinbeadlesmonthly/mode/2up.

Mallory, Michael. "The Mother of the American Mystery: Anna Katherine Green." *Mystery Scene*, no. 94 (Spring 2017). www.mysteryscenemag.com /article/1867-the-mother-of-american-mystery-anna-katharine-green.

The National Cyclopedia of American Biography, Vol. 9. New York: J. T. White Company, 1907.

Edward Caleb Randall

"Frontiers of the Afterlife: Edward C. Randall." Hove, UK: White Crow Books. Accessed April 18, 2023. http://whitecrowbooks.com/books/page/frontiers_of _the_afterlife/.

Funk, Isaac K. *The Psychic Riddle*. New York: Funk and Wagnalls, 1907.

Heagerty, N. Riley. *The French Revelation: Voice to Voice Conversations With Spirits Through the Mediumship of Emily S. French*. Hove, UK: White Crow Books, 2015. Kindle.

Moore, A. W. Quoted in *The Psychic Riddle*, by Isaac K. Funk, letter. New York: Funk and Wagnalls, 1907.

Randall, Edward Caleb. "Emily French and the Direct-Independent Voice Phenomena." Quoted in *The French Revelation: Voice to Voice Conversations With Spirits Through the Mediumship of Emily S. French*, by N. Riley Heagerty, Introduction. Hove, UK: White Crow Books, 2015. Kindle.

Randall, Edward Caleb. *The Dead Have Never Died*. N.p.: Palala Press, 2015.

Edward Streeter

Crowther, Bosley. "Screen: 'Mr. Hobbs Takes a Vacation': Edward Streeter Book Twists Family Life." *New York Times*, June 16, 1962.

"Edward Streeter, Humorist, Dies at 84." *New York Times*, April 2, 1976.

"Mrs. Charlotte Warren Streeter." *New York Times*, January 3, 1966.

30 Canandaigua

Austin Steward, John Chapin Mosher

The city of Canandaigua, on the shore of Canandaigua Lake, has a small-town, lakeside atmosphere, although the shoreline itself is distressingly overdeveloped and has been for generations. It was once a Seneca village, one of those burned to its roots by Gen. John Sullivan during the Revolutionary War. It was resettled by whites, and by the 1790s had a public school. Here, in 1873, at the Ontario County Courthouse, Susan B. Anthony was tried and convicted for the crime in Rochester of voting in the 1872 presidential election. As happens so often, the judge and jury were on the wrong side of history. It is also home to the New York Kitchen restaurant and cooking school and to Sonnenberg Gardens—all very much worth a visit.

Canandaigua is the birthplace in 1823 of Philip Spencer, a midshipman who in 1842 was hung with two other sailors aboard the USS *Somers* and buried at sea for the crime of conspiracy to mutiny, but without a legal court martial, which led to a scandal. He may have been the model for Herman Melville's *Billy Budd*. Melville had a relative aboard the ship, a cousin named Lieutenant Guert Gansevoort, so the author was certainly familiar with the incident. Spencer, son of John C. Spencer, President Tyler's secretary of war, was a noted rake and rogue. A Navy court exonerated the ship's captain, reasoning that had the men been merely confined aboard ship, they could have been sprung by other disgruntled shipmen and then mutiny would have ensued. Public opinion in the United States was outraged, but as everyone knows, outrage sputters out eventually.

Canandaigua was the birthplace in 1880 of Arthur Garfield Dove, known as America's first abstract painter, who kept a studio in the nearby city of Geneva.

This chapter covers graves in two locations in Canandaigua: West Avenue Cemetery and Woodlawn Cemetery.

Austin Steward (1794–1869): From Enslaved Person to Freeman

He was born into slavery in Prince William County, Virginia, in the last decade of the eighteenth century, and migrated with his master to Central New York before the War of 1812. While there, Austin Steward escaped bondage. His memoir, *Twenty-two Years a Slave and Forty Years a Freeman*, belongs among such great narratives of African American experience in the antebellum years as *The Narrative of Frederick Douglass, American Slave* and *Twelve Years a Slave*, by Solomon Northrop. It gives us a horrifying picture of enslaved life, but also a view of Upstate's early settlements from the perspective of a man in bondage, and later of a free man who took his destiny into his own hands. He became a businessman in Rochester and an active abolitionist, helping enslaved people flee to Canada via the Underground Railroad.

Steward was put to work in the fields at age seven, and later made a household enslaved person. His accounts of the lives of field enslaved people, of the thirty-nine lashes that one would receive with a heavy, lead-tipped whip allude to something even worse than senseless cruelty—an insane savagery in men who would have treated their horses and cattle gently. This brutality was more the norm than the exception, according to Steward, since lenient masters were despised by their neighbors. He relates details of an insurrection (years before Nat Turner) that occurred on a plantation when a patrol came to break up the enslaved people's Easter festivities, in which the three members of the patrol and two of the enslaved people were killed.[1]

Steward's plantation master, Captain Helm, loved his leisure activities: poker, booze, and racehorses, and eventually gambled himself into

1. Steward, *Twenty-Two Years a Slave*, 24–28.

penury. He sold his plantation and moved his household and enslaved people north to the recently settled Genesee Valley in New York State. Steward recalls that this was not good news to the enslaved people, who thought the Genesee to be beyond the pale of civilization, "where we should in all probability be destroyed by wild beasts, devoured by cannibals, or scalped by the Indians."[2] He writes:

> We traveled northward, through Maryland, Pennsylvania, and a portion of New York, to Sodus Bay, where we halted for some time. We made about twenty miles per day, camping out every night, and reached that place after a march of twenty days. Every morning the overseer called the roll, when every slave must answer to his or her name, felling to the ground with his cowhide any delinquent who failed to speak out in quick time.[3]

Steward does not say how many enslaved people made the journey, but it must have been a considerable crowd since he does not mention any left behind.

There wasn't much of a welcoming party at Sodus—only a single tavern. Captain Helm bought a large tract of land on both sides of the bay and ordered his enslaved people to clear the woods. But hunger set in. The Virginians had no idea how to feed their multitude in the unfamiliar place. Enslaved people found wild animal bones in the woods and boiled them to make broth.[4]

But things were different there in another significant way. Some of the enslaved people sensed that they now possessed a modicum of liberty in this new land. One day the overseer went into a cabin and found an enslaved person named Williams whom he was determined to whip. But Williams was having none of it. "Instantly Williams sprang and caught him by the throat and held him writhing in his vise-like grasp, until he succeeded in getting possession of the cowhide, with which he gave the overseer such a

2. Steward, 35.
3. Steward, 37.
4. Steward, 39–40.

flogging as slaves seldom get."[5] Shortly after, the monster quit his job and went back to Virginia.

Restless, Captain Helm moved them all back down the valley to Bath, where he used the proceeds from the sale of his plantation—$40,000, or around $800,000 in today's dollars—to found saw- and gristmills, which later proved unprofitable, and Helm began hiring out his enslaved people, including Steward. The nation was readying for war with Great Britain. While hired out to a man in Lyons, Steward witnessed troops training for war, a scene that became a carnival of drunken bedlam.[6]

Steward found a spelling book, and began teaching himself to read. However, he said,

> But here Slavery showed its cloven foot in all its hideous deformity. . . .
> I had been set to work in the sugar bush, and I took my spelling book
> with me. When a spare moment occurred, I sat down to study, and so
> absorbed was I in the attempt to blunder through my lesson, that I did
> not hear the Captain's son-in-law coming until he was fairly upon me.
> He sprang forward, caught my poor old spelling book, and threw it into
> the fire, where it was burned to ashes; and then came my turn. He gave
> me first a severe flogging, and then swore if he ever caught me with
> another book, he would "whip every inch of skin off my back," &c. . . .
> I found it just as hard to be beaten over the head with a piece of iron in
> New York as it was in Virginia.[7]

When Helm again fell into financial trouble, he began selling his enslaved people, while others simply walked away. Steward gained freedom with the help of members of the New York Manumission Society, who told him that by virtue of hiring Steward out, Helm had forfeited legal ownership of him in New York—a technicality in the state's 1799 Gradual Emancipation Statute. Dennis Comstock, of the Society, gave him money to help him get settled. Steward wrote, "the first thing I did after receiving it I went to Canandaigua where I found a book-store kept by a man named

5. Steward, 43.
6. Steward, 54–59.
7. Steward, 64, 84.

J.D. Bemis, and of him I purchased some school books."[8] Helm made one last grand effort to restore his wealth by attempting to kidnap his former enslaved people en masse and transport them back to Virginia to be sold. He threw a big party in Palmyra and invited them all; then, late at night, he closed in with a group of men to capture them. But it ended in a bloody battle, with many injured, including Steward's father who succumbed later to his wounds, and Helm and his confederates went away emptyhanded. Steward himself had sensed trouble and had stayed away.[9]

In 1816, Steward started a business in Rochester, on what is now West Main Street, selling produce and meat. He prospered despite some local resistance from whites, and soon became a property owner in Rochester and surrounding areas.[10] He married Patience Butler of Canandaigua.

The state of New York ended slavery in 1827, one of the last northern states to do so (although not until 1840 did a census find no enslaved people in New York). Steward, now active in the Underground Railroad, celebrated the occasion with a speech in Rochester's Johnson Square, exhorting former enslaved people to look forward to the hard work ahead as free people:

> Let not the rising sun behold you sleeping or indolently lying upon your beds. Rise ever with the morning light; and, till sun-set, give not an hour to idleness. Say not human nature cannot endure it. It can—it almost requires it. . . . Be watchful and diligent and let your mind be fruitful in devises for the honest advancement of your worldly interest. So shall you continually rise in respectability, in rank and standing in this so late and so long the land of your captivity.[11]

Later he was elected vice president of the first meeting of the National Negro Convention Movement, held in Philadelphia in 1831. That same year, he moved to Canada to join the Wilberforce Colony in London, Ontario, which had been founded for African Americans escaping slavery

---

8. Steward, 85–86. Bemis was a noted supporter of progressive causes. There is a Bemis Street in Canandaigua.

9. Steward, 88–89.

10. Lewis, "Austin Steward."

11. Steward, 112–17.

30.1: The grave of Austin Steward, his wife and four of their children, in Canandaigua.

and agents who crossed into Northern states looking for runaways. But he found the leadership of that colony corrupt, and in 1837 he moved back to Rochester, much poorer, and then to Canandaigua where he lived with his wife for the rest of their lives. His book *Twenty-two Years a Slave and Forty Years a Freeman* was published by William Alling in Rochester in 1857. Steward died in the winter of 1869 from typhoid fever.[12]

Finding the Grave

To find Austin Steward's grave in West Avenue Cemetery, take Exit 44 from the New York State Thruway, and head directly south on Route 332.

12. Heffer, "Austin Steward."

As you come into Canandaigua it becomes South Main Street. A bit less than nine miles from the tollbooths you will find West Avenue, where you will turn right. If you come to Canandaigua on Routes 5 and 20, turn north on South Main Street, and in a few blocks you will find West Avenue. Turn left. Shortly after your turn, you will see West Avenue Cemetery on the right, and you will find the front entrance where the hedge breaks. Or tell your GPS to take you to 100 West Ave., Canandaigua, NY, 14424.

Walk or drive in about fifty feet to an intersecting path, and turn to the right. The white granite spire for the Steward family, with footstones for him, his wife Patience, and several of their children, is about twenty-five feet ahead on the left.

John Chapin Mosher (1892–1942): At Twilight

Born in 1892 in Ogdensburg, New York, that distant town up on the St. Lawrence River, John Chapin Mosher joined the staff of the *New Yorker* in 1926 after serving in the medical corps in World War I, teaching English at Northwestern University, working as a freelance writer, and wandering merrily and aimlessly through postwar Europe. Noted for his articles on writers such as Willa Cather and F. Scott Fitzgerald, he was also the *New Yorker's* first regular film critic and the first reader of unsolicited manuscripts, known for his enthusiasm for writing rejections.[13]

About Fitzgerald, he wrote: "Scott feels that he is getting on in years, that he is no longer young. It weighs upon him, troubles him. He is almost thirty. Seldom has he allowed a person of such advanced age to enter his books."[14] Unsurprisingly this earned Fitzgerald's enmity.[15] Two of his plays, *Sauce for the Emperor* and *Bored*, were staged by the Provincetown Players in Greenwich Village, where he kept company with such other bright lights in that collective as Eugene O'Neill, Djuna Barnes, Edna St. Vincent Millay, and Wallace Stevens.[16]

13. Homestead, "Every Week Essays."
14. Mosher, "That Sad Young Man."
15. Brackett, *"It's the Pictures That Got Small,"* 401.
16. Kennedy, "Bored."

He was a summer resident of Cherry Grove on Fire Island, where he and his partner Philip Claflin were early property owners for an emerging gay community.[17] He wrote short fiction for the *New Yorker* about life on the island, collected in 1940 in a volume *Celibate at Twilight and Other Stories*, many of which focus on a very fastidious, middle-aged bachelor named Mr. Opal. It is not easy to lay hands on this book, as it is decades out of print, but it's worth the search; the stories are gems.

He died of heart failure September 3, 1942. His funeral service was held the following Saturday, September 5, in Memorial Chapel, Canandaigua, in the town where his maternal grandparents lived. And he is buried there in Woodlawn Cemetery in the Chapin family plot, but far from Fire Island. He was fifty, although his obituary in the Rochester *Democrat and Chronicle* listed his age as forty-nine.[18]

His sudden death shocked his many literary friends. Screenwriter Charles Brackett wrote in his diary, on Sept. 3, that he had received an urgent telegram from the editor of the *New Yorker*:

> "JOHN MOSHER DIED UNEXPECTEDLY THIS MORNING. HAROLD ROSS." Despite the profound inner conviction I have had ever since the first news of his heart trouble, it was a crushing blow. I'm afraid I bawled in the office, and as I drove home for luncheon cried all the way down Melrose and Wilshire. For myself again, because I'd begun to miss the wittiest, wisest friend I've ever had or will have.[19]

Finding the Grave

Take Exit 44 from the New York State Thruway, and head directly south on Route 332. As you come into Canandaigua it becomes South Main Street. A bit less than nine miles from the tollbooths you will find West Avenue, where you will turn right. If you come to Canandaigua on Routes 5 and 20, turn north on South Main Street, and in a few blocks you will

17. Homestead.
18. "Services Set for Writer, 49."
19. Brackett, 191–92.

30.2: The grave of John Chapin Mosher in Canandaigua.

find West Avenue. Turn left. Shortly after your turn, you will pass West Avenue Cemetery on the right. Continue west and take the next right onto North Pearl Street. In a short distance you will see the gates of Woodlawn Cemetery on your left. Or key into your GPS *130 N. Pearl St., Canandaigua, NY, 14424.*

John Chapin Mosher is in the far end of section 5 in Woodlawn. Starting at the cemetery gate, take the left road at the fork, and cross Sucker Brook. You will pass Woodlawn Chapel on the right, where Mosher's funeral services were held. Section 5 is on the right, but it is a very long one.

Turn right at the next intersection. You will pass a work shed on the right. Continue on the same path through the next intersection. The section to your right is still 5. Now make the next right turn. You will see a tall spire on the corner for McKechnie, and an ancient oak tree. When you turn the corner you will see a large mossy boulder on the right. The

Chapin family plot, which includes several Moshers, is to the right of the boulder. John Chapin Mosher has a small stone adjacent to his grandparents, John Bassett Chapin, MD, and Harriett Preston Chapin. Dr. Chapin was on the medical staff of the Brighton Hall Hospital for Mental and Nervous Diseases in Canandaigua, now closed.

Sources

Austin Steward

Heffer, Wendy. "Austin Steward, Abolitionist, Freeman, Father." Friends of Mount Hope Cemetery. Accessed April 18, 2023. https://fomh.org/austin -steward-abolitionist-freeman-father/.

Lewis, David. "Austin Steward (1793–1869)." BlackPast.org. Feb. 12, 2014. www .blackpast.org/african-american-history/steward-austin-1793-1869/.

Steward, Austin. *Twenty-Two Years a Slave and Forty Years a Freeman.* 1856. Project Gutenberg, 2004.

John Chapin Mosher

Brackett, Charles. *"It's the Pictures That Got Small": Charles Brackett on Billy Wilder and Hollywood's Golden Age.* Edited by Anthony Slide. Foreword by Jim Moore. New York: Columbia Univ. Press, 2015.

Homestead, Melissa. "Every Week Essays." University of Wisconsin Libraries. Accessed April 18, 2023. http://everyweek.unl.edu/view?docId=EveryWeeks EditorialStaff.html

Kennedy, Jeff. "'Bored,' by John Chapin Mosher." ProvincetownPlayhouse. Accessed April 18, 2023. http://provincetownplayhouse.com/bored.html.

Mosher, John Chapin. "That Sad Young Man." *New Yorker,* April 17, 1926. www .newyorker.com/magazine/1926/04/17/that-sad-young-man.

"Services Set for Writer, 49." *Democrat and Chronicle* (Rochester, NY), September 5, 1942.

31 Coldspring

Governor Blacksnake

Coldspring is a town in Cattaraugus County in New York's Southern Tier, part of which is in the Allegany Reservation of the Seneca Nation; it also includes the hamlet of Steamburg. The general area of Cattaraugus is one of New York's secret pleasures. Much of it is woods and winding roads, and it is home to Allegany State Park, which is deeper woods. The so-called Amish Trail takes you through farmland and cottage industries of cheese- and chocolate-making, custom woodworking, and of course quilting. Communities like Randolph have the nestled atmosphere you find in some villages in New Hampshire and Vermont, and in a harried America they seem to be in another time and dimension.

The Reservation, land designated in the Treaty of Canandaigua in 1794, spans the banks of the Allegheny River adjacent to the park (the river is spelled differently from the park). Only about 58 percent of residents are Native American because the city of Salamanca, with a majority population of whites, sits on land leased from the Senecas. These leases have not been without controversy: when they came up for renewal in 1990, the Senecas raised the rents, and when residents put up a kick it seemed for a time that the leases might not be renewed, as they were eventually.

A greater controversy erupted in 1961 when the Army Corps of Engineers began construction of the Kinzua Dam on the Allegheny River at a point across the border in Pennsylvania. The dam would prevent flooding in the Pittsburg area, supply that city with hydroelectric power, and create recreational waterways, but it would flood about a third of the reservation. Residents of the reservation fought this project bitterly, led by Seneca

Nation President George Heron, until their final pleas were rejected by President John Kennedy. Some six hundred families were forced from their homes; they lost rich farmland and a way of life for many Seneca who were living by traditional ways without electric power. Numerous cemeteries had to be moved.

The Allegany Reservation was home to Governor Blacksnake, a Seneca war chief, whose memoir of his century-long life tells us much about life among Native Americans in New York in the eighteenth and nineteenth centuries, and about their participation in the Revolutionary War.

Governor Blacksnake (1753?–1859):
Warrior, Leader, and Memoirist

His name was Tah-won-ne-ahs, but English-speaking Americans and British knew him as Chainbreaker, or Awl Breaker, and as Governor Blacksnake, although he was never a governor. He was born in the small village of Kendaia, a little southeast of the foot of Seneca Lake, on a date that has been a matter of conjecture by historians, but apparently in the early 1750s, probably 1753;[1] the Lewis Henry Morgan website places his birth circa 1749.[2] But all sources that I have found agree that he died in 1859, which would make him well over a hundred years old at his death, an unusually long life in any era. His gravestone claims his birth was in 1737, but few believe that he could have lived to 122, and Blacksnake's own accounts suggest a birthdate of 1753, since he said he was two years old when William Johnson defeated the French on Lake George.[3] Shortly after his birth, his family moved to Canawaugus, a prominent Seneca village across the Genesee River from present-day Avon, New York, then with his mother's family to Seneca village Jenuchshadago on the Allegheny River.[4]

---

1. Abler, *Chainbreaker*, 17.
2. Rochester Museum of Science Center Lewis Henry Morgan Website, "Blacksnake. Tah-won-ne-ahs."
3. Betts Jr., *Hatchet and the Plow.*
4. Abler, 21–22.

In that period the Senecas controlled a vast region from the Finger Lakes across Western New York and part of Pennsylvania and Ohio. The economy was hunting, trapping, and trading. The tribe was part of the Iroquois Confederacy of Six Nations, which by the eighteenth century also included parts of present-day Michigan, Illinois, and Indiana.

His uncles were Seneca religious leader and prophet Handsome Lake and warrior-diplomat Cornplanter (both of whom were born in Canawaugus), and his great-uncle was Seneca orator Gai-ya-sot-ha, so his birth alone was auspicious. All were members of the Seneca Wolf Clan.[5] Blacksnake sat at the council fires and was present at the signing of the Treaty of Big Tree (1797); he opposed a treaty with the Ogden Land Company in which several reservations were sold to investors, and he provided testimony in the New York State Court of Appeals which ruled that the land known as the Oil Spring Reservation (near the present-day town of Cuba) had not been given up by the Seneca in the Treaty of Big Tree and must be returned to them, although the final ruling came two years after his death.[6]

Blacksnake spoke little or no English. When he was in his late eighties, a Dr. Lyman C. Draper contracted another Seneca, Benjamin Williams, to take dictation from Blacksnake and transcribe his memoirs into English. Unfortunately, Williams was himself in poor command of the language, and thus the book is difficult to read, though fascinating. A good version is one from the University of Nebraska Press, edited by Thomas S. Abler, titled *Chainbreaker: The Revolutionary War Memoirs of Governor Blacksnake*, which covers a broad span of his life as well as the activities and councils of the Seneca tribe. Abler divides sections of Blacksnake's accounts between his own notes and commentary, which make it easier to read. Were it not so difficult, it might have become a more widely read book.

5. Rochester Museum of Science Center Lewis Henry Morgan Website, "Blacksnake. Tah-won-ne-ahs."

6. Rochester Museum of Science Center Lewis Henry Morgan Website, "Blacksnake. Tah-won-ne-ahs."

31.1: The grave of Governor Blacksnake in Coldspring, on the Allegany Reservation.

In the Revolutionary War he fought for the British with Mohawk warrior Joseph Brant,[7] but in the War of 1812 he fought for the United States, although the Six Nations of Iroquois were divided in that conflict.[8] Again, this contradicts information on his gravestone, but epitaphs can be confusing. He admitted to being bloodthirsty in war: "I have Killed how many I could not tell, for I pay no attention, or to Kept it, account of it, it was a great many. . . ."[9]

Finding the Grave

Governor Blacksnake is buried in Hillside Haven Cemetery on Bunker Hill Road on the Allegany Reservation of the Seneca Nation. The best approach

7. Abler, 58–63.
8. Abler, 219.
9. Abler, 131.

is from the Route 86 Southern Tier Expressway (formerly Route 17) which passes through the Reservation west of Olean, east of Jamestown.

Get off Route 86 at Exit 17 for Route 394, Steamburg. From the exit, turn north, travel less than a quarter mile to the first intersection, and turn right on Lebanon Road. Travel that road for about a mile to the end, passing the Seneca Training Center on the right side. After you cross a small bridge, turn left. There was no road sign there when I visited, but it is Bunker Hill Road. A sign sometimes partially obscured by brush will inform you that you are entering the Reservation. Hillside Haven Cemetery will be a half mile or so on the right side. Keying into your GPS Bunker Hill Rd., Coldspring, NY, should get you close.

The cemetery has one entrance; the flag of the Seneca Nation flies at the gate. Once inside, make an immediate right turn, drive up the hill, and stop by a small wooden footbridge that spans a shallow ditch. After walking across the bridge, look to your right. Governor Blacksnake is a couple hundred feet away in a cluster of stones, some of which are for others also named Blacksnake. His is the large, brown, unhewed stone, with a brass plate that reads:

The last resting place of

Tenh-Wen-Nyos

(Awl Breaker)

Governor Blacksnake

Born 1737–Died 1859

One of the greatest war chiefs of Seneca Nation

Warmly espoused American Cause in Struggle of 1776

Devoted his later years to work among his people

Absolutely honest and truthful and enjoying

entire confidence of Indian and Pale Face

Erected by

Seneca Nation of Indians

and State of New York

1930

The inscription of course contradicts Blacksnake's own account that he fought with the British in the Revolution.

When you enter Hillside Haven, you may wonder that such a broad expanse of well-kept lawn has so few gravestones spaced so far apart. But as you walk about, you will realize that it is a densely populated cemetery, the vast majority of interments marked with flat, uniformly rectangular markers, reading "Unknown" with a number, for Seneca people whose remains were exhumed by the state in 1964 to make way for the Kinzua Dam reservoir. Many interments went to a cemetery near Bradford, Pennsylvania. The contents of twenty-two cemeteries came here, and include Blacksnake and his heirs. A list of the names of the interred is on the cemetery's website, but in many cases the names could not be matched to individuals; thus the inscriptions "Unknown 267," etc.

A visit to Hillside Haven is a sobering experience.

Sources

Abler, Thomas S. *Chainbreaker: The Revolutionary War Memoirs of Governor Blacksnake as told to Benjamin Williams.* Lincoln and London: Univ. of Nebraska Press, 1989.

Betts Jr., William W. *The Hatchet and the Plow: The Life and Times of Chief Cornplanter.* Bloomington, IL: iUniverse, Inc., 2010.

"Blacksnake. Tah-won-ne-ahs. Wolf Clan. (1700–1798)." Rochester Museum of Science Center Lewis Henry Morgan Website. Accessed April 18, 2023. https://rmsc.org/exhibits/online/lhm/blacksnake.htm.

32 Fredonia

Grace S. Richmond, Olive Risley Seward

Fredonia's primary claim to fame nowadays is the State University of New York at Fredonia, formerly Fredonia Normal School, and before that the Fredonia Academy. The Chautauqua County village has in its history more than its per capita share of notable people. Forest Hill Cemetery on Lambert Street has two congressmen, Francis Smith Edwards and Warren Brewster Hooker, and Irish-born Capt. William Oliver Stevens who led a regiment in the Civil War and died of a bullet wound in 1863 at Chancellorsville. And then, there are the literary folks.

It is worth mentioning that Charles L. Webster (1851–91) and his daughter Jean Webster (1876–1916) were both Fredonians. He is buried in Forest Hill Cemetery; the whereabouts of Jean's remains are unrecorded. They were both literary people. She was a popular novelist, the grandniece of Mark Twain, and a close friend of Rochester poet Adelaide Crapsey;[1] in fact, it was she who saw to it that a few of Crapsey's poems were accepted by *Colliers* before tuberculosis claimed her life. According to scholar Karen Alkalay-Gut, "The irrepressible Jean did much to raise Adelaide's spirits. . . . They rode horses and bicycles together, co-wrote plays and operettas, travelled back and forth from Poughkeepsie [Vassar] to Rochester and Fredonia, and planned wonderful, fun-filled, and productive lives."[2]

---

1. See West, chapter 36, Rochester.
2. Alkalay-Gut, *Alone in the Dawn*, 83.

32.1: Jean Webster (left) and Adelaide Crapsey (right) at Vassar. Jean Webster Papers, Archives and Special Collections, Vassar College Library, Collection: Benedict / Folder 35.11.

Charles Webster, along with Twain himself, founded the Charles L. Webster Publishing Company in New York City, which published *Huckleberry Finn* and the *Personal Memoirs of Ulysses S. Grant*; both of which were, of course, very successful. The firm was flush with cash, and Twain wrote Grant's widow a check for $200,000,[3] more than two million in today's dollars. But later publishing projects sold poorly, including Pope Leo's autobiography and Elizabeth Custer's chronicles of her husband George the Indian-fighting general[4]. The business partners had a falling-out when the company hit the financial skids, the result of poor sales, but Charles Webster's health also relapsed. In 1888 he went home to Fredonia

3. "Business of Being Mark Twain."
4. "Business of Being Mark Twain."

where he died three years later, just shy of his fortieth birthday,[5] apparently from an overdose of pain medication for trigeminal neuralgia.[6]

Jean Webster's novels for girls were quite popular. Among them are *Daddy-Long-Legs*; *When Patty Went to College*; *Much Ado about Peter*; and *Dear Enemy*. Her stories reflected her social concerns, such as temperance, prison reform, and women's suffrage. She married lawyer Glenn McKinney in 1915. On their honeymoon at a camp in Canada, they were visited by former president Theodore Roosevelt who was hunting in the area and said that he'd always wanted to meet Jean Webster. She died in childbirth in New York City in 1916, only two years after Adelaide. And, like her father, she was only thirty-nine.

But two writers of note are buried in Fredonia's Forest Hill Cemetery, Grace S. Richmond and Olive Risley Seward.

Grace S. Richmond (1866–1959): The Art of Romance

Grace Richmond was born Grace Louise Smith in Pawtucket, Rhode Island, the daughter of Charles Edward Smith, a noted Baptist clergyman who later transferred to a church in Syracuse, and then to Fredonia Baptist Church. There, Grace was married to Dr. Nelson Guernsey Richmond.[7]

In her twenties she began publishing romance stories in the slick magazines of the day, such as *Ladies Home Journal*. Beginning with *The Indifference of Juliet* in 1902, she wrote twenty-seven romance novels, her last in 1934. One of her books, *Red Pepper Burns* (1910), was particularly successful and became a series, including *Mrs. Red Pepper*; *Red Pepper's Patients*; and *Red of the Redfields*. Many of her books feature the adventures of a physician, Dr. Pepper Burns. Her books are a cozy read, and not as formulaic as one might expect for a romance these days. By 1931, her publisher Doubleday, Doran and Co. reported her books sales had topped two and a half million.[8]

---

5. *Rediscovering Our Past* (blog), "Charles H. Webster."
6. Zullo, "Mark Twain's Publishing Firm."
7. Merriman, "Biography of Grace S. Richmond."
8. "Grace S. Richmond, Wrote 25 Novels," 21.

32.2: The Richmond family plot in Fredonia. Grace S. is second from foreground.

Finding the Grave

The quickest route to Fredonia from most places in the state is Thruway Exit 59 for Dunkirk and Fredonia. From the exit, turn left onto Route 60 and drive about six-tenths of a mile to a traffic roundabout where you will turn right on to Route 20, East Main Street. Then drive about a mile and a half into the village. From Main Street in the village, turn right on White Street north to Lambert Avenue, which will take you directly to the gate of

Forest Hill Cemetery. Or key into your GPS 55 Lambert Ave., Fredonia, NY, 14063.

Right after the main gate the paths split. Take the main path (not the two-track that curves left) for a short distance and make the first left. Follow that path until it comes to a T. At that point you will see, straight before you, a mausoleum for Newton-Campbell on a low ridge, and to its left a large tree with a sign for "J" plot. The Richmond family plot is a series of small footstones to the left of the mausoleum, and from the T you can walk straight up the ridge to it. Grace Richmond's stone is the second in the line from the mausoleum.

Olive Risley Seward (1844–1908): Companion, Philanthropist, Author

William H. Seward was an Upstate lawyer and politician of national prominence, President Lincoln's secretary of state, and survivor of a brutal attempt on his life the same night as Lincoln's assassination, which may have led to his wife's death from a heart attack three months later. He remained in President Andrew Johnson's cabinet, defending the hapless new president against Republican stalwarts who wanted his head for his reconciliation efforts with the South. He engineered the purchase of Alaska from Russia. He established informal relations between the United States and China and Japan. Seward was a monumental statesman, but in the years following the Civil War his health was in decline. Before he left the cabinet, he nearly died of cholera. And he returned home to Auburn, New York, in a weakened state.

Olive Risley was the daughter of a treasury department official, and from a prominent Fredonia clan; her grandfather Elijah Risley Sr. was a Revolutionary War veteran and an early settler in Fredonia when it was still called Canadaway. She was forty-three years younger than Seward, and beginning in 1868 she became his companion and helper, ever near at hand. When they traveled together tongues began to wag, as tongues often will, and even their families were worried that they might marry. But Seward was also a clever lawyer, and when he decided to do the honorable thing, he did what few would have predicted: he adopted her as his daughter. His own daughter Fanny had died recently from tuberculosis.[9]

Together, and along with Olive's sister Harriet, they traveled the world, and once they were back in Auburn, Seward and Olive sat down to write *William H. Seward's Travels Around the World*, working from her notes. He is listed as author, she as editor. But he died in 1872 before the book was completed, and Olive was left to finish the project, which, by the way, became a bestseller. In 1889 she published her own book of travels for young readers, the very absorbing *Around the World Stories*. Seward's house, which is now a museum, was left to his three sons. Olive inherited one-fourth of his estate of around $200,000.[10]

Olive moved to Washington, DC, after Seward's death, where she became active in philanthropic organizations and was one of the founders of the Daughters of the American Revolution, although she often summered in Fredonia. She spent several years in Rome where she converted to Catholicism.[11] There is now a metal sculpture of her by John Cavanaugh in Seward Square Park at 6th Street and North Carolina Avenue in Washington.

Finding the Grave

Take the Thruway to Exit 59 for Dunkirk and Fredonia. From the exit, turn left onto Route 60 and drive about six-tenths of a mile to a traffic roundabout where you will turn right on to Route 20, East Main Street. Then drive about a mile and a half into the village. From Main Street in the village, turn right on White Street north to Lambert Avenue, which will take you directly to the gate of Forest Hill Cemetery. Or key into your GPS 55 Lambert Ave., Fredonia, NY, 14063.

After the main gate, the path will split: the main path goes straight, and the lesser-traveled two-track secondary path branches off to the left.

9. Pohl, "Olive Risley Seward."
10. "Mr. Seward's Estate," 5.
11. "Olive Risley Seward Dead," 11.

32.3: The grave of Olive Risley Seward in Fredonia.

Take that left path for a short distance to where it curves again to the left. On the right you will see some stones under arborvitae trees; the more ornate stone, though not an imposing one, is Olive Risley Seward's grave, in the Risley family plot.

Sources

Charles and Jean Webster

Alkalay-Gut, Karen. *Alone in the Dawn: The Life of Adelaide Crapsey*. Athens: Univ. of Georgia Press, 1988.

"The Business of Being Mark Twain: Charles H. Webster." Cornell University Library. Accessed April 18, 2023. https://rmc.library.cornell.edu/twain/exhibition /webster/index.html.

"Charles H. Webster: Publisher of Grant's Memoirs." *Rediscovering Our Past* (blog). April 28, 2017. https://rediscoveringourpast.blogspot.com/2017/04/charles-l-webster-publisher-of-grants.html.

Zullo, Vonnie. "Mark Twain's Publishing Firm: Chapter 13." *Shapell Manuscript Foundation* (blog), November 18, 2001. www.shapell.org/blog/mark-twains-publishing-firm-chapter-13/.

Grace S. Richmond

"Grace S. Richmond, Wrote 25 Novels." *New York Times*, November 28, 1959, 21.

Merriman, C. D. "Biography of Grace S. Richmond." The Literature Network. Accessed April 18, 2023. http://www.online-literature.com/grace-richmond/.

Olive Risley Seward

"Mr. Seward's Estate." *New York Times*, October 17, 1872.

"Olive Risley Seward Dead." *New York Times*, November 28, 1908.

Pohl, Robert. "Lost Capitol Hill: Olive Risley Seward." The Hill Is Home, September 16, 2013. https://thehillishome.com/2013/09/lost-capitol-hill-olive-risley-seward/.

33 Geneseo

Carl Carmer

Sometime in the early 1980s when I was exploring my idea of becoming an antiquarian bookseller, someone told me that I should go to Geneseo and talk with a bibliophile there named Dante Thomas, and gave me his phone number. I called him (I was living near Batavia then), and he invited me to come down. He told me that he lived on the Wadsworth estate in the gardener's cottage with his wife Connie. It was autumn, a late afternoon, and as I circled around the estate I realized that this was a place so imposing that I would not have dared to venture there uninvited. But it was only later that I realized how much history converged here, James Wadsworth (1768–1844) and his brother William (1765–1833) having been land speculators in the settling of the Genesee Valley.

Dante, who taught at SUNY Geneseo, was standing inside his screen door surrounded by howling dogs, and he waved as I pulled up to the cottage. He was a short, intense man in his sixties who smoked Pall Malls unfiltered. Save for the kitchen and bath, every wall of the cottage was shelved and heavy with books. After a tour, we spent the evening talking about books and collecting, he jumping up occasionally to show me a volume by Kenneth Patchen, John Cowper Powys (I think Dante was the leading scholar on him), or Christopher Morley. Old bookstores, he made a point of telling me, were where revolutions got started, people sitting in the back room talking.

Before I left, he sold me the three-volume Grove Press edition of *The Rosy Crucifixion* by Henry Miller that he had bought years before from Anais Nin. I took them home and shook them out looking for any scrap of

271

paper that might identify them as having been in Nin's hands, but nothing. My guess is that they were free copies she had received from Grove, and she probably sold them to Dante because she already had a set from her friend Miller.

Geneseo is a college town with all the amenities. Its Main Street has a good independent bookstore called Sundance; good bars and restaurants, including the fabled Big Tree Inn; the Crickets Coffee Company; and the Buzzo record shop. And it had Dante Thomas. Although he is gone now (he lived to ninety-one), other bibliophiles are there, I am sure. Unlike some college towns, the university is right on its doorstep—take a short stroll down Bank Street and you're on the campus.

In the center of Main Street is a water fountain with the figure of a bear at its center, the gift of the Wadsworth family in 1888, in memory of Emmeline Wadsworth, one of the family's matriarchs. In my most recent visit, however, the fountain had been hit by mis-adventuring motorists three times in the previous months, the bear was out for repair, and the ceramic base had a sizable chunk missing, as if a real bear had taken a bite.

Buried nearby is Carl Carmer whose book *Genesee Fever* gave a vivid storyline to the settlement of the Genesee Valley.

Carl Carmer (1893–1976): Man from the Genesee

To talk about Carl Carmer, one has to address Upstate New York history, especially the settling of the Genesee region, and its folklore. Geneseo was the location of the Treaty of Big Tree where in late summer 1797 Thomas Morris negotiated the purchase from the Seneca of most of the land in New York State west of the Genesee River. Chief Red Jacket negotiated for the native tribe, aided by Mary Jemison, the famed White Woman of the Genesee. But the usual tricks were plied against the three thousand Seneca in attendance—booze and trinkets, and in the end Red Jacket signed away more than three million acres for $100,000 to be paid in installments of $6,000 per annum.

Carmer describes William Wadsworth, one of the biggest landowners (who hosted the delegations to the treaty), in imposing detail in his novel

Genesee Fever: "He wore a tricorn hat, white stock, and a long blue military coat that hung below the tops of his shiny black boots. . . . His face was thin and bold, and his beaklike nose was so prominent that it gave him resemblance to an enormous bird of prey."[1] Carmer's novel is set in the 1790s, amid land speculation, early farming, and the enmity between white and native, between those common tillers of the fields who carried the democratic spirit of the Revolution and the land barons who arrived bringing a new aristocracy and herds of enslaved people.

He is best known for his book *Stars Fell on Alabama*, his story of his time as a young man living in the South. Other books include collections of stories that come from the ground and blood of New Yorkers: *Listen for a Lonesome Drum*; *Dark Trees to the Wind*; *The Tavern Lamps Are Burning*, an anthology of literary New Yorkers from the seventeenth century to the twentieth; and *The Hudson*, a collection of tales and anecdotes from New York's most storied river. He belongs with the best chroniclers and storytellers of the state—Henry Clune, Arch Merrill, Edmund Wilson, Walter Edmonds, and Alf Evers. But his home region is really the Genesee. Like most of the best writers, his gravestone is modest, even humble. It carries the inscription, "Man of the Genesee."

Finding the Grave

If you are approaching Geneseo from the Thruway, or from the Southern Tier, take Interstate 390 to Exit 8, and turn west on Lakeville Road through the rolling hills and farmland. At about the four-mile point, where you will be entering the village, you will see the Temple Hill Cemetery on your right. Turn right onto the wooded Temple Hill Street, and after about a tenth of a mile make a right onto a gravel drive that looks for all the world like the driveway for a private home, but the looming white house is actually the association house for the cemetery. Or give the following address to your GPS: 111 Temple Hill St., Geneseo, NY, 14454. At the house's

1. Carmer, *Genesee Fever*, 104–5.

33.1: The grave of Carl Carmer, "Man of the Genesee," and his wife in Geneseo.

carriage port you will find, on one of its pillars, a cabinet with free maps of the grounds. Take one: you'll find it useful. You are looking for section E.

Proceed on the gravel drive, and in a short distance bear left onto a lesser path. Look for a stone under a grand red maple tree on your left marked "Barber," and stop. Walk under the tree to the other side. Four identically shaped flat stones mark the family plot for Carl Carmer, his wife Elizabeth Black, and family.

Sources

Carmer, Carl. *Genesee Fever.* New York: Farrar and Rinehart, Inc., 1941.

34 Kendall

Anthony Piccione

White settlers did not arrive in Kendall until 1812, and few stayed, probably due to forbidding swamps and dense forests. But in a decade, a saw-
mill and a schoolhouse were established. Slowly settlers moved in from
New England, Norway, and Wales. Accounts of early settlements abound
in descriptions of privations, yet the town was officially formed by 1837.
Today, with a population of just over 2,500, it still holds a rural ambience.
A poet moved here in the 1980s specifically for the quiet.

Anthony Piccione (1939–2001): The Poet Falling Outward

Long before I met Tony Piccione, I knew that he had a reputation among
his former students at SUNY Brockport as a kind of shaman, although I
do not think that he would have liked that term. What they were saying in
effect was that he not only taught the art and craft of poetry and prosody,
not only introduced students to poets that astonished them, whose books
(along with Tony's) would stay on their shelves for the rest of their lives, but
he taught that there was something elemental about being awake that was
essential to one's being and to one's poetry. His kind of poetry is a psychic
dialogue with the world, from a poet who struggled with what it means
to be humanly alert to the sensations of experience, having your hands in
the garden dirt, and always in search of truth. About this, and about many
things, he was one of the most uncompromising men I have ever known.
He said what he meant, and you didn't yank his chain.

He loved the Chinese mountain poets; he loved the contemplatives and the deep imagists. He didn't care for crowds and did few public readings, never went out on the reading circuit, didn't like conferences; and so his books did not sell as well as they probably would have if he'd played that game. Yet, people who read his books tend to buy extra copies and give them to friends.

I went to work at BOA Editions in 1985, a few years after the publication of Tony's first book, *Anchor Dragging* (selected for the press's New Poets of America Series by Archibald MacLeish). We brought out his second book, *Seeing It Was So*, and his third, *For the Kingdom*. His fourth, *The Guests at the Gate* (2002), appeared shortly after his death in November 2001. His best poems astonish at first, and in repeated readings tend to reboot your consciousness of what you thought you knew. One of my favorites I was happy to find inscribed on his gravestone:

Looking at the Stars and Falling Outward
We disappear into everything.
Atoms shudder and stir,
rock begins to speak its silence.
All is said, even our names.[1]

Robert Bly, in his Introduction to *The Guests at the Gate*, wrote that Tony was "as passionate for truth as a baby bear for honey." And he finished his piece with, "We have to say goodbye now to this sweet man, worthy of his family, his struggles and his language! Farewell!"[2]

Finding the Grave

From the Thruway, take the Leroy Exit 47, and drive north on Route 98, through Albion, to Route 104, then turn east and drive 5.9 miles, turning left on West Kendall Road. Or if you are coming from the northeast or

---

1. Piccione, *Seeing It Was So: Poems*, 66.
2. Bly, "Introduction," 11.

34.1: The grave of Anthony Piccione in Kendall.

northwest, 104 is a good direct route to West Kendall Road. In any case, turn north on West Kendall. You will find Beechwood Cemetery about seven miles ahead on the right. Or set your GPS for 1523 West Kendall Rd., Kendall, NY, 14476.

Woodchuck Lane, a gravel road, intersects there and runs along the north border of the cemetery. Turn there and drive straight back, and you will see that there is a second section of the cemetery that is hidden from the main road. Pass the stone chapel on the right side and turn right into the last entrance. Tony's stone is under the third tree, which is a massive maple. Half of his ashes are buried there. The other half is dispersed elsewhere. His plot is crowded with plantings, a stone Buddha, and mementos from his family, friends, and students.

Sources

Bly, Robert. "Introduction: Tony Piccione and the Woodstove." In *The Guests at the Gate: Poems*, by Anthony Piccione. Rochester, NY: BOA Editions, Ltd., 2002.

Piccione, Anthony. *Seeing It Was So: Poems*. Brockport, NY: BOA Editions, Ltd., 1986.

35 Mayville

Albion Tourgée

Just down the road from the revered Chautauqua Institution is the village of Mayville, one of the oldest and most charming communities in the area. Mayville has been the seat of Chautauqua County since the county was formed in 1810, but the village is actually much older. Chautauqua Lake's outlet is the *Chadakoin River* which flows into Cassadaga Creek, eventually into the Allegheny River, and thus it gave Seneca natives and early European traders access by canoe to the Ohio River. It was also a strategic encampment for French military, who were the first Europeans to arrive in significant numbers.

A log-cabin office of the Holland Land Company was established here in the early nineteenth century and functioned for twenty-six years. However, when hardy settlers did not like something, they could get ugly—and new investors gave them much to get ugly about, demanding cash payments on property instead of chickens and produce, and threatening to sell the land out from under the farmers. In 1836, a mob formed and broke into the office, destroyed furniture, broke down the door of the vault, and burned records. The stone vault still stands near the intersections of Erie and Chautauqua streets. Near that spot, in 1854, Susan B. Anthony spoke to a crowd trying to generate enthusiasm for women's suffrage. Here in 1919, Ellen Yates Miller was the first woman elected county clerk in New York State. When she took office, seven men resigned rather than work for a woman.

At the south end of the village, a hiking and bicycling trail in the path of the former Pennsylvania Railroad runs merrily into the hills. A sign along that trail points to a field below where, in the spring of 1835, the last public hanging in New York State took place. Thousands came to watch the execution of a Fredonia man named Joseph Damon who in a drunken rage had beaten his wife to death with an iron fireplace poker.

But Mayville's most prominent resident was a soldier, crusader for African American rights, journalist, diplomat, and novelist named Albion Winegar Tourgée.

Albion Winegar Tourgée (1838–1905):
Soldier Turned Civil Rights Activist Turned Novelist

Born into an Ohio farm family, Albion Tourgée enrolled at the University of Rochester to study law. His education was interrupted by the Civil War when he enlisted in the Union Army. Badly injured at the first battle of Bull Run, he was paralyzed and discharged. But his paralysis proved temporary, and he reenlisted in the 105th Ohio Infantry.[1] He was captured and spent months in a Confederate prison until freed in a prisoner exchange. The irrepressible Tourgée was back in the line of fire but, plagued by back pain from his original injury, he was forced to resign his commission, and he finished out the war as a journalist while continuing his studies, graduating with an MA from the University of Rochester.

Newly married at the close of the war, he traveled to Greensboro, North Carolina, with his wife Emma, where he threw himself into Reconstruction politics as a superior court judge and delegate to the state's 1868 Constitutional Convention where he argued for civil rights and black suffrage[2] in spite of legal opposition and threats from the Ku Klux Klan.[3] According to biographers Mark Elliott and John David Smith, Tourgée "founded one of the nation's first civil rights organizations, framed the nation's first successful antilynching law, and brought the first challenge to segregation before the United States Supreme Court in the 1896 case of *Plessy v. Fergusson.*"[4] In 1878, already one of the nation's most notori-

1. Elliott and Smith, "Introduction," 3.
2. Kickler, "Albion Tourgee (1838–1905)."
3. Elliott and Smith, 3, 6–7.
4. Elliott and Smith, 2.

ous advocates for equal rights, he ran for Congress, but lost. His political career was drawing to a close, but he continued to write a syndicated newspaper column, "A Bystander's Notes."

Now parents of a daughter, the Tourgées opted for a gentler milieu, and in 1881 they bought a home on Erie Street in Mayville, where he founded and ran a literary journal, the *Continent*, although it ultimately failed as literary magazines so often do. But he had another card up his sleeve. While still in the South, he had already become a bestselling novelist, and he continued his literary output in Mayville.

After a first novel published under a pseudonym, he found his first real literary success with A *Fool's Errand, by One of the Fools* (1879), a novel about Reconstruction. Its sales of over 200,000 made it a bestseller, followed by a sequel, *Bricks without Straw* (1880) which sold equally well. Although the failure of the *Continent* nearly broke him financially, he had many more books in him. His seventeen books of fiction include *Button's Inn* (1887), *Murvale Eastman: Christian Socialist* (1890), and *An Outing with the Queen of Hearts* (1894). His seven books of nonfiction include *An Appeal to Caesar* (1884) and *The Story of a Thousand, Being a History of the 105th Volunteer Infantry, 1862–65* (1896).

In 1897, he was appointed a consul to France at Bordeaux,[5] where he died in 1905.

Emma Tourgée left a sizable portion of the Tourgée estate to Mayville's public library—the Tuesday Club Library as it was then called since it evolved out of a small library that a women's book club kept. It has been located since 1975 on Erie Street, with a meeting room named for Albion Tourgée.[6]

Finding the Grave

To get to Mayville, take the Thruway to Exit 60. From the exit, take Route 394 southeast, which becomes Erie Street, Mayville. From Mayville's main intersection, Erie Street and Chautauqua Street, travel east on Chautauqua Street for about a quarter mile. The Mayville Cemetery entrance is on

5. Elliott and Smith , 15.
6. Taylor, *Mayville: View through Time*, 32.

35.1: The grave of Albion Winegar Tourgée and family in Mayville.

the left. Inside the entrance, make the first right. The path signs can be confusing, but stay with it as it curves right until it ends at an intersection. Turn right, and Tourgée's spire is a few yards ahead on the left where the cemetery borders on a field. His ashes are buried there with his wife Emma and daughter Aimee.

Sources

Elliott, Mark, and John David Smith. "Introduction." In *Undaunted Radical: The Selected Writings and Speeches of Albion W. Tourgée*. Baton Rouge: Louisiana State Univ. Press, 2010.

Kickler, Dr. Troy L. "Albion Tourgee (1838–1905)." North Carolina History Project. Accessed April 18, 2023. https://northcarolinahistory.org/encyclopedia/albion-tourgee-1838-1905/.

Taylor, Devon A. *Mayville: A View through Time*. Mayville, NY: The Mayville Library Association, 1993.

36   Rochester

Susan B. Anthony, Adelaide Crapsey,
Algernon Crapsey, Frederick Douglass,
Lewis Henry Morgan, Lillian Wald,
Edward R. Crone, Louise Brooks,
Henry Clune, Arch Merrill

A few years ago Rochester dropped off the list of the hundred largest US cities. This told Rochesterians what they already knew—that people weren't paying as much attention to the city as they had before. There still is a Kodak and a Xerox, though scaled down from their earlier grandeur. The fact is, however, that world-changing things happened here: flexible film made its debut, which put cameras in the hands of ordinary people (the digital camera too was invented at Kodak, but unfortunately they decided not to do anything with it), and Chester Carlson brought his invention of xerography here to manufacture (no more ugly mimeographing). One of the world's greatest suffragists, Susan B. Anthony, lived here, where she famously got arrested for casting a vote. Frederick Douglass, the most famous abolitionist and social reformer of the nineteenth century, made Rochester his home base. The University of Rochester, Rochester Institute of Technology, and the National Technical Institute for the Deaf are still world class, as is the Eastman School of Music and the Rochester Philharmonic.

In this chapter we will visit Mount Hope Cemetery, Holy Sepulcher Cemetery, White Haven Memorial Park, and Brighton Cemetery.

Mount Hope Cemetery

If you think you know Rochester, take a walk in Mount Hope Cemetery. Leave your car on one of its crisscrossing paths and follow your nose to the Civil War graves, the Spanish American War and World War I plots, the Jewish poor section with no individual markers, the Fire Department dead, the plot for the utopian Meggido settlement, and the Rochester Orphan Asylum graves. Walk in the ravines where forgotten graves and mausoleums of once-prominent citizens are choked in tall grass.

Founded in 1838, its 196 semi-forested acres rank among the loveliest urban walks in New York State, with more miles of paths than you can likely walk in a single day. On a weekday, there may be so few visitors that it will seem like you have the place to yourself.

In addition to the literary people in this chapter, here lie Hiram Sibley, founder of Western Union; three of Buffalo Bill's children; William Warfield, concert bass-baritone and actor; Frank Gannett, founder of the Gannett newspaper chain; Myron Holley, one of the principal builders of the Erie Canal; the pioneering Nathanial Rochester for whom the city was named; and John Jacob Bausch and Henry Lomb, founders of Bausch and Lomb, one of the world's great optical companies. And here lies Alexander Milliner (1760–1865) who was George Washington's favorite drummer boy and, at 105, was one of the last surviving Revolutionary War soldiers, and who lived to see his country turn against itself in Civil War. The cemetery is divided into numbered or lettered ranges. As of this writing, the street-name signposts in the cemetery are weatherworn and often illegible, but the directions herein will get you to the sites.

To reach Mount Hope Cemetery, if you live outside of Rochester, take the Thruway Exit 45 to Route 490 from the east, Exit 47 to Route 490 from the west, or Exit 46 to Route 590 from the south. All three routes lead to Route 390 and to Route 15, West Henrietta Road, which, two miles north, becomes Mount Hope Avenue. Just north of the intersection with Elmwood Avenue, you will see the main gate on the left. Or set your GPS to 1133 Mount Hope Ave., Rochester, NY, 14020.

Holy Sepulcher Cemetery

From the Thruway, take Exit 46 to Route 390 North about four miles to Interstate 590 North; stay on Route 590 to Route 104 West. Take Route 104 about 3.5 miles to Lake Avenue at the edge of old Kodak Park. Turn north on Lake Avenue and drive about 1.3 miles. Or set your GPS for 2461 Lake Ave., Rochester, NY, 14612. You will be just a few miles south of Lake Ontario. The main gate of Holy Sepulcher Cemetery, at a traffic light, will be on the left. The cemetery is an immense expanse of 332 acres, about 300,000 interments, or about 80,000 more people than now live and breathe in the city of Rochester.

White Haven Memorial Park

White Haven Memorial Park is in Pittsford, a suburb of Rochester. From the Thruway, take Exit 45 for Route 490 East; drive about five and a half miles and get off at Exit 26. Merge onto Route 31 toward Pittsford. Drive a half mile and turn right on Marsh Road. You'll see the grounds of White Haven in just over a mile. Or set your GPS for 210 Marsh Rd., Pittsford, NY, 14534.

Brighton Cemetery

Brighton Cemetery, dedicated in 1821, is one of the most curious and unusual places in Rochester. Located at the end of a short, shady, cul-de-sac called Hoyt Place, which you enter from the northeast side of the intersection of Winton Road and the 490 expressway, it seems a secluded world away from the rush of traffic and the Wegman's supermarket hardly more than a stone's throw away. It is called Brighton Cemetery because the lot was originally part of the town of Brighton before the expansion of Rochester's 21st Ward in 1905. It is also sometimes called the Dutch Cemetery because a number of the earliest graves are of people born in Holland. Certainly, many of the names on the stones are Dutch. It served as the cemetery for an adjacent Congregationalist Church. When the church burned down in 1867, the records of the earliest graves were lost, and consequently the residents of some of the unmarked graves are unknown.

The Erie Canal, in its original path, used to flow along its north side, which is now the expressway, and it is loud, but not quite enough to spoil the ambience of the place.

Drive to the north side of the Winton Road Bridge over Route 490, and turn east onto Hoyt Place. Or if you are coming from the west, take the Winton Road exit from the expressway (there is no exit coming from the east). At the light, drive straight across Winton Road to Hoyt Place. There are only a few houses on Hoyt Place, it is so short. You'll find a turnaround at the gate where you can park.

Susan B. Anthony (1820–1906):
The Name Synonymous with Women's Suffrage

Susan B. Anthony's name is stamped on reform in America; she fought the issues of slavery, temperance, and especially the rights of women in a rock-hard patriarchal society. In the matter of the women's vote she pointed out that it was protected under the constitution, and on Election Day in 1872 she cast a vote in Rochester and shortly after was arrested. She went to trial at the courthouse in Canandaigua and was convicted, but refused to pay the $100 fine. She considered it a cruel turn of fate when she realized that she would not live to see women granted the right to vote: the Nineteenth Amendment to the US Constitution was passed in 1920, fourteen years after her death.

She founded the Women's Suffrage Association—along with her friend Elizabeth Cady Stanton—in 1869. They also published a journal, *Revolution*. In an address near the end of her life she coined the now-famous phrase, "Failure is impossible."

On Election Day 2016, when most people anticipated that Hillary Clinton would win the presidency, Mount Hope Cemetery saw more visitors than ever before in its history, with women pasting their "I Voted Today!" stickers on Anthony's gravestone. TV cameras arrived; there were officers to direct traffic. But the reason the glass ceiling is so named is because sometimes you can't see it until you hit your head on it and receive the grim reminder that it is still there.

However, this book is about authors and authorship, and so we will turn now to *The History of Woman Suffrage*, which Anthony wrote along with her friends in the cause Elizabeth Cady Stanton, Matilda Joselyn Gage,[1] and Ida Husted Harper, four volumes of which were published during Anthony's life and the final two after her death, with the efforts of Harper taking the history to 1920.

For many historians, the book, despite its heft, was not the definitive history of the movement in the United States since enmity had arisen in the movement almost from the beginning, and it leaves out the efforts of another faction led by Lucy Stone and Julia Ward Howe. Few today have actually read it in its entirety. But these women produced it, and it is in libraries and available even if it is not quite the variorum that they meant it to be.

Anthony fell ill on her way home from the Women's Suffrage Convention in Baltimore, having to skip a banquet in her honor in New York City on February 18, 1906. On March 5 she came down with double pneumonia, which she nearly recovered from, but suffered a relapse on March 10. She died at her home on March 13, after being unconscious for twenty-four hours. She was not a wealthy woman, but what she had left she willed "to the cause." Reportedly she said to a friend, "To think I have had more than sixty years of hard struggle for a little liberty, and then to die without it seems so cruel."[2]

America continues to honor her. And in Rochester her name is displayed with Frederick Douglass on the main bridge spanning the Genesee River. Her home is now a national museum.

Finding the Grave

Enter Mount Hope Cemetery by the north gate on Mount Hope Avenue, easily noticeable with the stone gatehouse to its left. Directly facing you will be a triangular green space with the Florentine Fountain. Keep to the right and drive or walk uphill. At the top, turn right on Linden Avenue. Keep in mind that the road signs are often illegible. Drive to the bottom of the hill, and make your first left onto Maple Avenue. Pull over and stop.

1. See Central, chapter 12, Fayetteville.
2. Klos and Klos, "Susan B. Anthony."

36.1: The grave of Susan B. Anthony in Rochester.

On your left will be a gravel path and a brass plate on a post directing you to Anthony's grave. About seventy-five feet up that path you will find the Anthony family plot with a family monument and individual stones. Susan B. Anthony is in the front near the path, next to her sister Mary S.

Adelaide Crapsey (1878–1914):
Inventor of the Cinquain Stanza

It has been suggested that the famous heresy trial that the Episcopal Diocese of Western New York brought against the Rev. Algernon Crapsey, rector of St. Andrews Church in Rochester, hastened the death of his daughter Adelaide since she was reportedly distraught over her father being defrocked. In his trial, which was sensational news across the nation (what, *heresy*, in *this* day and age?), he was charged with preaching far afield of church doctrine, such as that the virgin birth of Jesus and his resurrection were fable, and that Christians ought to disregard those stories and simply follow His teaching. Certainly, the ridiculous medieval trial was hard on her. She was the only member of her family to attend it.

But I think that it is unlikely that the trial was responsible for Adelaide's decline. Algernon was convicted in 1906. Adelaide's tubercular meningitis appeared in 1908, and that was after accompanying her father to a peace conference in the Hague, followed by a walking tour of Wales. She died in 1914, after an extended time in a sanitarium in Saratoga Springs. In fact, her illness had progressed so slowly that she had begun to think it a misdiagnosis;[3] she went ahead and took a teaching post at Smith College, until the disease became undeniable. Tuberculosis was all too common in those days, and it was a virtual death sentence. But it was during her time in the sanitarium that some of her strongest verse was written.

Adelaide was a powerful poet, and inventor of the now well-known five-line cinquain stanza form of twenty-two syllables, influenced by the Japanese haiku and tanka forms, which according to her biographer Karen Alkalay-Gut is the only original American stanza form.[4] However, she did not live to see her poetry published, although her friend Jean Webster,[5] grandniece of Mark Twain, submitted poems for her when she did not have the strength herself, and one was accepted by a national magazine,

3. Alkalay-Gut, "Dying of Adelaide Crapsey," 230.
4. Alkalay-Gut, footnote, 225.
5. See West, chapter 32, Fredonia.

36.2: Adelaide Crapsey. Jean Webster Papers, Archives and Special Collections, Vassar College Library, Collection: Benedict / Folder 35.11.

Century Magazine, just before she died.[6] Rejections are disheartening to any struggling poet and Crapsey had her share, but she seems not to have let those disappointments discourage her.

But after her death, the mystic-architect-Theosophist Claude Bragdon, who lived in Rochester and was a friend of the Crapsey family, published her poems with his own company, Manas Press. Her posthumous book was titled simply *Verse* (1915). This was followed by A *Study in English Metrics* (1918), her book on prosody.[7]

Alkalay-Gut, who herself grew up in Rochester and now teaches in Tel Aviv, writes that when death was approaching, when the seriousness of her disease could no longer be denied, Adelaide wove her shroud in the form of a poem:[8]

Song
I make my shroud but no one knows,
So shimmering fine it is and fair,
With Stitches set in even rows.
I make my shroud but no one knows.

In door-way where the lilac-blows,
Humming a little wandering air,
I make my shroud and no one knows,
So shimmering fine it is and fair.[9]

To my eye, and to my body and soul, her strongest poems are her cinquains. In her poem "Amaze" she is already becoming estranged from her dying body. Her use of line-breaks for commas, or "half-commas," is a technique far ahead of her time. She was certainly one of the most original poets of the early twentieth century, when some of the Modernists were just learning to type.

---

6. Alkalay-Gut, *Alone in the Dawn*, 8.
7. For more on Bragdon, see Central, chapter 22, Pulaski.
8. Alkalay-Gut, "Dying of Adelaide Crapsey," 232.
9. Crapsey, *Verse*.

I know
Not these my hands
And yet I think there was
A woman like me once had hands
Like these.[10]

Finding the Grave

See "Finding the Grave" for Algernon Crapsey in this chapter.

Algernon Crapsey (1847–1927): The Last Heretic

Algernon Crapsey was more than an Episcopalian minister. After grad-uating from General Theological Seminary, he served as a deacon at St. Paul's Chapel of Trinity Parish, New York City, where he worked among the poor and denounced the conspicuous wealth of churches in poverty-stricken areas. In 1879, he came to Rochester to serve as the first rector of the new St. Andrew's Church, on the corner of Ashland Street and Averill Avenue,[11] where he remained for twenty-eight years. He was a friend and colleague of the renowned social gospel theologian Walter Rauschenbusch of Colgate Divinity School in Rochester.[12] He established a training school for kindergarten teachers called the School of Practical Knowledge and Recreation, and he was one of the founders of City Club, a forum for discussion of community matters.[13]

But it was also in Rochester that he got himself in trouble. As men-tioned in the paragraphs on his daughter Adelaide, he ran afoul of the Episcopal Diocese for his liberal interpretation of scripture and insistence that such doctrines as virgin birth and resurrection be reconsidered, and that the church should function as an agency for social reform. In 1906,

10. Crapsey, *Verse.*
11. Swanton, "Doctor Algernon Crapsey," 1–4.
12. Episcopal Church Domestic and Foreign Missionary Society, "Crapsey, Alger-non Sidney."
13. Swanton, 5.

36.3: The grave of Adelaide Crapsey.

he was brought to trial thirty miles away at St. James Church in Batavia, much as a criminal trial is often moved to another city today to prevent local opinion from influencing the proceedings. But the sensational trial drew such crowds that the proceedings were moved to the larger Batavia Court House. He was convicted and defrocked.[14]

But he went on lecturing and writing, his most significant book after his trial being *The Last of the Heretics* (1924), which is, of course, his version of events.

Finding the Graves

To find the graves of Algernon and Adelaide Crapsey, enter Mount Hope Cemetery by the main gate, then turn left on Fifth Avenue (yes, that is the real name of the road); go all the way to the south fence and turn right on

14. Swanton, 16–19.

36.4: The graves of Algernon Crapsey and his wife also named Adelaide.

South Avenue. The corner lawn is range 1. Continue on South Avenue; after you pass the next intersection, range 2 will be on your right. About 150 feet ahead you will see a prominent stone for Jennings McCord; a little before it and to the right is a small, plain, marble cross for the Crapsey family plot. There are three rows of modest individual footstones for the family. Algernon is in the first row next to his wife (also named Adelaide), and their daughter Adelaide the poet is in the third row with her siblings.

Frederick Douglass (1818–1895):
A Man Who Altered America's Conscience

Everyone in America should read *The Narrative of the Life of Frederick Douglass, American Slave*. Not that his is the only authentic narrative of an enslaved person in the antebellum South, but Douglass's, while it is horrifying in many places, is also particularly eloquent, as are his two other autobiographical works, *My Bondage and Freedom* and *Life and Times of Frederick Douglass*, which makes his story all the more powerful.

36.5: Frederick Douglass. traveler1116/DigitalVision Vectors via Getty Images.

Few people have had a greater effect on our national conscience. He was the most photographed American of the nineteenth century, and was certainly a prophet in his time.

He was born Frederick Augustus Washington Bailey about 1818 in Tuckahoe, Talbot County, Maryland.[15] Records of enslaved child births were rarely kept, and he was never sure of his exact age.[16] The special privileges granted him, as well as his extraordinary powers of observation,

15. Blight, "Frederick Douglass's Childhood of Extremes."
16. Douglass, *Narrative of Life of Frederick Douglass*, 31.

indicate that he was an especially bright young man.[17] His father was a white man, probably his master. Shortly after his birth he was separated from his mother and sent to be raised by his grandmother, a day's walk from his birthplace.[18] He would be moved several times more, and witness savage beatings, but a kindly wife of a slave owner named Auld taught him to read and write, until her husband intervened.[19] However, the die was cast.

One day when he was sixteen, while working for a master named Covey and after a prolonged series of beatings, he fought back and beat the white man. "This battle with Mr. Covey was the turning-point in my career as a slave," Douglass wrote. "It rekindled the few expiring embers of freedom, and revived within me a sense of my own manhood."[20]

While working as a ship caulker in Baltimore, he managed to escape north by train after borrowing the seaman's papers of a free black man. For a time, he worked as a caulker in New Bedford, Massachusetts. In 1838 he married Anna Murray, a free black woman, and at last had a solid home and family.[21] But he was destined for a life as an abolitionist, social reformer, orator, supporter of the Underground Railroad, and writer. He began attending abolition meetings and speaking widely. According to Blight:

> Douglass's autobiographical representation of his early life as a slave is a thoroughgoing abolitionist manifesto, a penetrating portrait of the inner and exterior worlds of both slaves and slaveholders. And he may, indeed, have seen or certainly heard a good deal about all that he wrote. The blood that flows in what he called his "chapter of horrors" [in *My Bondage and Freedom*] is full of philosophy as well as psychology.[22]

17. Blight, 1.
18. Douglass, 32–34.
19. Douglass, 53.
20. Douglass, 81.
21. Frederick Douglass National Historic Site, "Frederick Douglass."
22. Blight, 2.

One of his early champions was famed abolitionist William Lloyd Garrison, who encouraged him to publish his *Narrative of the Life of Frederick Douglass*. This became a bestseller, but the publicity brought unwanted fallout and he had to sail to Europe for a time to avoid being recaptured and returned to slavery. The North may have been free states, but slave owners had the right to cross borders to track down their legal property. Often they sent a bounty hunter, sometimes called a soul-catcher. While he was in England, British sympathizers raised funds to purchase his freedom, and thus he was able to return to the United States.[23]

He moved to Rochester in 1847 after his return from Europe, where he founded and published a newspaper, the *North Star*, so named for the star that escaping enslaved people used to guide them north—although the paper was overburdened with debt almost from the start.[24] And he continued to lecture. He attended and spoke eloquently at the first women's rights convention in Seneca Falls, New York. But he had a falling-out with his friend Susan B. Anthony and some other women suffragists for supporting the Fifteenth Amendment to the Constitution, which granted the vote to African American men but not to women of any race. It was a political move. He knew Congress would not grant the vote to both women and black citizens at the same time.[25]

His speech, "What to the Slave Is the Fourth of July?" was delivered at Rochester's Corinthian Hall on July 5, 1852, and is one of the masterpieces of American oratory.[26]

After Anna's death he married Helen Pitts from Honeoye, New York, a feminist and social reformer; this caused controversy and a breach with both his family and hers because she was white, and younger than him by two decades. But after a tortuous route to freedom, he was not going to be restrained by such silly hangups.

He was living in Washington when he died suddenly of a heart attack. But he had lived longer in Rochester than anywhere else, and it was his

23. Frederick Douglass National Historic Site, "Frederick Douglass." 7–9.
24. Fassett, "*North Star*, 1847–1849," 1–2.
25. Gordon, "Fraught Friendship."
26. *We The People Podcast*, "What to the Slave Is the Fourth of July?"

36.6: The grave of Frederick Douglass in Rochester.

most familiar ground, so his remains were returned by his family to Mount Hope Cemetery.

Finding the Grave

There are several ways to approach Frederick Douglass's grave, and one of the Mount Hope Cemetery Pocket Guides may prove useful to decide which way is best for you. However, if you like to walk, here is the way I usually go: Enter via the North Gate, and turn left at the Florentine Fountain. Take the next left onto Lawn Avenue, which will take you along the Mount Hope Avenue fence. Very quickly you will come to a fork in the road. To the right is Prospect Avenue. Straight is East Avenue, blocked off to traffic by post barriers. Park there and continue on East Avenue on foot. In a short distance you will see a post with a brass plate directing you uphill to Douglass's grave. Walk about fifty feet up that path, where another post will direct you to the right; the Douglass family plot is about fifty more feet on your left. He is buried next to his wife Anna, their daughter Annie, and his second wife Helen Pitts.

Lewis Henry Morgan (1818–1881): Groundbreaking Anthropologist and Social Theorist

Among the fraternal and civic organizations in early Rochester was one called the Grand Order of the Iroquois, founded by a railroad lawyer and politician named Lewis Henry Morgan to advocate for Iroquois rights to their land on which white settlements were rapidly encroaching.[27] He went to court and traveled to Washington on their behalf.[28] This work drew him into a deepening study of Iroquois life. The University of Rochester has for many years held a distinguished visiting lecture series in his name, since Morgan is now acknowledged as one of the founding fathers of modern

27. Launay, "Lewis Henry Morgan."
28. Frank and McKelvey, "Rochesterians of National Distinction."

36.7: The mausoleum of Lewis Henry Morgan in Rochester.

anthropology, which in his own time was roundly disparaged.[29] In fact, his 1851 book, *League of the Ho-de'-no-sau-nee (or Iroquois)* is considered by some to be the first work of American anthropology.[30]

According to historians Meryl Frank and Blake McKelvey, "His researches uncovered unsuspected family relationships and led to illuminating books not only on the Iroquois but also the strange consanguinity of systems of other tribes and distant peoples."[31] He believed that original human social systems, like that of the Iroquois, were matrilineal and not patriarchal. His ideas of social evolution, based on advances in technology, progressive government, property, and family, influenced Marx and Engels.[32] Other books include *Ancient Society* and *Houses and House Life of the American Aborigines.*

Finding the Grave

To find Lewis Henry Morgan's mausoleum, enter Mount Hope Cemetery by the north gate. Turn left at the green space with the Florentine Fountain. Park near the stone chapel. To your left are barrier posts to prevent vehicle traffic from a brick paved road called Ravine Avenue. It is a short walk up that road to Morgan's stately mausoleum, one of the cemetery's grandest structures.

Lillian D. Wald (1867–1940): Friend to the Poor

She was a pioneer of the modern urban settlement movement and organizer of the Visiting Nurse Service in New York City, the first nonsectarian one in the world,[33] as well as a force behind numerous social reforms. Lillian Wald's famous Henry Street Settlement, founded in 1893, was a haven for the homeless, indigent, and just plain poor with all the maladies born of hunger.

29. Launay.
30. Iglinski, "Lewis Henry Morgan at 200."
31. Frank and McKelvey , 16.
32. Launay.
33. "Lillian Wald Dies," 15.

Lillian Wald was born in Cincinnati in 1867 to a German Jewish family and grew up in comfortable middle-class circumstances in Rochester,[34] where she was schooled at Miss Crittenden's English and French Boarding School for Young Ladies. Her first "ah-hah!" moment (as Joseph Campbell might put it) came when a nurse came to care for her ailing sister and encouraged her to train as a nurse. Thus inspired, she entered New York Hospital, graduating as a nurse in 1891.[35]

Shortly after graduation, she was led by a terrified child to a miserable tenant room where her critically ill mother was suffering a hemorrhage. This might be called her second and greater "ah-hah," since from this experience—and the terrible need she saw in grim, smoky, and filthy East Side tenements, where the poor had no access to medical care, or even parks to go to—grew all that she established in her long career in the service of the poor.[36] Thus, enlisting the help of another nurse, Mary Brewster, the Henry Street Settlement was founded. This place of light blossomed into the Visiting Nurse Service and into educational outreach to homes and schools. She worked hard to establish parks and playgrounds. According to her *New York Times* obituary, "The immigrant, the sweatshop worker, the street peddler, the unemployed, all found her a friend."[37]

Her first book, *The House on Henry Street* (1915), requires a bold heart to read, with its descriptions of the debased and brutal living conditions that she encountered in the slums of New York's lower east side. This was followed in 1934 by *Windows on Henry Street*, written during her long final illness. Both books are now considered classics in their genre. She took a stand as a pacifist during World War I, which was an unpopular position at the time and earned her public rebukes.[38] But, in retrospect, she was right. That war proved nothing by sending millions of people into its meat-grinder to satisfy the vanity of kings and military strongmen and fill the pockets of munitions manufacturers.

34. Feld, "'An Actual Working out of Internationalism,'" 122.
35. "Lillian Wald Dies," 15.
36. Wald, *House on Henry Street*, chapter 1.
37. "Lillian Wald Dies," 15.
38. "Lillian D. Wald: 1867–1940," 756.

She advocated for the establishment of the US Children's Bureau, and was a strong advocate of child labor legislation.[39] For her endorsement of Socialist candidates, her vocal support of the Russian Revolution, and her friendship with Emma Goldman and other radicals, she was included in a list of sixty-one persons in a document addressed to the US Judiciary as an "undesirable."[40]

But even while bucking the system she had visits from influential friends, including presidents Theodore Roosevelt and Woodrow Wilson, President Franklin and Eleanor Roosevelt, and even Albert Einstein. On her seventieth birthday she was feted at a celebration in New York City at which messages streamed in from FDR and Eleanor, New York Governor Lehman, and New York City Mayor LaGuardia.[41]

After her death, LaGuardia said, according to the *Social Service Review,*

> It is comforting to us who knew and loved her that she lived to see the full realization of her plans and dreams. The idea of home nursing has developed into great public health services in every city of the country. Her dream of proper housing for all the people is now shaping itself into low-cost housing all over the country. Her wish for parks and play-grounds she lived to see fulfilled in her city.[42]

The Henry Street Settlement is still going strong, with far-reaching programs for the poor in its community. Its elaborate website stands in marked contrast to Wald's humble grave site in Rochester.

Finding the Grave

Enter Mount Hope Cemetery by the main gate, turn right, and make the first left onto Grove Avenue. After crossing the intersections with Second,

39. "Lillian D. Wald: 1867–1940," 756.
40. Jewish Women's Archive, "Lillian Wald—Red Scare Resistance"
41. "Lillian Wald Dies," 15.
42. "Lillian D. Wald: 1867–1940," 757.

36.8: The grave of Lillian Wald in Rochester.

First, and Greentree avenues, you will have range 3 on your left, and you will find the Wald family plot near the path, directly across from the Carl F. Lomb mausoleum. I found Lillian's grave to be charmingly well kept with plantings.

Edward R. Crone Jr. (1923–1945): The Real Billy Pilgrim

All of the gravesites in this book belong to authors—save one. The grave of Edward R. Crone is included here because, although he was not a writer, his contribution to American literature is undeniable. He was not aware of it, however. Crone graduated from Brighton High School near Rochester in June 1941, seven years after another literary light in the same school, Shirley Jackson. The following December the United States entered World War II. Crone was drafted and served with the 106th Infantry, was captured in Belgium, and became a prisoner of war in Dresden.[43] He survived the dreadful Allied bombing raids that destroyed the city, but died nearly two months later, according to some sources, of starvation and a broken heart. But one of his fellow prisoners was the future novelist Kurt Vonnegut, and Crone became the model for the character Billy Pilgrim in *Slaughterhouse-Five*.

In 1995 Vonnegut was invited to speak at the Rochester Arts and Lecture Series. During his stay, the two women who ran the series, Susan Feinstein and Rosemary Mancini, told him that Crone was buried in Mount Hope Cemetery, and asked if he would like to visit the grave. Mancini, now Rev. Rosemary Lloyd at the First Church in Boston, related in a sermon Vonnegut's startled reaction, "But he's in Dresden. I saw him buried myself—in a paper suit—because there wasn't enough fabric to bury him in a suit of clothes."[44] They told him that they'd learned from a local reporter that the Crone family had gone to Germany after the war, had their son disinterred, and brought him home to Rochester for reburial in

43. McDermott, "Oct. 26: Edward R. Crone Was Born in 1923."
44. Lloyd, "A Dream of Peace."

36.9: The grave of Edward R. Crone, the model for Billy Pilgrim, in the Crone family plot in Rochester.

the family plot. Reverend Lloyd said, "So we drove to the cemetery and left Mr. Vonnegut at the gravesite for a private cigarette and talk with Ed. Walking back to the car he said, heavily, 'Well, that closes the book on WWII for me.'" That evening, she said,

> He waxed about life and meaning and absurdity. Musing about his own eventual death, he said he hoped that when he died people would look up to the sky and say, "Well, I guess he's in heaven now. . . ."[45] I like to think that [Vonnegut] is up there shooting craps with Billy Pilgrim, and telling old stories.

45. Lloyd.

Finding the Grave

This one is easy. Enter Mount Hope Cemetery by the main gate, make a left, and turn right at the first intersection. The Crone family plot is just a few paces on the left.

Louise Brooks (1906–1985): Lulu from Pandora's Box

She was a silent film star, but she wanted to be a dancer. And later, a writer. While still a teenager, Louise Brooks danced for civic organizations in Cherryville, Kansas, where she was born in 1906. She joined the Denishawn Dance Academy in New York, touring with them from 1922–24, and in 1925 was hired by Ziegfeld for the *Follies* where she gained a reputation for insubordination—always a rebel, often walking away from success just because she was bored. Louise started playing bit parts for Paramount when the studio was still on Long Island, and soon she was a rising star in Hollywood with her trademark helmet-hair (the style went viral in the 1920s).[46]

She made three of her best films in Europe—two for legendary German director G. B. Pabst, including the role of the alluring, deadly, Lulu in *Pandora's Box* (1929), the film she is best known for, which created a stir in European cinema. According to Barbara Hales, critics saw in Brooks's Lulu a demonic character. "The popular reception of Lulu's monstrous sexuality reveals a widespread trend in Weimar Germany to stamp the sexual woman as criminal."[47] It's one of the great silent films, one that bears watching any number of times. A. O. Scott, in an appreciation of *Pandora's Box* in the *New York Times* in 2006, wrote, "With each viewing, a new dimension of Lulu's personality (and Brooks's) seems to emerge, and yet the film remains as indelibly strange as ever, capable of inspiring some critics to babbling gush—and reducing others to awed silence."[48]

---

46. Tynan, "Introduction," *x–xiv*. This intro was originally published in the *New Yorker* as "The Girl in the Black Helmet," which stirred up new interest in Brooks.

47. Hales, "Woman as Sexual Criminal," 101.

48. Scott, "Louise Brooks, a 'Pandora'," E25.

36.10: Louise Brooks. George Grantham Bain Collection, Library of Congress, Prints and Photographs Division, LC-DIG-ggbain-32453.

Though Pabst pleaded with her to stay in Germany, she sailed for the United States again. But it was the era of the talkies now, and Brooks never made an easy transition—primarily because she didn't want to. On the other hand, Hollywood in those days was full of silent film actors who found themselves in strange territory when talkies came in. She made her last film in 1938 in an early John Wayne vehicle, *The Overland Stage Raiders*.[49] The posters for the film show Brooks's name in small font in the third tier of the cast. Then she quit, but she had lost her enthusiasm for films and Hollywood long before.

"Why did I give up the movies?" she said in answer to a question from British theater critic Kenneth Tynan. "I could give you seven hundred reasons, all of them true."[50]

Sometime in the 1950s, George Eastman House film curator James Card rediscovered her living poor in Manhattan. According to Rochester journalist and syndicated film reviewer Jack Garner, "Card eventually persuaded Brooks to come to Rochester, where she could indulge her recently discovered passion for writing essays about filmmaking by using the resources and films of the Eastman House collection."[51] In Rochester, she said, "I could study old films and write about bits of my rediscovered past."[52] Card also took her to Paris to introduce her to cinema preservationist and director of the *Cinémathèque Française*, Henri Langlois, who, according to Jan-Christopher Horak, "declared her a saint after Card insisted he view a print of *Pandora's Box*."[53] With his typical flamboyance, Langlois said, "There is no Garbo. There is no Dietrich. There is only Louise Brooks."[54] She was on her way up again, but not as an actor.

She turned out one book, the autobiographical *Lulu in Hollywood*, which is still considered one of the best books on the movie industry in the silent era. But, according to Garner, arthritis set in, and in her last

49. Garner, *From My Seat on the Aisle*, 190.
50. Tynan, xxxiii.
51. Garner, 190–91.
52. Brooks, *Lulu in Hollywood*, 39.
53. Horak, "The Dreamer," 207.
54. Documentary of a Lost Girl, "Louise Brooks from A to Z."

years she could no longer use her typewriter, and she wasn't interested in dictation. Her writing career, short as it turned out, was over.[55] But *Lulu* has gone through a number of editions and has sold well in the United States and Europe. Many have commented that Brooks was an autodidact, who read constantly. Garner remembered a two-volume edition of Proust's *Remembrance of Things Past* on her shelf that was so crammed with her marginal notes that there was virtually no white space between its covers.[56] Unquestionably, she'd taught herself to write, the same way she'd learned to act.

Louise Brooks lived out the rest of her life in a one-bedroom apartment on Goodman Street in Rochester, sometimes the object of pilgrimages by the luminaries of the entertainment world. "In the sixties, many schoolboys wrote to me and came to see me," she wrote. "Most of them knew only my name and had never seen any of my films. They approached me with wildly uninformed flattery . . ."[57] She had special visitors: actresses Luise Rainer, Sylvia Sydney, and Joan Rivers; actor Richard Arlen; Tynan, who wrote about his several visits in an article for the *New Yorker*, "The Girl in the Black Helmet," which later became the Introduction for an edition of *Lulu in Hollywood*; and a small number of Rochester friends such as Garner.

But she lives on in popular culture. One of her best films, *Beggars of Life*, was re-released in 2017 in a Blu-ray edition. Many of her other films are available on DVD. Before I visited her grave, I watched *Pandora's Box*, *Diary of a Lost Girl*, and *Prix de Beaute* (her one French film). And I reread *Lulu in Hollywood* in one long, pleasant evening. She was a natural writer just as she was a natural actor—with a flow of very natural voice, what most writers struggle to attain.

She died of a heart attack in her apartment in 1985.

Why do so many visit her grave? Certainly because she was a great actor and film star, an icon of pop culture, and one of the loveliest women on the silver screen. And, I think, because she was a rebel, a woman who

55. Garner, 192.
56. Garner, 191.
57. Brooks, 72.

36.11: The grave of Louise Brooks in Rochester.

had success and fame, had worked hard for it, but found the doors closed
to her ultimately because she refused to surrender her soul and dignity,
which, by her account, was what Hollywood studio heads wanted of her.
But also, for me, because she saw another life beyond that: *she wanted to
be a writer, she wanted to be a very good writer.* She only had time to write
one book, but it is one very good book.

Finding the Grave

Once inside the main gate of Holy Sepulcher Cemetery, circle to the right
around the grass-island Golgotha with the brass Pieta and the three crosses.
You can park in the office parking lot, but there is plenty of room along the
roads to park. From the parking lot, take the south road. As you continue
south, you will pass the Christ Our Light Mausoleum on your left and the
All Saints Mausoleum on the right. The second section from the end of
the road on the right side is Garden Section 33 South, well-marked and

pleasantly landscaped with trees and plantings. Turn right onto the south side of that section, where you will see gravestones clustered prettily around small shrub plantings. About half-way to the next intersection, look for a stone for Popina. Stop there and walk directly north to the stone for Mastri, and turn left. You will see a cluster of modest flat stones in three rows. Louise Brooks's ashes are interred nearby in the third row. Once, when I visited, someone had left a photo of her in a plastic sleeve. The next time, there were two withered roses. People still love Louise.

Henry Clune (1890–1995): He Always Liked It Here

In this century it may be too easy to regard Henry Clune, even to write him off, as a regionalist. Certainly two of his later books, *I Always Liked It Here* and *The Rochester I Know*, would draw few readers beyond the Genesee Region. Not that there is anything wrong with being a regionalist, and to be fair, he sometimes referred to himself as a homebody writer: he found the capitals of Europe impressive and World War I was a big deal (he covered the war for the Rochester *Democrat and Chronicle*),[58] but they weren't Rochester. Every city needs such a writer. But he was actually a popular novelist in his time, especially with *The Good Die Poor (1937)*, which almost became an Edward G. Robinson-Bette Davis flick, and *By His Own Hand (1952)*, loosely based on George Eastman, which his editor at Macmillan thought would sell as big as *Gone with the Wind*.[59] It didn't reach that pinnacle.

One of the extraordinary things about him is that he lived to 105; he was 100 when his last book came out, which makes me wonder if I should switch from wine to martinis since that was his drink even in his advanced years. His books have an easy eloquence rare in letters of any time or place, or at any age. I did not know him—I wish I had. But I have tried to follow his advice to younger writers: *glue your ass to a chair.*

He was a veteran newsman in Rochester where he was a colleague of Arch Merrill, where he knew George Eastman (his mother was one

58. "Henry W. Clune, Writer, 105," B7.
59. Kauffman, "Oldest Living Novelist Tells All."

of George's first twelve employees) and Louise Brooks (who referred to him as "a goddamn bourgeois,"),[60] and where he covered anyone of consequence who came into town, such as Winston Churchill who kicked him out of his hotel room for asking impertinent questions. But being Rochesterian myself, I love his accounts of the old neighborhoods before World War I, when fresh raw milk and ice were delivered to the door in a wagon, and when news of a murder shocked everyone in the city.

Clune married Charlotte Boyle, an athletic swimmer, in 1921, almost immediately after they met. She was a world recordholder in the 150- and 200-yard and 200-meter distance swimming events, who had taught swimming to the Prince of Wales;[61] and the wedding, in New York City, was crowded with women swim athletes.[62] They settled not in Rochester but in Scottsville, a bedroom community ten miles south of the city. But there was more of interest in Charlotte's background. Her father, Joseph Boyle, was an almost mythological character, and like many larger-than-Rushmore men, a great deal of information about him is scattered across the internet, some contradictory and speculative. A Canadian, he was a highly successful gold and lumber prospector in the Yukon; during World War I he worked to reorganize the Russian railroads until the Bolsheviks established control; then, forming a liaison of a mysterious nature with the Queen of Romania, he arranged for Romania to reclaim national treasures from Russia. By the end of the war Russia, Romania, and France awarded him medals.[63] But to me, Clune is more interesting than his father-in-law.

Finding the Grave

Henry Clune and Charlotte are buried at White Haven Memorial Park. From the road it looks more like a golf course than a cemetery, since all the grave markers are one-size, uniform brass plates flat on the level earth,

60. Kauffman, "Henry and Louise."
61. "Charlotte Boyle to Wed," 17.
62. "Charlotte Boyle Married," 16.
63. "Happy Birthday Joe Boyle."

36.12: The grave of Henry Clune in Rochester.

so that a riding lawnmower can cut the grass without breaking its stride, and no one has to come along with little clippers and trim around the base of hundreds of stones. Well, death is the great leveler anyway; we're all brothers and sisters across the river.

Clune is in section H, lot 397, which also is the resting place of his parents. Drive in the front gate, turn right at the roundabout, and drive south. Section B will be on your right, G on your left. H, as you might guess, follows G, also on your left. In the middle of H is a tall monument to four US Army Chaplains who gave up their lifejackets, and thus their lives, when on the night of February 3, 1943, their troopship was torpedoed with a loss of more than six hundred lives. But the monument is also your anchor. If you go to the monument and walk directly west, back toward Marsh Road, count fourteen rows and you will find the author, next to Charlotte and near his parents.

Arch Merrill (1894–1974): The Upstate Rambler

Arch Merrill wrote for Rochester newspapers, mostly for the *Democrat and Chronicle*, from 1923 to 1974. In 1939 he started writing features on Rochester and Upstate history, geography, and points of interest—with an affinity for the well-honed yarn—which ran in the *Sunday Democrat and Chronicle*, continuing even after his retirement in 1963. Many of the columns were collected in some twenty-four books, most of them slim, quick reads. And they're still available for purchase online and in used bookstores. He was sometimes called the Poet Laureate of Upstate New York, yet his love played favorites: the Genesee Valley, its river and tributaries, its small towns and back roads. He was a man who could work in the newsroom all day and pound his typewriter all evening at home.

He loved Upstate, its people, its color and history. His first book, *A River Ramble* (1942), is his account of walking the entire length of the Genesee River, 157 miles from its source over the border in Pennsylvania to Rochester's harbor on Lake Ontario—not bad for a cigar-puffing man pushing fifty. Others include *Land of the Senecas* (1949); *The White Woman and Her Valley* (1961), about Mary Jemison, a white woman captured as a girl in an Indian raid on a Pennsylvania settlement and raised in the tribe in New York State, later settling in a cabin in what is now Letchworth Park; *Slim Fingers Beckon* (1963), about Central New York's Finger Lakes; and *The Underground: Freedom's Road and Other Upstate Tales* (1963), about the Underground Railroad, the clandestine route that enslaved people traveled to freedom. Twenty-four books in all, published between 1943 and 1969, all of them considered collectable. In Upstate, one often meets people who own them all and have read them many times.

According to James P. Hughes, Merrill's books "leave a unique literary legacy of those who left their mark on the land—hardy pioneers, noble Indians, politicians, soldiers, industrialists and crooks. In short, his body of work creates a tapestry of the places and characters that define the region, the big and the small, the celebrated and the unfamiliar."[64] They were never intended to be scholarly treatises. Reading through them, I

64. Hughes, "Down-Home Bard."

36.13: The grave of Arch Merrill and family in Rochester.

was struck not only by how much Upstate has changed, but how much the rural countryside is the same as in Merrill's time. Sure, there are fewer dirt roads. Some of the once prosperous towns need a coat of paint. Mom-and-pop groceries have been pushed over a cliff by corporate convenience stores. Too many diners have died so that McDonald's might live. But farming is still the biggest deal, or at least it takes up the most space. And the people seem much like those he met in his travels. Plus, you can still get very lost.

Born in Sandusky, in Cattaraugus County, New York, he served with the army in France in World War I. He came to Rochester with his wife Katherine Marie Towell after work stints in Washington, DC; Detroit; and New York City.[65] He had come to the right place.

65. Hughes.

Finding the Grave

At Brighton Cemetery, walk through the gate—or around it, since it is chained to prevent unauthorized vehicle traffic. Walk straight down the gravel path, about seventy-five feet, and take the first right. A corner bush will be on your right and a Watson family monument on your left. Walk straight for about another sixty feet. You will see a trio of modest flat stones on your right, one each for Arch Merrill 1894–1974, his wife Katherine T. 1994–1981, and their daughter Marion L. 1923–1981.

Sources

Susan B. Anthony

Klos, Dr. Naomi Yavneh, and Stan Yavneh Klos. "Susan B. Anthony." Accessed April 18, 2023. https://www.susanbanthony.net.

Naparsteck, Martin. *The Trial of Susan B. Anthony: An Illegal Vote, a Courtroom Conviction and a Step toward Women's Suffrage.* Jefferson, NC: McFarland and Co., 2014.

Adelaide Crapsey

Alkalay-Gut, Karen. "The Dying of Adelaide Crapsey." *Journal of Modern Literature* 13, no. 2 (1986): 225–50. http://www.jstor.org/stable/3831493.

Alkalay-Gut, Karen. *Alone in the Dawn: The Life of Adelaide Crapsey.* Athens: Univ. of Georgia Press, 1988.

Crapsey, Adelaide. *Verse.* Foreword by Jean Webster. Preface by Claude Bragdon. New York: Alfred A. Knopf, 1922. Kindle.

Algernon Crapsey

"An Episcopal Dictionary of the Church: Crapsey, Algernon Sidney." Episcopal Church Domestic and Foreign Missionary Society. 2018. Accessed April 18, 2023. www.episcopalchurch.org/library/glossary/crapsey-algernon-sidney.

Swanton, Carolyn. "Doctor Algernon Crapsey: Religious Reformer." *Rochester History*, ed. Joseph W. Barnes. Vol. XLII, no. 1 (January 1980).

Frederick Douglass

Blight, David. "Frederick Douglass's Childhood of Extremes." Black Perspectives. African American Intellectual History Society. November 27, 2018. www.aaihs.org/frederick-douglasss-childhood-of-extremes/.

"Frederick Douglass." Frederick Douglass National Historic Site. Accessed April 18, 2023. https://www.nps.gov/frdo/learn/historyculture/frederickdouglass.htm.

Douglass, Frederick. *The Narrative of the Life of Frederick Douglass, American Slave*. Orinda, CA: SeaWolf Press, 2020.

Fassett, Will. "The *North Star*, 1847–1849, Based on Evidence Found in the Paper's Ledger." University of Rochester Frederick Douglass Project. Accessed April 18, 2023. https://rbscp.lib.rochester.edu/2524.

Gordon, Ann D. "Fraught Friendship: Susan B. Anthony and Frederick Douglass." National Park Service, June 4, 2020. www.nps.gov/articles/000/fraught-friendship-susan-b-anthony-and-frederick-douglass.htm.

"What to the Slave Is the Fourth of July?" *We The People Podcast*. July 2, 2020. https://constitutioncenter.org/interactive-constitution/podcast/what-to-the-slave-is-the-fourth-of-july.

Lewis Henry Morgan

Frank, Meryl, and Blake McKelvey. "Some Former Rochesterians of National Distinction." *Rochester History* XXI, no. 3 (July 1959).

Iglinski, Peter. "'Lewis Henry Morgan at 200' Reintroduces a Landmark Scholar." *Newscenter*. University of Rocester. December 21, 2018. www.rochester.edu/newscenter/lewis-henry-morgan-at-200-reintroduces-a-landmark-scholar-355942/?msclkid=120b2578cfa711ec88b1e18e35206153.

Launay, Robert. "Lewis Henry Morgan." Oxford Bibliographies. January 11, 2012. Accessed April 18, 2023. https://www.oxfordbibliographies.com/display/document/obo-9780199766567/obo-9780199766567-0050.xml.

Lillian Wald

Feld, Marjorie N. "'An Actual Working Out of Internationalism': Russian Politics, Zionism, and Lillian Wald's Ethnic Progressivism." *Journal of the Gilded Age and Progressive Era*, no. 2 (2003): 119–49. http://www.jstor.org/stable/25144325.

"Lillian D. Wald: 1867–1940." *Social Service Review* 14, no. 4 (1940): 755–57. http://www.jstor.org/stable/30014699.

"Lillian Wald Dies; Friend of the Poor." *New York Times*, September 2, 1940.

"Women of Valor: Lillian Wald—Red Scare Resistance." Jewish Women's Archive. Accessed April 18, 2023. https://jwa.org/womenofvalor/wald.

Wald, Lillian. *The House on Henry Street*. New York: Holt, 1915. Kindle.

Edward R. Crone

Lloyd, Rev. Rosemary. "A Dream of Peace." Sermon given at the First Church in Boston, April 15, 2007.

McDermott, Meaghan M. "On This Day in Rochester History. Oct. 26: Edward R. Crone Was Born in 1923." *Democrat and Chronicle* (Rochester, NY), October 23, 2013.

Louise Brooks

Brooks, Louise. *Lulu in Hollywood*. Introduction by Kenneth Tynan. Univ. of Minnesota Press, 1982.

Chabot, Charles, and Richard Leacock, directors. *Louise Brooks*, documentary. BBC Arena, 1986. 57m.

Garner, Jack. *From My Seat on the Aisle*. Rochester, NY: RIT Press, 2013.

Hales, Barbara. "Woman as Sexual Criminal: Weimar Constructions of the Criminal Femme Fatale." *Women in German Yearbook* 12 (1996): 101–21. http://www.jstor.org/stable/20688838.

Horak, Jan-Christopher. "The Dreamer: Remembering James Card." *The Moving Image: The Journal of the Association of Moving Image Archivists* 1, no. 1 (2001): 203–10. http://www.jstor.org/stable/41167048.

"Louise Brooks from A to Z: L for Langlois, Lotte, 'Louder, Please,' London, Lulu in Berlin, and Lolita." Documentary of a Lost Girl. Accessed April 18, 2023. www.documentaryofalostgirl.com/.

Scott, A. O. "Louise Brooks, a 'Pandora' Who Transcended Categories." *New York Times*, June 16, 2006.

Tynan, Kenneth. "Introduction." In *Lulu in Hollywood*, by Louise Brooks. Expanded ed. Minneapolis: Univ. of Minnesota Press, 1982.

Henry Clune

"Charlotte Boyle Married." *New York Times*, October 19, 1921.

"Charlotte Boyle to Wed." *New York Times*, October 14, 1921.

"Happy Birthday Joe Boyle: Celebrating a 'Larger than Life Klondike Hero." CBC News, November 6, 2017. Accessed April 18, 2023. https://www.cbc.ca/news /canada/north/klondike-joe-boyle-birthday-whitehorse-fraser-1.4385107.

"Henry W. Clune, Writer, 105." *New York Times*, October 13, 1995.

Kauffman, Bill. "Henry and Louise in the Lair de Clune." *Crooked Lake Review*, February 1992. Accessed April 18, 2023. www.crookedlakereview.com/articles /34_66/47feb1992/47kauffman.html.

Kauffman, Bill. "The Oldest Living Novelist Tells All." *Los Angeles Times*, November 11, 1990. Accessed April 18, 2023. https://www.latimes.com/archives /la-xpm-1990-11-11-bk-5967-story.html.

Arch Merrill

Hughes, James P. "Down-Home Bard, Finger Lakes Great, Arch Merrill." *Life in the Finger Lakes*, Winter 2008. April 21, 2017. https://www.lifeinthefinger lakes.com/home-bard-finger-lakes-great-arch-merrill/.

37 Rushford

Philip Wylie

I know this area of the state to be beautiful countryside, but on the April day that I went to Rushford looking for Philip Wylie's grave, a fog lay so dense on the land that visibility was like a heavy snowstorm. Rushford itself is an old agrarian town, very much like dozens of other Central New York towns and villages, especially pretty in summer. Nearby Rushford Lake, which is now crowded with cottages and docks, was created by Rochester Gas and Electric Company in 1927 by damming Caneadea Creek, with the result that the old communities of East Rushford and Kelloggsville now sleep with the fishes.

Nearby Caneadea was once the location of an important Seneca long-house. And it was in Rushford that a boy named Calvin Fairbank came to a tent revival meeting with his parents. They lodged in town with a family of runaway enslaved people. The stories of enslavement in the South that they heard from their hosts made such a profound impression on Calvin that he vowed to fight. Before the Civil War he—as Rev. Fairbank—conducted almost fifty enslaved people to freedom in the North, for which he was eventually caught and locked up in a Kentucky prison where they made an example of him with regular lashings. He was released finally in 1864.

Rushford is also the burial place of one of the last century's most schismatic writers.

Philp Wylie (1902–1971): A Fiery and Iconoclastic Intellect

Philip Wylie was born in Beverly, Massachusetts, in 1902, the son of a Presbyterian minister and the brother of writer Max Wylie. They were distantly related to Jonathan Edwards and Aaron Burr. After the death of his mother in 1907, the family moved to Ohio, where, after his father remarried, Philip began to distance himself from his family. He went to Princeton for three years but left without a degree. Soon after, he joined the staff of the *New Yorker* and became friendly with a pantheon of New York authors such as Dorothy Parker, James Thurber, and Theodore Dreiser. After leaving the magazine in 1927, bristling with creative energy he hired a literary agent. He was on his way.

Wylie was certainly prolific (he wrote thirty-four novels and thirteen volumes of nonfiction), but he also hopped genres with apparent ease. Early in his career, he was most influential as a science fiction writer, and his plots and characters are said to have influenced comic strips such as Superman.[1] In the 1930s he wrote screenplays for Hollywood flicks such as *King of the Jungle* and *Island of Lost Souls*, an adaption of H. G. Wells's *The Island of Dr. Moreau* (a very good film, with Charles Laughton, Bela Lugosi, and Richard Arlen). Later, some of his own novels were made into movies, such as *When Worlds Collide* (coauthored with Edwin Balmer, 1951) with Richard Derr, Barbara Rush, and Peter Hansen. *Night unto Night* (1949) was set in Florida during World War II, a fine novel and a genuine B-movie with Ronald Reagan, Viveca Lindfors, and Broderick Crawford.

But it was for a single episode of the TV series *The Name of the Game* that he wrote the screenplay *LA 2017* (1971), directed by a young Stephen Spielberg, and starring Gene Barry, Barry Sullivan, and Edmond O'Brien, which proved him prescient.[2] An early supporter of the conservation movement, he used this futuristic story to warn of civilization-destroying pollution and global warming. He had considerable practice writing eschatological nightmares. When I was a kid, around the time of the Cuban Missile Crisis in 1962, I read his dystopian novel *Tomorrow* (1954), which had been reissued in paperback, about the after-effects of a nuclear war. It scared the hell out of me, especially because the present

1. Yardley, "Generation of Vipers Loses Its Bite."
2. Newman, "The Name of the Game."

world seemed on the brink, although later I realized that Wylie had greatly underestimated the probable effects—but then, he was working with information that was publicly available in the mid-'50s.

None of these works caused anything like the notoriety or, more precisely, infamy, that he earned with *Generation of Vipers* (1942), in which he goes on the attack against the institutions that Americans hold dear, including religion (Christianity in particular), our political system and leaders, and motherhood (he coined the term "momism"), bringing out his fiery and bombastic intellect. Some of the ducks in his shooting gallery are ones that Mark Twain might have aimed at with satirical humor. But Twain did not possess Wiley's malevolence, and Wylie wasn't joking. Wylie's book was, according to Jonathan Yardley, "a veritable Mississippi of bile, churning out word upon word to a total of some 100,000, just about every one of them quivering with rage—though whether real or simulated rage remains unclear to this day." Yet, Yardley says, *Vipers* did hit a few nails squarely on the head: "Then as now, American hypocrisy about sex was near universal—'The people, common or self-important,' Wylie wrote, 'are engaged in a violent vocal repudiation of that which they are simultaneously engaged in doing.'"[3]

For a taste of the controversy caused by the book, his televised interview with Mike Wallace in 1957 is available on the website of the Harry Ransom Center, University of Austin, Texas, where you'll meet the restless, contrarian writer, chain-smoking and sparring, twisting in his chair, making statements that must have outraged his audience in the staid, conservative America of the time. In fact, as he says in the interview, he received thousands of nasty letters after the publication of *Vipers*.[4]

And yet, he claimed to be an optimist. "I'm an optimist who is taken for a pessimist," he told an interviewer. "My jokes are taken straight, and my irony is taken literally."[5] Well, maybe.

3. Yardley.
4. Wylie, *Mike Wallace interview*.
5. Breit, "Talk with Philip Wylie," 44.

An avid deep-sea fisherman, he was an officer of the International Game Fish Association (IGFA), and his articles in the *Saturday Evening Post* introduced saltwater fishing to a generation of Americans.[6]

He died in Miami on October 25, 1971, of a heart attack while visiting friends. Rushford was his second wife Federica's hometown, and they had lived there together for a time. Hawaii had been home for three years prior to his death,[7] but, in the end, home is where the family plot is. Theirs was a large Georgian-style house surrounded by a wrought-iron fence on Lower Street, the last house before you turn the corner onto Brooks, only a few hundred feet from his grave.

Finding the Grave

Rushford is a bit out of the way.

Take Route 19 north from Route 17/I-86. In Caneadea, turn left on Route 243, where a sign points to Rushford and Rushford Lake. After about six miles, turn left onto a rural road that calls itself Main Street. The volunteer fire department is just up a hill on the left. Follow Main Street around a couple curves, which will lead you to the village. Turn left from Main Street onto Lower Street, and after a couple hundred feet make a right onto Brooks Avenue. Old Rushford Cemetery at the edge of the village, where Philip Wylie is buried, is just a short distance up the hill to the right. Or else, and especially if you are coming from any other direction, set your GPS for Brooks Avenue, in the town of Rushford.

My GPS called it Rushford Cemetery, but according to Russell Heslin, the town assessor, who has an office at the town hall, it's called First Cemetery. I had seen a sign in a picture online that read "First Burying Ground Cemetery," which is what the Allegheny County Historical Society calls it on their website, although when I arrived the sign was gone from its iron hanger. Maybe someone objected to the name. The town

6. Arnold, "Philip Wylie, Author, Dies," 44.
7. "Author Philip Wylie Dies," 72.

37.1: The grave of Philip Wylie and wife in Rushford.

historian Becky Cole calls it the Old Rushford Cemetery, so in deference to local authority, that is what I am calling it. There is no parking area, but a generous shoulder to pull off on. The graves farthest from the road are the oldest, and there I found some going back to 1837, but records show burials as early as 1820. Wylie is in the row nearest the road with most of the modern dead, close enough that if he is a light sleeper, he can hear the farm machinery rumbling by. He lies beside Frederica, and another family member, Edmund Kiskaddon.

Sources

Arnold, Martin. "Philip Wylie, Author, Dies; Noted for 'Mom' Attack." *New York Times*, April 26, 1971, 44.

"Author Philip Wylie Dies." *Observer-Reporter*, December 25, 1971, 72.

Breit, Harvey. "Talk with Philip Wylie." *New York Times*, July 3, 1949, 44.

Newman, Kim. "The Name of the Game LA 2017 (1971)." TV review. Accessed April 18, 2023. https://johnnyalucard.com/2022/01/16/tv-review-the-name-of-the-game-la-2017-1971/name-of-the-game-la-2017-3.

Wylie, Philip. *Mike Wallace Interview*. May 12, 1957. Harry Ransom Center, University of Austin, Texas.

Yardley, Jonathan. "Generation of Vipers Loses Its Bite." *Washington Post*, July 30, 2005.

Steven Huff is the author of two story collections, *Blissful and Other Stories* (Cosmographia, 2017), and *A Pig in Paris* (Big Pencil Press, 2007), as well as three books of poetry, *A Fire in the Hill* (Blue Horse Press, 2017), *More Daring Escapes* (Red Hen Press, 2017), and *The Water We Came From* (Foot-Hills, 2003). He is editor of *Knowing Knott: Essays on an American Poet* (Tiger Bark Press, 2017). Autobiographical essays have appeared in the *Gettysburg Review* and the *Solstice Literary Magazine*. He is a Pushcart Prize winner in fiction, and teaches creative writing in the Solstice Low-Residency MFA Program at Lasell University in Boston. The former publisher/managing editor at BOA Editions, Ltd., he served as publisher at Tiger Bark Press from 2006 until 2022. He lives in Rochester and Forestville, New York.

Printed in the USA
CPSIA information can be obtained
at www.ICGtesting.com
LVHW091306251123
R17978900001B/R179789PG764281LVX00001B/1